**A FUN AND SEXY GUIDE TO FINDING AND
KEEPING THE LOVER OF YOUR DREAMS**

You finally did it! You bought *Sex, Stars and Seduction*! Well
done and have fun! You have reserved your place on a voyage
of romantic adventure and erotic discovery that will totally
transform your love life . . .

Finding your perfect lover is rather like buying a new car. You
first have to decide what kind of car you are looking for . . .
This book will not only act as your personal guide, but will
also give you the secret key to the zodiac's devastating sexual
power . . . Amongst other things, you will discover how to
entrap and seduce your lovers, how to satisfy them in bed, how
to hold on to them and how to get rid of them.

ABOUT THE AUTHORS

Barbara Dunn and Archie Dunlop are both graduates of the London School of Economics. They have extensive experience in the teaching, practice and lecturing of astrology. They are directors of the London School of Traditional Astrology.

Barbara and Archie each hold a diploma from the Faculty of Astrological Studies and the Olivia Barclay School of Horary Astrology. Their experience in this field has afforded them membership of the Association of Professional Astrologers. They are also delegates on the Advisory Panel for Astrological Education.

Barbara Dunn is widely known as a media astrologer and is currently the astrologer for the *Today* newspaper. She has also made frequent appearances on radio and television shows in the United Kingdom.

Their first book on astrology, *Life, Love and Destiny* (1994), is available in Signet.

SEX, STARS AND SEDUCTION

A Fun and Sexy Guide to Finding and
Keeping the Lover of Your Dreams

by Barbara Dunn and Archie Dunlop

A SIGNET BOOK

SIGNET BOOKS

Published by the Penguin Group
Penguin Books Ltd, 27 Wrights Lane, London w8 5tz, England
Penguin Books USA Inc., 375 Hudson Street, New York, New York 10014, USA
Penguin Books Australia Ltd, Ringwood, Victoria, Australia
Penguin Books Canada Ltd, 10 Alcorn Avenue, Toronto, Ontario, Canada m4v 3b2
Penguin Books (NZ) Ltd, 182–190 Wairau Road, Auckland 10, New Zealand

Penguin Books Ltd, Registered Offices: Harmondsworth, Middlesex, England

First published 1995
10 9 8 7 6 5 4 3 2 1

Filmset in 10/12½ pt Monophoto Plantin
Typeset by Datix International Limited, Bungay, Suffolk
Printed in Great Britain by Clays Ltd, St Ives plc

A CIP catalogue record for this book is available from the British Library

This book is dedicated to X, in the hope that it helps her find a stunning multi-millionaire who has the physical and financial stamina to satisfy her ferocious lust.

CONTENTS

ACKNOWLEDGEMENTS

Rob Dunlop for the illustrations.

Susie Montagu for ensuring that this book reaches every corner of the known world.
Luigi Bonomi for his unbending faith in the authors.
Simon Trewin for his continual support and encouragement.
Victor Downer for his creative assistance.
Monica and her colleagues for their technical support on Chapter Six.
Sandra for her co-operation on Chapter Eight.

INTRODUCTION

You finally did it! You bought *Sex, Stars and Seduction*! Well done and have fun! You have reserved your place on a voyage of romantic adventure and erotic discovery that will totally transform your love life.

As you travel through jungles of unexplored passion, this book will not only act as your personal guide, but will also give you the secret key to the zodiac's devastating sexual power. *Sex, Stars and Seduction* will indeed show you how an understanding of the twelve signs of the zodiac can massively improve your love life.

You will find out how a person's Sun sign reflects their personality and their sexuality. So, when you have relationships in future, find out your lover's Sun sign and then consult this book. Amongst other things, you will discover how to entrap and seduce your lovers, how to satisfy them in bed, how to hold on to them and how to get rid of them.

When reading *Sex, Stars and Seduction*, you can be confident that you are in the hands of experts. We – Barbara Dunn and Archie Dunlop – are two of the world's best astrologers, have twenty-five years of astrological experience between us and are specialists in the astrology of relationships. We are also Diploma holders of the Faculty of Astrological Studies and the élite Qualifying Horary Diploma Course. Our first book, *Life, Love and Destiny*, is widely regarded as the most accessible introduction to serious astrology ever written.

Sex, Stars and Seduction represents the culmination of many years of astrological research and practice. The romantic and sexual experiences of thousands of people have been gathered together and then grouped according to their Sun sign. So, when you read that Taureans can be seduced by gâteaux and trifles and that Sagittarians are noisy lovers, you can rest assured that our statements are based on real, live cases, rather than dry theory.

In cases where we found our own data to be unbelievable, we sought second opinions from experts in other fields. They confirmed that our findings were, indeed, true to life. Unfortunately, these experts insisted on their anonymity, so we cannot acknowledge them.

If you follow our advice in *Sex, Stars and Seduction*, we are sure that your love life will improve no end. However, we do ask that you use common sense – before you take any initiative, first check that it is morally acceptable. For example, you might decide that it's unethical to seduce Leos with non-stop sexual flattery and immoral to upset Virgos by emptying ashtrays on their heads.

None the less, it is your decision what you do with this book and we must stress that we can take no moral, legal or karmic responsibility for your actions or for their consequences.

Now that we've got that disclaimer out of the way, we would remind you to make *Sex, Stars and Seduction* your constant bedside companion. It will never let you down and will always be there to ensure that you make the very most of your love life.

Chapter One

FINDING YOUR DREAM LOVER IN THE STARS

Finding the perfect lover is rather like buying a new car. You first have to decide what sort of car you are looking for. You might, for example, want a family saloon that is safe, reliable and cheap to run. It may not be the fastest, or the most exciting car on the road, but you know it will give you years of trouble-free motoring.

However, if you want to live dangerously and enjoy the risk and the adventure of the fast lane, you might decide to buy a flashy Italian sports car, which has amazing manoeuvrability and can top a hundred and fifty miles an hour. Unfortunately, this car is expensive to maintain and has a phenomenal fuel consumption. It also has a mind of its own and, if you don't watch out, you'll find yourself driving into the back of a juggernaut.

So, do you get the message?

If you're looking for a lover, you should first of all decide what kind of relationship you want. Do you want a fast and furious one-night stand, which will be history by tomorrow lunchtime? Or are you looking for a lifetime of wedded bliss?

Once you are clear in your mind about what you are looking for, you can then use the magic of astrology to help you find the man, or the woman, of your dreams.

The importance of knowing what you want is illustrated by the following letter that was recently sent to us:

Finding the perfect lover is rather like buying a new car.

Dear Barbara and Archie,

I wonder if you can help me. I am a Gemini, born on 6 June 1961. I am an attractive, vivacious woman, but I am always unlucky in love.

I have been to many different astrologers, palmists and tarot readers, asking them when I am going to find a man who is caring and considerate, who I can spend the rest of my life with.

They always tell me that someone is going to turn up, but he never does. Sometimes I meet someone who seems to be right, but when I get to know him I find him boring and I start looking for someone more exciting, and more passionate.

My sister says it's something to do with me being a Gemini, but I have many Gemini friends who are happily married. What should I do?

Yours sincerely,

Jane

Jane's problem is that she can't make up her mind. She is looking for someone special to whom she can get married. Yet she gets bored quickly and is obviously looking for variety. She even hints that she is looking for sexual variety. If sexual variety is what she wants, then it might be a good idea for her to accept that, right now, she is not ready to commit herself to one person.

She should see relationships instead as temporary affairs that only have a limited shelf life. However, if it is really important for her to settle down and get married, she should count her blessings and make the most out of her chosen man – even if he does turn out to be a little boring.

In theory, there is a third choice. She could get married, with the full intention of having affairs on the side. We don't see it as our role to encourage adulterous behaviour, so we would advise her to give that possibility a miss.

To help Jane and anyone else who is unsure what they are looking for in a relationship, we recommend the following little exercise. Perhaps you'd like to try it out for yourself. You may find that it will help clarify your current romantic goals. Start off by looking at the following ten things which a relationship can give you.

1 Passionate sex
2 Fascinating conversation
3 True love
4 Perfect understanding
5 Unfailing reliability
6 Endless variety
7 Breathless excitement
8 Masses of money
9 Rock-solid stability
10 Power and status

Now think about the relationship you are in, or the relationship you would like to be in. Which of these ten things is most important to you? Which is the second most important? Which is the least important?

If you think that passionate sex and endless variety are most important to you and that true love is least important, then this is a sure sign that you are not looking for a permanent relationship. On the other hand, if true love and rock-solid stability head your list, this would indicate that you are well and truly ready for marriage – provided, of course, that you can find the right marriage partner.

There is no doubt that astrology can help you to find the right lover, which is why we have written this book, so that we could share our expert knowledge of the various Sun signs with you. We have found, in our many years of experience as consultant astrologers, that certain signs have special qualities and special problem areas. For example, our exhaustive research has revealed that Scorpio men and Scorpio women are undoubtedly the best sexual performers in the zodiac. So, if you had listed passionate sex as your main priority in a relationship, you might think that your ideal partner would be a Scorpio.

Although a Scorpio might well be your best bet, there are other things to consider. It may be that the only Scorpio you know is absolutely disgusting and has the sex appeal of a stuffed wart-hog. Alternatively, he or she may be the latest reincarnation of the Boston Strangler, in which case, you'll have to be satisfied by someone else. Fortunately all the signs, not just Scorpio, have secret sexual depths and, if you read Chapter Five, you will discover how to plumb these depths.

It may be that sex isn't your number one priority. Perhaps you are looking for rock-solid stability and unfailing reliability. It is certainly true that Cancer and Taurus are the most reliable and stable signs and are, therefore, the easiest to hold on to. However, when you move on to Chapter Seven, which tells you how to hold on to your lover, you will discover that it is possible to keep any lover hooked for life. All you have to do is look up their Sun sign and lock into their sexual and astrological soft spots.

As astrologers, we are always being asked about which pairs of signs are compatible. In our experience, some pairs are more compatible than others. For example, Geminis tend to get on very well with Leos, but not quite so well with Capricorns. So, on balance, it is probably best to choose a lover whose Sun sign is compatible with your own.

To help you with this choice, you will find, in Chapter Three, a comprehensive guide to compatibility, with a special emphasis on sex. This tells you how the twelve signs relate to each other and it gives warnings about problem combinations. We expect that you will find Chapter Three both interesting and useful, although we don't want it to rule your love life. After all, there are times when you've just got to go for it, regardless of what sign your intended partner is.

So, if you are a passionate Scorpio and you are desperate to go to bed with the adorable Leo who works across the corridor, don't let us put you off. Just bear in mind that having good sex with this person may not be easy and it may require plenty of patience and understanding before you are finally fulfilled.

Astrology is not just useful for starting relationships: it can help you end them. Right now, as you read this first chapter, you're probably more interested in finding or keeping a partner than getting rid of one. However, we live in the real world and have to accept that sometimes we grow out of people. Or, to put it more bluntly, we get sick of them. So, when you have finally outgrown your lovers, turn to Chapter Eight, and we'll tell you how to get rid of them.

You can also use Chapter Eight for fending off unwanted advances. If, for example, you find that your drooling boss keeps asking you out for candlelit dinners, all you have to do is find out what his or her Sun sign is. Armed with this vital information, you'll be able to pour cold water over your admirer's tiresome sex drive.

Sex, Stars and Seduction is an important book that can benefit all aspects of your love life. Whether you are single or married, courting or divorcing, make sure that you regularly consult its wisdom-packed pages.

To make use of *Sex, Stars and Seduction*, you need only two pieces of information: your Sun sign and your lover's Sun sign. If you don't know what they are, then look at the following approximate list. You simply take your birthday, or your lover's, and read off the corresponding sign.

Sun sign	Birthday
Aries	21 March – 19 April
Taurus	20 April – 20 May
Gemini	21 May – 20 June
Cancer	21 June – 22 July
Leo	23 July – 22 August
Virgo	23 August – 22 September
Libra	23 September – 22 October
Scorpio	23 October – 21 November
Sagittarius	22 November – 21 December

Capricorn	22 December – 19 January
Aquarius	20 January – 18 February
Pisces	19 February – 20 March

Once you know your lover's Sun sign, you will be able to take full advantage of our advice. Indeed, it won't be long before you are playing him or her like a violin. If you are not in a relationship, then you will be able to use the secrets of the twelve signs to seduce and entrap whomever you like.

So, whatever your romantic intentions, good luck, and good hunting!

Chapter Two

SIZING UP YOUR DREAM LOVER

Astrology can definitely improve your love life and it can definitely help you to find a dream lover. None the less, you have to be realistic. If, as you read this book, you are alone on a desert island, two thousand miles away from the nearest Aries sex machine and four thousand miles away from the nearest dreamy Pisces, then there is very little we can do to help. If you write us a nice letter, put it in a watertight bottle and throw it into the ocean, we'll make sure that you get your money back by return of tide.

Those of you who are not marooned in the South Pacific will have access to other people. You'll work with them, study with them and meet them in supermarket queues. Many of these people will be attractive and desirable and you'll be wondering how to size up their romantic potential. Like Christopher, who wrote the following letter to us:

Dear Barbara and Archie,

I am a 21-year-old student, studying English Literature. I am an introverted Aquarius, who has never had a serious relationship before.

Recently I started doing a course in North American drama. It's very interesting, but I have become distracted by this amazing girl, called Natalie, who is also on the course. She's stunningly beautiful, is outward-going and seems quite friendly.

I have talked to her several times and I think she likes me. I would really like to ask her out, but I feel I don't know anything about her. I don't know about her real personality and I don't know what she wants from relationships. Most importantly, I don't know whether or not she's interested in me. What clues should I look for? She's says she's a Libra.

Yours sincerely,

Christopher S.

Christopher's problem is very common. There is a beautiful girl in his class and he is desperate to know if there is any chance of a romance. Natalie's not giving any clues away and Christopher is terrified of making a fool of himself. Fortunately, he knows that she's a Libra. This means that Natalie is a cultivated person, who is very good at dealing with other people. She knows how to make them feel at ease, which may be why Christopher thinks that she likes him. Indeed, Libran women have a reputation for being flirts, so Christopher has to watch out that Natalie doesn't lead him up the garden path.

The case of Christopher and Natalie shows how important it is to size up your romantic target before you take action. Astrology is an excellent way of doing this. Whatever Natalie says, however much she flits and flirts, she will not be able to hide the truth about her Sun sign.

In this chapter we answer the kind of questions that Christopher was asking in his original letter. We tell you about each sign's personality, about the things they look for in a relationship and the way they treat their partners. Most importantly, we describe the special clues that each of the twelve signs gives when he or she is interested in you.

By the time you have finished reading this Chapter, you will know how each sign approaches relationships. This means that when you next contemplate a romantic attachment, you will be able to make a sensible and informed decision.

ARIES

The Aries personality

The Rams are exciting and dynamic people who have a reputation for impulsive and reckless behaviour. They go steaming into arguments and fights without a second thought for their own or other people's safety, so it is hardly surprising that they make excellent riot police, nightclub bouncers and kamikaze pilots.

It's also worth noting that Aries soldiers tend to do very well. Their acts of mind-blowing heroism become legendary and they quickly notch up a string of posthumous awards for gallantry. This underlines the fundamental Aries philosophy: life is there to be lived, enjoyed and experienced. It is far better to die fighting, in a hail of machine-gun bullets, than to live a long, uneventful and ultimately meaningless life, which is only punctuated by a marriage, a couple of children and a retirement party.

All Rams, whether soldiers or bank clerks, regard spontaneity as being vital. Once they have decided to do something, they want to do it immediately. This character trait has its advantages. An Aries businesswoman will see an opportunity to make a fortune and will seize it before her rivals have time to get in on the act. Alternatively, the Ram may be sitting around with friends on a wet Saturday evening. Everyone's bored, and no one knows what to do. Suddenly the Ram will zoom into action and announce the he's going to organize a huge all-night party. An hour later, two hundred guests have arrived and there's a karaoke machine installed in the kitchen. And, to make matters even better, the Ram is completely unaffected by the neighbours' complaints. This is because Aries is one of the most selfish and egocentric signs of the Zodiac.

However, very few Aries people will admit to being selfish. They often claim that they are dedicated to a set of higher, humanitarian principles, which they will live for and, if necessary, die for. Rams tend to inflict these principles on friends, neighbours, lovers and any passer-by who crosses their path.

So, if you're happily minding your own business, eating a hamburger, an Aries vegetarian may come storming up to you and tell you how disgusting your habit is. You may be told that you are encouraging the slaughter and torture of animals and that if everyone stopped eating meat, world starvation would be wiped out overnight. Although the Ram is probably right, it might be better if he or she were a little more diplomatic.

When it comes to their love lives, the Rams are complete barbarians. They are always on the look out for fresh conquests and they never take no for an answer. It is hardly surprising

When it comes to their love lives, the Rams are complete barbarians.

that both Attila the Hun and Bodicea had Aries as their Sun sign. Going out with Aries lovers can indeed be an exciting, as well as a barbaric, experience and many people enjoy the thrill of having their sexual and emotional resources pillaged by these Vikings of the bedroom.

However, you must be careful. The Rams get bored easily and once you've lost your novelty value, you run the risk of being discarded like a used con. . .tact lens.

What Aries wants from a relationship

You might expect Rams to want submissive partners, who enjoy being kicked around. While it's true that Aries people are good at putting the boot in, you should appreciate that they hate weakness. They might humour a weak partner for a month or two, but eventually they will yearn for a strong lover, who can stand up to them because, at heart, Rams are looking for a challenge. This means that you must be careful how you handle arguments with your Aries lover. If you want to be respected and appreciated, then make sure that you stand up for what you believe in and that you don't hold back from aggressive behaviour.

Women in particular shouldn't be afraid of telling the Ram to go f— himself; such candour will really turn him on. If you're a man and you want an Aries woman to love and admire you on a permanent basis, then remember to be a REAL man. Be assertive, and let her know that you're the boss. If she starts being argumentative, or tries to claim the moral high ground, make sure that you can shout louder than she can.

How Aries behaves in a relationship

It's up to you how the Aries behaves. If you don't assert yourself and allow Aries to call all the shots, then you'll find that he or she rampages all over you. The Ram will make demands that become increasingly unreasonable and you will soon be driven to the brink of despair and madness.

You might, for example, be told that you look like a haystack. As a result you spend a fortune on a new wardrobe, and visit the most expensive hairdresser in town. Aries will then tell you that you are over-dressed, and that your appearance should be more casual.

Despite all this, it is worth bearing in mind that these people do have a generous streak. When you are most exasperated by your Aries lover, when you feel that you can take absolutely no more, you will be surprised and delighted by an unexpected present or treat. However, don't be totally taken in. If you allow yourself to forgive the Ram's previous excesses, there is no guarantee that he or she won't misbehave in the future.

How Aries shows romantic interest

You'll be pleased to know that it is very easy to tell whether or not Aries is interested in you. Both male and female Rams find complicated courting games tedious. Once you are in their sights, they'll get to the point as quickly as possible.

Aries chat-up lines tend not to be very subtle. Examples include 'I like your body. Let's go to bed' and 'Your place or mine? Or would you prefer it behind the nearest bush?' Sometimes these people don't have the patience to string together coherent chat-up lines. Instead, they put their foot on the sexual accelerator, and ram-raid your unsuspecting body. By the time you know what's happened, it's the morning after. You're completely pulverized, but hopelessly in love.

TAURUS

The Taurus personality

Taurus is a luxury-loving sign that enjoys the good things in life. Good food and good wine are usually very important to these people and they always know where to find the best restaurants in town.

The Bulls insist that their food is made from the best ingredients; they avoid anything which is preprocessed or comes out of a can. Taste alone is often not enough – many Taureans like to feel, touch and caress what they eat. So, if you're in a restaurant and see Bulls eating with their bare hands, don't be surprised. They are being sensual rather than bad mannered.

The concept of beauty is close to every Taurean's heart. The Bulls love beautiful clothes and jewellery; their greatest joy is expensive shopping trips to London, Milan and Paris. This is particularly the case for female Taureans, although the male of the species won't lose too much sleep about spending three thousand pounds on a designer Italian suit.

The Bulls also put a lot of effort into the decoration of their homes. They buy the best wallpaper and the best furniture and, if possible, they stuff their homes with valuable works of art. This love of beauty can become obsessive – many Taureans whose incomes don't stretch to Canaletto or Matisse become international art thieves.

Despite their love of beauty, the Bulls are somewhat unsophisticated. They have a disgustingly crude sense of humour, especially the males, and once they get down to the serious business of enjoying themselves they don't care what other people think. So, if you're at a party and you see someone smashed out of his brains, with a bottle of wine in one hand, a chicken leg in the other and a food-splattered Picasso strapped to his back, you'll know for certain that you're dealing with a Bull.

While we're on the subject of mindless debauchery, it is an interesting fact that all the best orgy organizers in Ancient Rome were Taureans. They knew how to indulge their guests' wildest fantasies and never allowed good taste to spoil a good party.

When it comes to relationships, the Bulls regard beauty as being absolutely essential. They judge potential partners by their appearances and have utter contempt for those that are incapable of looking after their bodies. This attitude may seem rather hypocritical when you consider that many Taureans (almost always male Taureans) are world famous for their sloth and their gluttony, but that's the way it goes. On the plus side, you can regard it as a major compliment if the Bull picks you from among the many delicacies on offer. It means that you are regarded as being stunningly attractive, and well and truly fit to join his or her collection of beautiful objects.

Overall, it is probably true to say that Taureans are fairly straightforward animals. They know what they want out of life and they enjoy having a good time, in beautiful surroundings, with beautiful people. However, very occasionally, you will come across Bulls who have no apparent vices and have absolutely no sense of humour. Watch out! You're almost certainly dealing with a psychopath, whose real vices include religious mania and a fanatical desire to rule the world. Give him an inch, and he'll take a continent.

What Taurus wants from a relationship

Most Taureans have simple tastes. They want a beautiful partner, who will be completely reliable and trustworthy and who will give them plenty of sex and plenty of money. Female Taureans are particularly concerned about their partner's income and career prospects. They know that money does buy happiness and that fur coats and handmade Belgian chocolates don't grow on trees. If you are planning on asking one of these creatures out, make sure that you have available full details of

15

If you are planning on asking a Taurean out, make sure that you have available full details of your personal wealth.

your personal wealth, as well as accounts for the last three years.

Having a rich partner is not quite so important for male Taureans: they are more interested in sex and physical contact. You'll probably find that once the Bull starts dating you, he'll expect 24-hour access to your body. If you find this kind of demand too hard to handle, then it is probably a good idea to get out of the relationship as soon as possible.

How Taurus behaves in a relationship

When it comes to love, Taureans are fairly traditional. Once they commit themselves to a relationship, they see it as a long-term venture; if you're a 'one-night stand' sort of person, you would be advised to avoid these people and choose a less stable sign, such as Aries or Sagittarius.

Taurean lovers are certainly dependable and, if you're meeting one for a date, you can count on his or her punctuality. But you must bear in mind that Taurus, like Cancer, is an extremely possessive and jealous sign. They want to have you all to themselves and they don't like the idea of you having an independent life.

However, unlike Cancerians, Taureans have a gullible streak and will usually believe your lies. This means that you can carry on being unfaithful to your Taurean lover, provided that you have a reasonably good alibi.

How Taurus shows romantic interest

Taureans will spend a lot of time looking at your body. They will be mentally undressing you, in an attempt to get a picture of what you look like in your natural state. So, if you catch them gazing at your bulging biceps or your heaving breasts, then this is a sure sign that they are interested in you, particularly if they are simultaneously drooling at the mouth.

Male Taureans often show their affection by stroking your hair, or by putting a friendly but uninvited hand round your waist. If you don't stop them there and then, they'll quickly start exploring other, more intimate, parts of your body.

Female Taureans are not afraid of making such gestures, but usually they first test the water with a few searching questions, just to make sure that you really are a suitable partner. These questions might include 'How much do you expect to be earning in ten years' time?' and 'Is now a good time to be investing in the property market, or would oil be a better bet?'

GEMINI

The Gemini personality

Gemini is arguably the most intelligent sign of the Zodiac. It is associated with super-fast brains and an ability to solve the most difficult of problems, which means that if you ask a Gemini a question, you will always get a useful and informative reply. So if you're stuck on the North Pole and you're looking for fresh mangoes, find an Eskimo who was born between 21 May and 20 June. He'll take out his mobile phone, make a couple of calls and tell you which trading stations have them in stock. If you can give the Eskimo your credit card number, he'll also arrange for the mangoes to be flown out to you by helicopter.

This underlines the point that Geminis are excellent communicators. They are able to hold their audience's attention with their wit and their versatile intelligence. And those of you who are lucky enough to have a long conversation with a Gemini will almost certainly find the experience orgasmic. Two of the greatest Gemini communicators were John F. Kennedy and Marilyn Monroe. They were able to use the mass media to project their sexuality and to launch themselves as immortal sex symbols.

So far, the picture looks pretty good for Geminis. Perhaps you, the reader, are beginning to suspect that the authors of this book are biased in favour of them. Well, it is true that one of us is a Gemini, so it is possible that a bit of bias has crept in. However, we are honest enough to admit that there are a few flaws in the Gemini personality. For one thing, Geminis are two-faced. They may appear to be warm and friendly as they chat away to you on the phone, but the second they put the receiver down they'll hiss 'bastard' or 'bitch' under their breath. Geminis are also terrible gossips. They love hearing all the dirt about their friends and colleagues, and they get a real kick out of slagging people off behind their backs.

There is a certain tendency for Geminis to regard themselves as superheroes.

Another problem with Geminis is that they tend to live in their heads. The Twins pride themselves on their logic and rationality and often have complete contempt for people who are over-emotional. There is therefore a certain tendency for Geminis to regard themselves as superheroes who are beyond the everyday cares and worries of the rest of humanity.

The truth is somewhat different. The Twins find it very difficult to express real emotion and they secretly know that this is a crippling weakness. They do their best to mask the problem, by avoiding emotionally charged public events such as weddings, football matches and Barry Manilow concerts.

As far as relationships are concerned, they can present a range of problems. The Twins' inability to deal with heavy emotion can make them unexpectedly vulnerable to manipulation and sexual power games, particularly when confronted with intense partners who are at home with their feelings.

However, it should not be forgotten that Gemini can be an insensitive and inconsiderate sign, which can be quite oblivious to other people's emotional needs. So, if you are weak or naive, don't rush into a relationship with a Gemini. Take your time and make sure that you don't take his or her promises too seriously. You should also remember that Geminis are accomplished liars and frequent bigamists.

What Gemini wants from a relationship

Geminis have a narcissistic streak and they quite enjoy looking at their youthful good looks in the mirror. Sometimes, as they look at themselves, they dream of finding a lover who is just as intelligent as they are. On reflection, the Twins realize that this is an impossible dream. After all, they are the most intelligent being in the universe, without any rival.

There are other times when the Twins fantasize about having a relationship with their complete opposite. They dream up, or should we say blow up, a moody Cancerian, with the IQ of an inflatable doll. As a result of this uncertainty, Geminis can come to two possible conclusions. One group of Geminis decide that they don't want any relationship at all and that they'll stick to their own brilliant company. Another group decide to have two lovers at once. One lover will be a moronic hunk of meat, with a vocabulary of three grunts, while the other will be chosen for his or her brain power. Which one are you? Well, you're reading this book, so you must be the one with the brain power.

How Gemini behaves in a relationship

Geminis won't spontaneously buy you flowers, or decide on the spur of the moment to whisk you off to Paris for a weekend of steamy passion – instead, they will carefully think everything through. So if you are lucky enough to receive a bouquet of roses from your Gemini lover, then it is likely that he or she will have spent weeks wondering whether or not it was the right thing to give you. The Twins will have analysed your psychological profile and will have asked their computer to calculate the statistical chances of you being impressed by this apparent act of generosity.

Yes, Geminis can be rather cold and calculating in relationships, but at least they are able to keep their cool. They won't throw tantrums if you either misbehave, or cast your eyes at another man or woman. At the same time, Geminis are always prepared to listen to their partner's point of view. They will even gracefully admit defeat, if you are clever enough to beat them in an argument.

How Gemini shows romantic interest

Geminis are so out of touch with their feelings that, when they fall in love, they are the last ones to know it. And when they do realize that they've fallen in love with someone, they are often too embarrassed to do anything about it.

None the less, there is one sure way to find out whether Geminis are romantically interested in you. Ring them up at four o'clock in the morning and keep the telephone conversation going for as long as possible. If they terminate the call after an hour, it's a sure sign that they're not interested in you. If you're on the phone after two hours, then there is a possibility. If the conversation is still going strong at seven o'clock, then you can be sure that you've got the Twins hooked.

CANCER

The Cancer personality

Crabs are sensitive animals who need to be handled with care and attention. They are affected by your every word and your every movement and if you say or do the wrong thing they will quickly take offence. They will scream and shout at you for a few hours and then fall into a prolonged sulk. If Cancerians are in a position of power, this can be a dangerous time. King Henry VIII, for example, was a Cancerian. When his partners upset him, he had no hesitation in beheading them. So, when you are dealing with a Cancerian, you must tread carefully and avoid taking risks.

However, we don't want to dwell on the vindictive traits of Cancerians. Despite their inability to forgive and forget and their psychopathic obsession with settling old scores, these people have hearts of gold. The Crabs always look after their friends and family and they have a soft spot for those who are worse off than themselves. If you are in trouble and are desperately in need of help, then find a Cancerian. The Crab will patiently listen to your problems, before sorting them all out. Given this altruistic character trait, it is hardly surprising that many Cancerians are priests, nurses and psychotherapists.

Cancerians can also do well in professions that involve the arts. This is because they are extremely imaginative and are able to express their powerful feelings in the form of painting, music and literature. Even if the Crab appears to be an uncouth Philistine, he or she should still be encouraged to paint water colours of the local church and to write sonnets in praise of nature. With patience and practice they will eventually tune into their hidden creativity.

The home is important to every Cancerian. They put large amounts of money and effort into making their homes comfortable and always make sure that nothing threatens their domestic bliss. As a result, the Cancerian home is surrounded by surveillance cameras, razor wire and packs of pit bull terriers. People who visit Cancerians should always make sure that they've got an appointment, otherwise they risk serious injury.

On a slightly different note, the Crabs are good at doing domestic chores, such as washing, cooking and ironing and will often do more than their fair share of the housework so, if you're planning on moving in with one of them, you can rest assured that you won't have to spend all day with your hands in the sink.

If you deal with Cancerians on a regular basis, you will have to get used to their sensitivity and their moods. There are many things which affect the Crab's emotional balance; it is impossible to keep track of them all. However, one thing you can take notice of is the Full Moon, which has a powerful influence on all Cancerians. If your favourite Crab has been quiet and withdrawn in the week preceding a Full Moon, he or she may suddenly become lively and optimistic. Alternatively, the Full Moon may plunge the Cancerian into an unfathomable silence. Given this connection, it is hardly surprising that a recent poll has shown that 65.7 per cent of werewolves were born between 21 June and 22 July.

What Cancer wants from a relationship

Cancerians take relationships very seriously, so watch it! They are not interested in 'open relationships' in which both partners lead different and independent lives and have different friends and interests. No, the Crab wants a partner who can be loved, trusted and, above all, possessed. Once you date a Cancerian, you must start sacrificing many of the freedoms which you had previously taken for granted, like going to the shops on your own and choosing the channel you watch on TV.

If you want to get a really good idea of what your special Cancerian wants from a relationship, then meet and observe his or her family. The male Crab is looking for someone just like his mother. If you cook and behave like she does, then you can't go too far wrong. The female Crab, on the other hand, is looking for a father figure. Watch carefully how her father treats her. If you treat her in the same way, then she'll never let go of you.

How Cancer behaves in a relationship

The Crabs are extremely romantic – in fact, some would say too romantic. Their mushy sentimentality can be overpowering; if you are on the receiving end of it, you may have to reach for the sick-bag. But, like it or not, the Crabs will give their lovers regular demonstrations of their undying affection. They will send hideous, heart-shaped Valentine cards and fly aeroplanes trailing ghastly messages such as, MANDY, MARRY ME ON TUESDAY – KEVIN.

At the same time, the Crabs will not hesitate to take you out to your favourite restaurant, remember your birthday, look after you when you are sick and even wash and iron your underwear. Although this behaviour is impressive, it is important that you are not taken in by it. Cancerians understand romance better than any other sign, and will use romantic gestures as a means of enticing you into their lair. Every time you accept a gift from a Crab, whether it be a pink carnation or a pink Cadillac, you are becoming increasingly indebted. Eventually, the Crab will make an offer you cannot refuse. And then it's a life sentence.

How Cancer shows romantic interest

Crabs decide very quickly whether or not they are interested in you, usually within five seconds of the first meeting. From then on they will do everything they can to seduce you. Once the Crab is after you, it should be obvious, because these creatures find it impossible to hide their feelings. However, if you are one of the less sensitive signs, such as Gemini or

The female Crab pounces on her victim and then drags him by the tie around furniture shops.

Aquarius, you might find it helpful to watch out for a few extra clues.

When a male Crab is on your case, he will trap you in a dark corner and force you to look at photographs of his family. At least half of these photographs will be of his beloved mother. The female Crab is even less subtle. She pounces on her victim and then drags him by the tie around furniture shops. By the end of this shopping trip he will have been forced to buy a three-piece suite and a fitted kitchen, as well as their eventual marital bed.

LEO

The Leo personality

Leos are proud people who have an extremely high opinion of themselves. They believe that they are gifted and beautiful and destined to be rich and famous. Although it is undeniable that many of the Lions are beautiful and talented, it is also true that they expect too much from the world. They tend to think that, whatever they do or do not do, they will inevitably be recognized by a talent scout. Aspiring Leo actors, supermodels and footballers will often spend their summers on the beach, waiting for instant stardom. It goes without saying that fame eludes them; by summer's end, they are left with nothing but a sun-frazzled complexion and a shattered ego.

That's rather a cruel thing to say, but we hope it motivates our Leo readers and encourages them not to take their eventual success for granted.

If Leos are prepared to push themselves, then there is no doubt that they can achieve great things. In the world of entertainment, both Mick Jagger and Madonna are Leos who succeeded through a combination of star quality and sheer hard work. Other Leos find power fascinating and do all in their power to achieve positions of leadership – many Leos end up as presidents and dictators. Examples of famous Leo leaders include Fidel Castro, Benito Mussolini, Napoleon and Bill Clinton. However, there is some doubt as to whether Leos make *good* leaders, unless they've got an ambitious Scorpio partner called Hillary to help them out. They often spend too much time building up their public image and putting up statues of themselves. They forget about the boring details of their countries' economies and, as a result, inflation and unemployment go out of control.

Whatever their faults, the Lions are an uncomplicated group of people and it is usually very easy to get on with them. All you have to do is follow a very simple set of ground

Examples of famous Leo leaders include Fidel Castro, Benito Mussolini, Napoleon and Bill Clinton.

rules. You must always make sure that you agree with them, particularly if you are dealing with a male Lion. If they come up with ideas which are completely insane, and which are a sure recipe for disaster, then you must still be enthusiastic, otherwise you'll be branded as a dangerous troublemaker.

It is also worth flattering the Lions as much as possible. Tell them that they are complete geniuses, have superb bodies and are also amazing lovers. This will make them purr with satisfaction. If you continue with your flattery, Leos will eventually turn over and allow you to tickle their tummies. Another thing to bear in mind about the Lions is that they are incredibly generous animals. They like to shower their friends and lovers with money and gifts; all they want in return is a bit of love and appreciation.

As a result of this character trait, Leos can be very easy to manipulate and are frequently taken to the cleaners by conmen and conwomen. They take other people at face value and will fall for lines such as, 'You're so brilliant, you're so wonderful, you're so generous, you're so gorgeously sexy. Now lend me ten thousand pounds, and I'll love you for ever.' On balance, Leos have to be a little more careful who they trust; in particular, they have to make a greater effort to question other people's motives.

What Leo wants from a relationship

Leos get a special kick out of knowing that there is one person out there who is devoted to them and who will follow them to the ends of the earth just to kiss their feet. However, devotion and slave-like subservience may not be quite enough to win the Leo's heart. Leos are concerned about their public image and want partners who can boost this image. They are unlikely to be interested in you unless you are prepared to be a prestigious fashion accessory whom they can show off to their friends and colleagues. This means that Leos' lovers have to think very carefully about their appearance.

The male Lion will want his woman to look beautiful, but not so beautiful that she outshines him. This shouldn't be too much of a problem, because it is difficult to outshine a Leo. However, if you've got the looks and the physique of Helen of Troy (she was the one whose face launched a thousand ships, remember?) then smudge your lipstick before going out with the Lion, or else damage your figure with a prolonged chocolate binge. When it comes to the Lionesses, they have a physical streak and it may not be enough for their escort to be well dressed. He must have a good body, and be bulging in all the right places.

How Leo behaves in a relationship

There is some difference between the behaviour of male and female Leos. The male Lion is more arrogant than the Lioness and he expects his partner not only to agree with him, but also to obey his every word. However, his roar is louder than his bite and with a bit of skill he can be tamed. This is particularly the case if his woman is strong-minded and enjoys a good argument.

The Lioness is a quieter animal. She doesn't boast so much about her qualities, because she regards them as being self-evident. None the less, she is a prima donna who expects to be admired and to be treated like major royalty. In the early stages of a relationship, don't expect her to lift a finger to keep the thing going. It will be up to her lover to do all the work and to prove that he is genuinely worthy of her attention. A final point about the Lioness's behaviour is that she is slow to anger. However, if her man ignores her, or humiliates her in public, she will never forgive him.

How Leo shows romantic interest

It rather depends on gender. The Lioness doesn't fall in love easily and it is up to the men around her to earn her love. However, if she's allowed you to take her out for a dozen expensive meals, has agreed to go to the Bahamas with you for a fortnight's holiday and has accepted your gift of a penthouse in Manhattan, there's a very good chance that she likes you. Male Leos are less subtle than their female counterparts. If the Lion regards you as being a suitable mate, he will swagger up to you and tell you how lucky you are to be talking to him, then spend the next half-hour telling you about his many achievements. If that doesn't impress you, he'll reel off some staggering statistics about his manhood and his sexual prowess.

VIRGO

The Virgo personality

As every astrologer will tell you, Virgos are obsessed by details. They notice everything and are quick to spot faults in other people's dress and appearance. If you are planning on impressing a Virgo, make sure that you are dressed to perfection and are not wearing odd socks or odd earrings. This may seem an obvious point, but you should also make sure that you and your environment are spotlessly clean, because most Virgos have a horror of dirt. They usually carry around bottles of bleach and disinfectant; and if you offer them a cup of coffee,

If you offer a Virgo a cup of coffee they will first sterilize the cup and then check your kitchen for cockroach infestation.

they will first sterilize the cup and then check your kitchen for cockroach infestation.

Another Virgo obsession is routine. To illustrate this, one Virgo we know claims to always: get up at 7.30 a.m., have two slices of toast and one glass of orange juice for breakfast, be at work at 9.05 a.m., have lunch at 12.30 p.m., leave work at 5.30 p.m., have pasta and pesto sauce for supper at 7.30 p.m., and go to bed at 11.30 p.m. Furthermore, this person finds it impossible to have sex, except between the hours of 10.00 and 11.00 p.m.

If you want to know why Virgos have such obsessive personalities, then you have to look at their early childhoods. You will invariably find that they were permanently traumatized by the experience of being toilet-trained. Anyway, that's the bad news about Virgos. On the plus side, they are very intelligent people who are often mistaken for Geminis. However, there is a big difference between the intellectual approaches of the two signs. Geminis know a bit about everything, without concentrating on any one subject. Virgos, on the other hand, are perfectionists who are aware of their limitations. They choose one specific area and become world experts on it. If they don't have knowledge about something, they are quite honest about it.

Virgos can therefore be trusted to give good advice, particularly when it comes to money and health. The Virgo stockbroker will have an in-depth understanding of the market, and the portfolio of shares that he selects for you will perform beyond your wildest expectations. The Virgo doctor will make a real effort to make you better; but, if he has the slightest suspicion that your complaint is outside his area of expertise, he will immediately transfer you to a specialist.

Virgos have a certain reputation for modesty. It is probably true that about two-thirds of them are modest and don't have delusions of grandeur. However the other third are insufferably arrogant. They have utter contempt for the rest of humanity and their favourite pastime is criticizing other people. When these Virgos are in an argument with someone who knows more than they do, they will pour scorn on this person's knowledge. The Virgo might, for example, say, 'Oh, so you're a scientist. I know nothing about science and the revolution has no need for scientists. Send him to the guillotine.' None the less, the caustic humour of this kind of Virgo can be very effective: they make excellent critics and stand-up comedians.

What Virgo wants from a relationship

Virgos are very self-critical. They feel that however hard they work at something it's never quite good enough. We can think of a three-year-old Virgo child, straining away on his potty, desperate to impress his parents. At root, the child is looking for reassurance and acceptance. This need continues into adult life when the Virgos look for reassurance and acceptance from their partners.

Given the obsessiveness of most Virgoans, it might also be expected that they want lovers who are tidy and well-organized people. Well, our research indicates that this is not always the case. Virgos often have relationships with chaotic and disorganized lovers, who have the decorum and poise of walking bomb-craters. The reason for this curious fact is quite clear. By getting involved with messy partners, Virgos are deflecting attention from their own deficiencies.

How Virgo behaves in a relationship

Virgos try hard to be romantic. A fortnight before the first date with a new lover, they will write out a check-list of the things which need to be done like booking the right restaurant, ordering the flowers and chocolates, carefully selecting the champagne and buying tickets to an appallingly over-sentimental Hollywood movie.

Unfortunately, Virgos are so concerned about the details of this first date that they lose sight of their ultimate goal. So, rather than whisper sweet nothings at the end of a wonderful meal, the Virgos spend all night arguing with the waiter about the bill. They had probably gone through the bill with a fine-tooth comb and noticed that they had been charged for one glass of mineral water too many. Despite these shortcomings, Virgos mean well and they should at least be given seven out of ten for trying.

How Virgo shows romantic interest

Virgos worry about whether they are eating the right things; when they get ill, it's panic stations. They also worry about the physical well-being of the people they care about most. So, if a Virgo tells you that you look ill and need to change your diet, it is a sign that he or she is interested in you. When Virgos are really keen on someone, they start giving them life-saving presents like vegan cook-books and gift-wrapped bottles of vitamin pills!

Virgos are petrified of catching diseases and have to be absolutely sure that their sexual partners are contamination free. This obsessive health-consciousness makes it easy to tell when Virgos are carnally interested in you. Just before their lust overwhelms them, they will hand you a twenty-page questionnaire, containing searching questions about every conceivable aspect of your sexual history. One hint – if you answer 'don't know' to question ninety-four, your Virgo lover will immediately dump you.

LIBRA

The Libra personality

Most Librans are civilized people, who do everything in their power to avoid arguments, fights and confrontations. They are careful to phrase their words in such a way as not to cause offence and, if by accident they do upset someone, they are quick to apologize. This character trait has advantages. Librans can be excellent diplomats; if two people are having a fight, it is always a good idea to bring one of them in to mediate.

However, Librans can be a little too diplomatic and have a particular aversion to breaking bad news. So, if you are planning on sinking thousands of pounds into launching your musical career and everyone knows that you have no musical talent and no hope of success, your Libran lover won't tell you. Instead he or she will agree with you that you are a musical prodigy and allow you to make a complete fool of yourself.

Before we go any further, it is worth pointing out that about twenty per cent of Librans are quite untypical of their sign. One example is Margaret Thatcher, the former British Prime Minister. She enjoyed a good fight; when the Argentinians invaded the Falkland Islands in 1982 she appeared impatient of diplomacy and sent the troops in as soon as possible.

Other, less conservative Librans enjoy shocking society and do their very best to attract the attention of the tabloid press. This usually means indulging in animal sacrifice, black magic and assorted acts of unmentionable sexual depravity. However, we must emphasize that these Librans are in the minority. If you lead a normal life and avoid satanists and prostitutes, you will never come across them.

There is no doubt that Librans have excellent social skills and a natural understanding of what makes other people tick. This means that they are good at careers which involve the media and the general public. They make good TV presenters and chat-show hosts and do very well in advertising.

Librans are also brilliant at hosting and organizing parties. They know exactly who to invite and they will ensure that none of the guests feels lonely or left out. Which brings us to the subject of matchmaking: Librans are wonderful matchmakers and have an uncanny knack of tracking down people's dream lovers.

Librans are wonderful matchmakers and they have an uncanny knack of tracking down people's dream lovers.

As we have already suggested, most Librans hate upsetting people. They also hate turning people down, so double-glazing salesmen always get a warm welcome in a Libran home. Librans will listen to what they have to say and tell the salesmen how amazing their products are. However, when it comes to signing on the dotted line, the Librans will somehow manage to fudge the issue. They might, for example, say, 'I'd love to sign the contract. However, my astrologer says that today's an unlucky day. Come back tomorrow.'

Librans who are being pestered by an over-keen admirer suffer from the same indecisiveness. They neither refuse his or her advances, nor give into them. Instead, Librans resort to their usual delaying tactics. They are particularly fond of saying things like 'let's meet up next century' and 'I'm free for sex on 31 February'.

What Libra wants from a relationship

Librans spend a lot of time thinking about relationships and when they are without a partner they feel that there is a great hole in their lives. None the less, Librans are rather unsure about what exactly they want from a relationship. They talk about finding the ultimate partner, who can give them an eternity of passionate love, but in reality they find the idea of being emotionally close to one person abhorrent. This is not surprising, because Librans are fascinated by other people; in a lifetime they want to experience as much variety as possible. Indeed, many Librans are sexual connoisseurs, who travel the world looking for new partners and new heights of orgasmic delight.

So, if you are having a relationship with a Libra, make sure that you regularly change both your personality and your sexual style. If you're up to this challenge, then we wish you the very best of luck.

How Libra behaves in a relationship

Once Librans have decided to commit themselves to someone, their behaviour is usually immaculate. They know what is expected of them; if they really love you, they'll make a real effort not to embarrass you, unless they're one of the dreaded twenty per cent whom we discussed earlier. These Librans will, of course, do everything to upset and humiliate you.

Anyway, assuming you haven't made a terrible error of judgement, you can take your devoted Libran partner anywhere, whether it be for tea with your mother, or for tea with the Queen.

When dealing with Librans, you should be aware that there is a difference between weak and strong Librans. A weak

Libran is very weak and you can do pretty much what you like to him (it's usually a him, not a her) and he'll still forgive you. Strong Librans appear to be sweetness and light on the surface, but as you get to know them better, you will discover that you have ruthless manipulators on your hands. Once you've fallen for them, they'll take you for everything you've got, emotionally, sexually and financially.

How Libra shows romantic interest

This is a difficult question, because Librans show superficial interest in practically everyone. Words like 'I love you for ever' and 'let's get married' roll off their tantalizing and seductive tongues every few minutes; nine hundred and ninety-nine times out of a thousand they are being completely insincere.

Another problem with Librans is that they often share certain character traits with the Whore of Babylon. This means that if they're bored one afternoon, or want a special favour out of you, they'll quite happily sleep with you. From a romantic point of view this sexual act won't mean a thing, and once you've sated the Librans' greed, lust and curiosity, they'll have no further interest in you.

So, how do you tell whether or not a Libran is romantically interested in you? Well, Librans talk a lot; if they're really keen on you, you'll eventually hear about it on the grape-vine.

SCORPIO

The Scorpio personality

Scorpios are heavy-duty people who should never be underestimated. They have strong desires; once they have decided that they want something they invariably get it. The reason why many Scorpios are so successful is that they are able to focus all their energies on one thing, without allowing themselves to be side-tracked by irrelevant details. If, for example, Scorpios want a job, they will make a mental list of all the things which need to be done to achieve their goal: first, find out which person in the target company needs to be contacted; second, find out how many other people are applying for the job; third, find out what the names and addresses of these other people are; fourth, destroy their lives and their reputations; finally, get the job.

However we don't want to imply that Scorpios are always ruthless. They are often great humanitarians, who really care about other people's suffering. Rather than do everything in their power to benefit themselves, they will throw their resources into raising money for charity, or doing voluntary work in their community. Another positive trait of Scorpios is that they hate injustice. When they see someone being unfairly discriminated against, they will personally intervene. Scorpios also get upset when they see animals being mistreated and frequently take direct action – indeed, many Scorpios are hunt saboteurs and anti-vivisection campaigners.

Scorpions are very private creatures. They avoid the brightness of the midday sun and spend as much time as possible chilling out under rocks. Human Scorpios are rather similar. They don't want other people to know about their private lives and are just as careful to conceal their positive characteristics as their negative ones. Scorpios are therefore not prepared to discuss either the millions they donate to charity, or the millions they spend fuelling their crack habit. They also keep quiet about their spirituality. On the surface they may not seem particularly spiritual people, but underneath they have a profound faith in God and an unshakeable belief in the eternal salvation of the human soul.

When it comes to forgiving, Scorpios are more easygoing than Taureans and Cancerians. A person who hurts them a couple of times will be forgiven. After all, mistakes do happen and people do make occasional errors of judgement. However, when dealing with Scorpios, you are advised not to push your luck. After the fourth or fifth insult or snub, Scorpios snap and from then on you're an enemy for life; at every available opportunity, the Scorpio will then try to get back at you. Occasionally this revenge will be direct – for example, getting a dozen puff adders stuffed through your letterbox. But usually it will be more subtle. The Scorpios will use their influence to insure that your life goes absolutely nowhere. So, if you have been applying for the same promotion for the last twenty consecutive years, it's a good bet that the Scorpio you upset in the late 1960s is sleeping with the personnel officer.

However, Scorpios are even-handed. If you do them a favour, they will always return the favour, measure for measure.

What Scorpio wants from a relationship

The Scorpios are a group of extremely passionate animals who take relationships very seriously. They are uninterested in casual flings and are unimpressed with the idea that a partner can be a 'friend as much as a lover', who is always available for sympathy and intelligent conversation. If Scorpios want casual sex, they can always buy a sex aid; if they want intelligent conversation, they can always make an obscene phone call to the speaking clock. So you can now see that Scorpios regard relationships as being intense experiences, which go beyond a one-night stand with a vibrator in a telephone booth. They want a relationship which can be so powerful that it enables them to transcend reality in an upward spiral of cosmic passion. This means that Scorpios will see regular and intense sex as being important components of any relationship. However, it is not the only thing they require.

At heart, Scorpios know that they are emotional time bombs, waiting to explode. They are therefore looking for a partner strong enough and stable enough to contain the blast. You should not get involved with Scorpios unless you are very sane and very down to earth. You should also remember that once the Scorpios choose you, these vampires of the zodiac want to control your mind, your body and your soul. If you are unable to stand up to them, they will suck you dry.

How Scorpio behaves in a relationship

Scorpios are control freaks who get turned on by controlling and anticipating the movements of their friends, colleagues and lovers. They also have pronounced psychic powers, which enable them to lock into people's thoughts and feelings.

When it comes to relationships, Scorpio's strategy has two stages. The first happens before the relationship starts. The Scorpios observe their targets from a distance, so as to build up a detailed psychological profile. It is at this stage that

The Scorpio observes her target from a distance.

Scorpios get an idea of what a person's soft spot is. In the second stage, when the relationship starts in earnest, Scorpios act quickly to gain the upper hand. They repeatedly sting their target with a powerful emotional poison, for which there is no known antidote.

How Scorpio shows romantic interest

The Scorpios are subtle creatures and, at first, it is not easy to tell whether they are interested in you. However, if you are in their firing line, you can be sure that an enormous amount of emotional and telepathic energy will be focused on you. As a result, the first hint can be a particularly vivid dream. You might, for example, wake up in a cold sweat one night, having just dreamt that you are being chased by a frighteningly attractive monster, with sexy horns and an exciting tail.

Sometimes Scorpios will be more direct. Like when they ask you to meet them for a picnic, at midnight, in the blood bank of the local hospital. In case you want to know, Count Dracula was born on 31 October, which makes him a Scorpio.

SAGITTARIUS

The Sagittarius personality

Sagittarians are exciting and dynamic people who are full of energy and enthusiasm. They enjoy life and really know how to have a good time. If you are having a party, make sure that you invite as many Sagittarians as possible. They will make sure that the party never sags and that everyone is kept amused. However, you shouldn't be surprised if your Sagittarian guests go over the top. These people have an over-the-top sense of humour and very little taste or sophistication. Sagittarians' idea of a hysterically funny joke is lacing everyone's drinks with fast-acting laxatives and then super-gluing the lock on the lavatory door.

Freedom and space are very important to every Sagittarian because they want to be able to do what they want, when they want. They do best at jobs that involve travelling, so good choices of career for Sagittarians include mountaineer, explorer and mercenary. At the same time, many of them have a love of animals, particularly those Sagittarians born after 5 December. The reason for this is that the symbol for Sagittarius is a centaur who is half man and half horse. The front half represents the human side and the back half the animal. If you date a Sagittarian who was born after 5 December and he or she also keeps animals (particularly dogs and horses), then make sure that these animals are got rid of, otherwise you may not be able to count on your Sagittarian lover's undivided attention and loyalty.

One of the greatest strengths and greatest weaknesses of Sagittarians is their complete honesty. They find it very difficult to tell lies; if you ask them a straight question, you'll invariably get a straight answer. If you proposition a Sagittarian, you won't be fobbed off with a 'maybe' or a 'perhaps'. You will be given a clear 'yes' or a clear 'let me introduce you to my six foot six boyfriend, who's just been made heavyweight boxing champion of the world'.

However, there is a fine line between honesty and tactlessness, which Sagittarians frequently cross. They seem to believe that the truth is more important than other people's feelings and they have a nasty habit of finding each sign's Achilles heel. Sagittarians will therefore tell Leos that they are not only useless in bed, but that they're also physically repugnant. Geminis will be told that they're boring, while Taureans will be told that they're fat pigs who eat too much.

Another problem with Sagittarians is that they are terrible gossips who find it extremely difficult to keep a secret. You must, therefore, be very careful about confiding to a Sagittarian – you might well be confiding to the whole world. You might, for example, open your Sunday paper one day and find that your favourite Sagittarian has written an in-depth story about all the sordid details of your private life, with photographs included.

He or she will be quite open about this breach of confidence and will say something like 'I thought you wouldn't mind' or 'does anyone really care what you look like in bondage gear, particularly at your age?'

What Sagittarius wants from a relationship

Sagittarius wants an easy-going partner who is spontaneous and who will give up home and career for the sake of an impossible dream. To illustrate this, one Cancerian we know got home one evening from her job in a bank, to be told by her Sagittarian husband that they were flying to Greece the next morning to start up a goat farm. She carried on banking, he went to Greece and they divorced.

If you are planning a long-term relationship with a Sagittarian, then you need patience and understanding as well as spontaneity, because Sagittarians occasionally fall into dark depressions, during which they need someone to hold their hand and keep them amused with dirty jokes. Fortunately, these depressions seldom last for very long. The moment they are invited to the next non-stop, extra-fun, super-fabulous party, they soon cheer up.

How Sagittarius behaves in a relationship

This section of the book had to be rewritten, because our editor is a Sagittarian. He thought that our original description of Sagittarians' behaviour in relationships was 'dreadful'. Well, we can reassure you that most Sagittarians behave very well in relationships. They are kind and considerate, they always look after you when you are ill and their wonderful sense of humour will ensure that you never have a dull moment.

"Ello, darling, look at my Sagittarian beer gut.'

Another point about Sagittarians is that they will always let you know where you stand with them. If they regard you as a bit of fluff on the side for whom they'll never leave their husband or wife, then they'll be honest with you. However, if you are the one and only love of their lives, then their romantic spontaneity will speak louder than words.

The only real problem with Sagittarians' behaviour is that it can be a bit unpredictable, particularly at the beginning of a relationship. They are quite capable of turning up on your doorstep uninvited because they're bored and want instant amusement. When you're dating Sagittarians, expect such interruptions, and always make sure that you're well stocked with fireworks, blue videos and fancy dress costumes.

How Sagittarius shows romantic interest

Sagittarians who are interested in you not only tell you, but they also describe in intricate detail what they want to do to you. The reason they do this is because they are honest people who say what they feel. This is particularly the case with male Sagittarians. The female of the species is a fraction more restrained.

When Sagittarians are on holiday in hot climates, their chat-up lines become gross, unsophisticated and unprintable; if you're going away this summer, avoid them at all costs. English Sagittarians are the worst, especially when England has just gone down 7–0 to the San Marino 'B' team. They drown their sorrows with 20 pints of lager and then expect ''ello, darling, look at my beer gut' to be enough to get you into bed with them.

CAPRICORN

The Capricorn personality

The Goats are reserved animals, who keep themselves to themselves. They have very few friends and will go to great pains to avoid public attention. The reason for this approach to life probably has something to do with trust. Capricorns find it difficult to trust other people and if you try to befriend them they start questioning your motives. They might think that you're after money, a promotion, or perhaps sex. So if you want to get close to Capricorns, keep your distance, and give them time to get to know you.

It is a common mistake to underestimate Capricorns. They seem to be rather unspectacular people who are unlikely to ever set the world on fire. However, beneath their modest exterior, the Goats are extraordinarily ambitious. They want to be fantastically successful in their career and they are also looking for considerable amounts of power and status. They are patient animals and are prepared to work hard over a period of years to achieve their goals. To get a picture of the Capricorn personality, think of a slow, but sure-footed, mountain goat, who eventually reaches the summit of the mountain. Other animals can climb up the mountain faster, but in their haste they lose their grip and fall to their deaths.

If you have ever played around with tarot cards, you will probably know that the tarot card associated with the sign Capricorn is The Devil. This is not surprising, because the Devil is always depicted in horror films as having a goat's head. The Devil represents an obsession with material wealth and power, at the expense of spiritual growth. It is the idea that short-term material pleasure is what life is all about and that one shouldn't worry about things like God, the soul and an afterlife – because there's no guarantee that any of them exist.

Although we are not suggesting that all Capricorns are godless hedonists, some Capricorns are overly concerned with material success. They don't have any higher reason for making money, like feeding the starving or restoring the tower on the local church. Instead they just do it for the sake of it. When you ask them about their spiritual needs, they just shrug their shoulders and ask a waiting servant to fetch a piece of nubile young flesh from their personal harem.

Capricorns are often compared to good wine. If you drink them while they're still young, you may be disappointed and feel that they lack that certain *je ne sais quoi*. Only when Capricorns grow older do they acquire a rich and rounded flavour; indeed, as they age they often become more daring and more adventurous. In their early years they are cautious and conservative and find it difficult to let go. It is only when they reach middle age that they loosen up and develop the capacity to have a really good time.

From the point of view of career, Capricorns are seldom successful in their early years and may not come into their own until their late thirties and early forties. On a purely physical level, Capricorns are extremely fortunate. They have a natural beauty (in particular the women), which ages well and which doesn't have to be supplemented with cosmetics, face-lifts or liposuction.

What Capricorn wants from a relationship

Capricorns are materialistic and want relationships which can improve their finances and their status. This is particularly the case with female Capricorns, who regard love and money as being intimately connected. To illustrate this attitude: one Capricorn we know was talking about her love for her boyfriend. She seemed touchingly sincere as she talked about her plans for future romantic bliss. However, when asked whether she would love him if he had no money, she looked confused. When the question was repeated, she said 'no', because his wealth was an essential part of his personality.

Male Capricorns often have a very low opinion of themselves. They feel that they are rotten to the core and are not worthy members of the human race. You can just imagine how Stalin (who was a Capricorn) felt as he signed a hundred death warrants over breakfast. To get over their guilt, male Capricorns seek out partners who can reassure them that, despite their crimes against humanity, they are still lovable, kind and considerate people with hearts of gold.

How Capricorn behaves in a relationship

Capricorns don't rush into relationships. They take their time and double-check to make sure that their calculations are correct. Female Goats have to be absolutely sure that they know how much their lover is worth, while male Goats need guarantees that they won't be rejected.

Once Capricorns enter relationships, they take things one step at a time. They first have to get to know their partners. At this stage the Goats won't show much passion and they may even appear disinterested. However, once Capricorns have slept with you a few times and got used to the kinks and curves of your body, you will notice a change. They will lose their early reserve and start living up to their reputation of being one of the most sex-charged animals of the Zodiac. This is particularly the case with male Capricorns. After all, in many ancient cultures the goat was a symbol of fertility, virility and primal lust.

How Capricorn shows romantic interest

Many Capricorns dislike spending money, so if they are prepared to splash out on you, it is a sure sign of their romantic interest.

However, you must bear in mind that the Goats want a return on their investment. So if they buy you an expensive piece of jewellery, it is never enough to give them a kiss and say thank you. You will have to do something very special for them in return.

A few Capricorns will show their interest by asking for business advice. They might, for example, ask you whether they should close down the ship-building arm of their multi-national corporation, with a saving of eight hundred million dollars and a loss of fifteen thousand jobs. While they won't listen to your advice, you can at least take their question as a hint that one day they might half trust you.

AQUARIUS

The Aquarius personality

Aquarians are very independent-minded. They have a unique way of looking at the world and are not easily swayed by other people's opinions so, if you are a politician, don't waste

If a Capricorn buys you an expensive piece of jewellery, he will want a return on his investment . . .

time trying to persuade Aquarians that your party has all the answers. This is because Aquarians invariably make their minds up in their own way, at their own pace; and once they have come to a decision, they stick to it, come hell or high water.

When making decisions, the Water-carriers tend to be objective and, wherever possible, they avoid emotional considerations. This means that Aquarians often have the strength of character to walk out on partners who they are passionately in love with. They will have analysed the relationship and realized that it was not only too loving, but that it was also cramping their style and their creativity.

When talking to Aquarians, you may be amazed how tolerant and accepting they are. They will listen to what you have to say and they may even agree with you, even if you are talking out of your oesophagus. However, it is important to appreciate that the Water-carriers are by nature friendly and curious and like to hear other people's opinions – even if these opinions are offensive rubbish. When Aquarians nod their heads in agreement at your wild statements and assertions, they are just being polite. Privately, they probably think you're a complete moron.

Astrology books are often very enthusiastic about Aquarians who, they say, are idealistic and want to do something to help humanity. Well, Genghis Khan and Pol Pot may have been idealists who wanted to help humanity, but this didn't prevent them from killing millions of people. It should also be borne in mind that Aquarius is a sign which is strongly associated with communism and fascism and that many totalitarian governments come to power between 20 January and 18 February. Under these circumstances, it is not surprising that many Aquarians are total fanatics who believe that they have the answers to all the world's problems.

Aquarians who are clever fanatics get involved in politics and run ruthlessly efficient police states. Those who are less clever may decide that the only way to change society is to blow it up; as a result, they become terrorists. These Aquarians have some early successes, fuelled by their sign's natural flair for making bombs and handling automatic weapons. However, the security forces always catch up with them – usually because their Sagittarian comrades can't keep their mouths shut in public places.

Whatever their faults, Aquarians do very well in the astrological beauty contest. They are often very attractive, being almost as stunning as Capricorns. From a physical point of view, Aquarians have an excellent bone structure and sparklingly beautiful eyes. When it comes to behaviour, their cool rationality can be quite irresistible. Aquarians will talk away about Tantric Buddhism or the latest political crisis in the Balkans, without being aware of the devastating effect being wrought by their icy sexuality. The Water-carriers are then shocked and confused when they are propositioned by six different people in the space of ten seconds.

What Aquarius wants from a relationship

Aquarians regard friendship as being just as important as love. As a result they often have long friendships with their eventual partners before there is any sign of romance. Once a romance does start, Aquarians tread carefully and are always on their guard. If things get too hot and there is a danger of an emotional meltdown, they will act quickly to diffuse the situation.

At the same time, Aquarians don't want relationships which in any way restrict their freedom, so don't ever think that you can possess or control these people. In fact, the moment you tell an Aquarian to give up his or her private space programme and to get a pension plan and a proper job instead, you'll find yourself blasted off on a one-way ticket to Mars. Also bear in mind that, although Aquarians appear modest and unassuming, they actually have a burning need for praise and attention. They will be particularly gratified if you tell them that the booster rocket on their spaceship looks and feels fantastic.

How Aquarius behaves in a relationship

Aquarians are slow to express their feelings, particularly at the beginning of a relationship. They avoid being over-sentimental and will do their best to hide their real feelings so, if you're in a relationship with one of these people, don't expect extravagant displays of romantic love. Aquarians do have feelings, though, which they would like to share with their partner. Once they have found someone special, who they can really trust, these feelings will slowly come to the surface.

One small thing you might like to remember when dating Aquarians is that they find it difficult to show lasting interest

Aquarians find it difficult to show lasting interest in other people's creative and cultural life.

in other people's creative and cultural life. So if their partner is a ballet buff, the Water-carriers might go to the ballet once, just to show how open-minded they are. They will then say that ballet is utterly boring, and of no use to humanity.

How Aquarians show romantic interest

As we have already said, Aquarians usually find romance by means of a friendship. They find someone they can talk to and whose intelligence they respect. When love does eventually blossom, it is almost a side-product of the friendship. So, if an Aquarian finds you interesting and starts cultivating a friendship with you, it is possible that he or she is romantically interested in you. However, you must appreciate that Aquarians have many friends, the vast majority of whom they don't sleep with. So don't get too excited if a handsome Aquarian sidles up to you at a party and asks you leading questions about life, love and the universe.

Still, the Water-carriers do occasionally give clues away. If they take you home and show you the secret plans for their latest invention, then you know that you're on the right tracks. They might also be interested in you if they address you as 'Comrade', and ask you to join the revolution.

PISCES

The Pisces personality

Pisceans are often compared with pieces of drift-wood, floating in the middle of the Pacific Ocean. They have no motivation of their own and instead go where the current takes them. Occasionally Pisceans get washed up on dry land, but this is by accident rather than design. None the less, these people are survivors and, however waterlogged their lives get, they never entirely sink. No one quite knows the reason for this. Perhaps Pisceans have particularly sympathetic guardian angels, who are always there to lend a celestial hand when things get difficult. Alternatively, Pisceans may have a sixth sense, which alerts them to hidden dangers, such as Scorpios, icebergs and Aquarian terrorists.

Whether or not the Fish have psychic powers, they certainly have an uncanny knack for being in the right place at the right time. They are able to spot new crazes and fashions years before anyone else and, as a result, are often very successful entrepreneurs; so don't laugh when you see Pisceans standing on a street corner selling green, plastic, pulsating armadillos for fifty pounds each. However, if you also hear these Pisceans claim that their armadillos can recite the complete works of Jackie Collins backwards, be on your guard. The Fish are

Don't laugh when you see Pisceans standing on the street corner selling green, plastic, pulsating armadillos.

notorious liars who aren't afraid of twisting the truth in order to make a quick buck.

It has been suggested that there are two kinds of Fish. One type are ruthless operators who use their slippery intuition to hack into other people's vulnerabilities. These sharks have no compassion and regard everyone as fair game. They often become criminals or telephone salespeople. The latter will ring you up and tell you that there have been ten burglaries in your road over the last week (all committed by his or her brother-in-law, who also happens to be a Pisces) and that, if you don't buy an expensive security system, your home will be next.

The other type of Pisces is very different. They are completely unmaterialistic and often spend a lot of time helping other people. With a bit of practice, they may even find that they have healing abilities and that they can do very well as faith healers, reflexologists and aromatherapists.

Like Scorpios, Pisceans are very spiritual. They pick up all kinds of weird vibrations, which convince them that super-natural forces exist. As a result, the Fish are interested in paranormal phenomena and have a strong belief in ghosts, UFOs and astrology. But some Pisceans are too credulous and accept everything that they're told at face value. If you stop them on the street and tell them that you're Jesus and that the twelve people waiting for a bus across the road are all your disciples, they'll believe you. In fact, they'll go so far as to take out a copy of the New Testament, and ask you to sign it.

On a more serious note, the Fish have to be careful that their gullibility in spiritual matters doesn't get the better of them. They are suckers for cults and fringe religions and are easily taken in by lines such as 'we're having an informal prayer meeting on Tuesday evening and we'd really like you to come along'. The Piscean says yes and by Wednesday morning he is a happy convert, with the brain-power of a lobotomized pumpkin.

What Pisces wants from a relationship

Most Pisceans feel a great need to be in a relationship. They realize that their lives lack grounding and they see relation-ships as being a means by which they can find lasting stabil-ity. Indeed, Pisceans often fantasize about finding a strong and domineering partner, who will force them to stay in one place. Our lengthy researches actually indicate that a high proportion of the Fish want to be physically restrained by their partners. We'll tell you more about these findings later in the book.

It is also important to appreciate that the Fish are emotional animals and once they are in a relationship they want to express the full power of their feelings. Sex and passion are, therefore, going to be important and they will expect their partners to be sexually and emotionally uninhibited.

How Pisces behaves in a relationship

Pisces is the most unreliable sign of the Zodiac. They find it difficult to turn up to meetings on time and very often don't turn up at all. One reason for this is that the Fish are easily sidetracked. They might pass a cinema on the way to see you and decide to pop in and watch a film. Or they might stop off at a bar for a couple of drinks and after an hour find that they're too drunk to move. If and when they do show up for a meeting, their speech slurred and their breath reeking of alcohol, Pisceans will be full of good excuses. They might say, for example, that they had fallen asleep in a traffic jam and that by the time they had woken up they'd driven halfway from Paris to the Moon. Whatever excuses Pisceans do come up with, you can be fairly sure that they're either lying, or grossly distorting the truth.

Now for a bit of good news about Pisceans. If you, the reader, are a thoroughly unpleasant person, then you'll find that Pisceans are unusually tolerant people. They won't mind about your disgusting habits, and if you're really lucky, they'll even join in.

How Pisceans show romantic interest

Male and female Pisceans differ in the way they show affection. Males find it difficult to hide their feelings. If one of them is interested in you, you'll quickly notice his hands wandering and his mouth slobbering. The female is more discreet. She knows she's highly desirable and that in relationships she doesn't have to make much of an effort. If you want to get any clues out of her, you'll have to pay careful attention to her body language. If she copies your every movement, such as crossing her legs when you cross yours, or picking her nose when you pick yours, then it is likely that she is falling in love with you.

Another way of finding out how keen Pisceans (of both sex) are on you is to observe their punctuality. If, miracle of miracles, they turn up five minutes early for a dinner date, then this is a sure sign that they're crazy about you.

Chapter Three
....

ASSESSING YOUR DREAM LOVER'S ROMANTIC AND SEXUAL COMPATIBILITY

INTRODUCTION

Over the years we have done an enormous amount of research on the question of romantic and sexual compatibility. We have persuaded people to tell us about their love lives, often in explicit detail. It wasn't long before we started getting a clear picture: some pairs of Sun signs are more compatible than others. For example, Aries and Leo are a more compatible pair than Aries and Scorpio.

We also found that there are differences in the way the twelve signs express their sexuality. If we take the example of Gemini, we find that seven out of ten Geminis believe that group sex would improve their love life. However, signs such as Taurus, Cancer and Scorpio are far more conventional in their sexual tastes and in most cases they would be horrified if their partner organized a husband- or wife-swapping party.

Sexual compatibility really is important and is something that you should think very carefully about before you make lasting romantic commitments. However, it's not the end of the world if you can't find someone who is astrologically compatible. It is indeed possible for two people who have completely incompatible Sun signs to have a sexually fulfilling relationship. In the same way, two people who have well-matched Sun signs can have an absolutely catastrophic relationship. However, it is more likely that you and your lover will get on and have good sex if you are astrologically compatible.

To give you an idea of the questions that people ask about astrological compatibility, we enclose the following letter from a girl called Anne.

Dear Barbara and Archie,

I loved your book *Life, Love and Destiny*. It was really fabulous. However, I have a problem with my love life, which I wonder if you could help me with. I'm really crazy about my new boyfriend, Dave. He is an Aries, six foot three, and a swimming instructor. I'm a Scorpio.

I know there can be problems between Aries and Scorpio, but so far things haven't been too bad, except for the time when I found him talking to another woman in a restaurant. That time I forgave him but next time I don't know what I'll do. Anyway, what I really want to know is whether or not we are compatible and whether we can have a long-term relationship.

Thank you,
Anne G.

If Anne was reading this chapter and wanted to find out about her compatibility with Dave, she would simply look up our description of the Aries–Scorpio relationship. As you can see, our description of Aries–Scorpio is on page 63.

Anne's relationship with Dave will have its up and downs. From a sexual point of view, the combination between Aries and Scorpio is extremely exciting, although a considerable amount of rivalry should be expected between them. Anne the Scorpio may feel threatened by Dave the Aries' need to take the initiative and she may attempt to restrain his freedom of action. This was clearly shown by her reaction to Dave talking to another woman. Overall, this is a turbulent relationship and it is probably true that these signs are not very compatible – unless they are only interested in sex.

When we wrote back to Anne we didn't tell her to abandon Dave. Instead we pointed out the areas of tension and told her that if she wanted to keep Dave she would have to be less jealous. Anyway, enough of Anne and Dave.

What about your relationship? Are you and your lover totally compatible with each other? Or are there problem areas which need to be ironed out? If you want to hear our expert opinion on your relationship, then read on.

COMPATIBILITY BETWEEN THE SIGNS

Aries – Aries

These two Rams will steam in quickly with little forethought or restraint. Aries people are after a conquest and, once the battle is won, initial interest could wane. Even so, this is a highly sexual combination and hot fiery passion will keep this affair at boiling point for a few days (or hours). As a solid romantic bet, the odds are poor, but neither party is looking for long-term love.

Aries – Taurus

While Aries is raring for action, Taurus is pondering the financial advantages of the affair. The Rams want to leap into the sack, but the Bulls are slow in coming forward – at least until they are sure that there is something in it for them (and not just sex)! However, the ardour of Aries mixed with the sensuality of Taurus will make for a very sexual relationship.

Aries – Gemini

An unusual coupling, but on the whole, Gemini prefers to talk about sex and could frustrate the Ram to such an extent that

Aries and Aries is a highly sexual combination and hot fiery passion will keep this affair at boiling point.

the affair never gets off the ground. Aries enthusiasm and sexuality will be analysed to death by Gemini, at which point one partner's sex drive withers and confusion reigns supreme. Gemini can be a bit cold and won't respond in bed in the servile way that Aries expects (if they get that far)!

Aries – Cancer

A volatile, but stimulating match. Cancer's sex drive mixed with Aries impulsiveness will take these two on wild sexual adventures. Aries gets very excited by Cancer's unusual manoeuvring in bed and Cancer reacts quickly to Aries initiatives. Such a brilliant sex life will keep things together in the short term, but Aries will eventually become bored with Cancer's hypersensitivity and Cancer will fail to understand why Aries can't commit.

Aries – Leo

A highly emotional relationship that could burn itself out quickly. Although both parties are looking for much the same thing sexually, the danger seems to be of too much hot air and too little substance. Leo expects to be on top (both in bed and out), but Aries won't take Leo's nonsense lying down. Clashes and battles are inevitable but, if one party can compromise just a little, the long-term odds are good.

Aries – Virgo

Virgo's attention to detail and highly critical nature will drive the Ram round the bend. Climactic moments of passion could be ruined by Virgo not wishing to stain the sheets. Aries spontaneity will be severely tested and it's possible that the Ram's confidence and sex drive will take a battering under the sharp Virgo tongue. The Aries idea of heaven is a lot of sex, but Virgo prefers to hoover the bedroom. Not a match made in heaven.

Aries – Libra

A tantalizing but demanding mixture. Libra's erotic desires and Aries lust are a bit too much for either party to handle. This affair will swing up and down in a confusion of passion and hot air. Libra is likely to back out when things get too intense, but Aries will want to keep the momentum going and could end up disappointed.

Aries – Scorpio

Scorpio is filled with desire for Aries and finds it difficult to get a perspective on the situation. Aries people tease deliberately and might, if they are not careful, be the victim of revenge attacks by Scorpio. Wounded pride and anger could result if the affair is not handled more sensitively by Aries. But this is a highly charged combination and both parties will benefit from long, steamy sex sessions.

Aries – Sagittarius

Both parties will meet their match here. Ardour, enthusiasm and abandon are qualities they have in common. Romantically and physically this is a stunning combination. However, if Aries takes the affair too seriously, Sagittarius will get claustrophobic and may start resenting the limitations that Aries seeks to impose. Freedom to experiment with other sex partners may be part of Sagittarius's demands and Aries might have to put up with it.

Aries – Capricorn

This combination of Aries fire and spontaneity, and Capricorn's practicality and stability usually results in a rather cool sort of union. But, on occasion, Capricorns live up to their reputation as a very erotic and tactile sign. In this case, an extremely exciting affair takes off, with both parties fighting uncontrollable desires. With enough understanding and sensitivity, a very serious relationship could emerge out of the flames of passion.

Aries – Aquarius

Sexually this affair could be a non-starter. Aries wants too much too quickly, but Aquarians prefer to analyse the implications of their actions. This annoys Aries, who is likely to go off in search of pastures new. Of course, to Aquarius, this confirms their initial doubts. If they do end up in bed, the broad-minded Aquarian could have a few surprises in store for Aries, who was only expecting a routine sort of night!

Aries – Pisces

A very interesting coupling. Pisces is more into experimentation than Aries could have imagined in their wildest dreams. Ever the master of subtlety, the Fish will weave silent webs around trusting Aries, until the Ram is caught in a deadly trap of sex, sex and more sex. Not that Aries won't enjoy it, but he or she might feel out of control. Together they will enjoy a tempestuous sex life.

Taurus – Taurus

By putting together these two super-physical people, the result will be a hot romance and a scalding sex life. What more could you ask for? Well, the Bulls' degree of sexual interest is evenly matched by their degree of interest in money, stability and security. And each of these Taureans will be looking to the other to fill that financial gap. However, if at least one party can come up with the goods, that will be enough to keep them together forever.

Taurus – Gemini

Whilst Taurus fantasizes about a life filled with sex, money and material things, Gemini fantasizes about writing books, being creative and of being with more than one lover. There is little common ground and it would be a rare Taurus who could stomach a long-term affair with such a person. Gemini too will find the basic needs and desires of the Bull quite distasteful. However, Taurus could teach Gemini a thing or two about making love and Gemini could teach Taurus some restraint.

Taurus – Cancer

A meeting of souls and bodies. Both parties are into touch in a big way. The Crab responds brilliantly to the Bull's sexual demands and need for intimacy. Cancerians will allow Taureans to have their way in bed and will be particularly sensual and supportive lovers. Both will feel nurtured by the affair. The Crabs' touch is spine-tingling and they will find a very appreciative lover in tactile Taurus.

Taurus – Leo

The Lions want to be in supreme control of all aspects of this affair. If they've got plenty of material back-up, Taurus might let them get away with it. Sex will either be magnificent or disastrous. The Bull's desires are very strong, but the Lions won't respond unless they are given the attention and flattery they deserve. Taurus dislikes playing second fiddle and might decide to opt out at the pre-sex stage.

Taurus – Virgo

A very intense and satisfying coupling. Virgo envelops Taurus with warmth and confidence and in this fertile atmosphere the affair will blossom quickly. Bodily needs are perfectly understood and each party will be continually available for sex. These practical earth signs are not into playing mind-games: they prefer sex games. This, above all else, will keep them together for some time.

Taurus – Libra

Libra is a little too sophisticated for Taurus, who has certain requirements that Libra finds revolting. The Bull's sexual athletics don't cut any ice with Libra, who generally prefers the theatre and the arts to a riveting sex life. Taurus is likely to get extremely frustrated by these continual put-downs and may eventually seek out a more basic and down-to-earth partner. However, with compromise and effort, this affair might work.

Taurus – Scorpio

A dynamic attraction of opposites. Very substantial performers in bed, they will go out of their way to totally satisfy each other. Although Scorpios are demanding partners, they won't ask for more than they can give. Taurus sex energies blend perfectly with Scorpio's recklessness and both have extraordinary talents for the sexual act. In the longer term, the Bulls' need for security will be fulfilled, as well as their need for undying love.

Taurus – Sagittarius

The earthy desires of Taurus may not blend well with the Archer's more spiritual quests. Sagittarius tends to find foreplay a bit boring and can occasionally be obsessed by self-gratification. Taurus is likely to be disappointed by all the hot air and inaction. The Bulls will be upset by the great liking that Sagittarius has for new flesh and they could easily end up playing second fiddle in the Archer's sexual orchestra.

Taurus – Capricorn

A very satisfying union. Harmony of movement and total consistency in love will keep these two together for a long time. Both are convincing during sex and know how to make each other feel wanted and needed – things that are vital to these security-minded people. Taureans will give themselves completely to the Goats who will, in turn, exercise astonishing selflessness when dealing with the Bulls' insecurities and vulnerabilities.

The Bulls will be upset by the great liking that Sagittarius has for new flesh.

Taurus – Aquarius

Unsatisfactory physical contact is likely here. Aquarius finds the rather basic nature of the Bull somewhat gross, while the latter cannot understand why Aquarius doesn't want to get closer. These two are chasing different dreams. Aquarius will flirt constantly and enjoy quick sex romps, whereas Taurus is into serious sex and serious relationships. Love doesn't come easily.

Taurus – Pisces

The Bull would be advised to take the Fish with a pinch of salt. Pisces is a notoriously slippery customer. But in the first flush of sexual expression Taureans could easily lose their heads and will believe everything they are told. Pisces finds the Taurean sex appeal to be quite mesmerizing, but once the novelty has worn off, the Fish are at their most fickle and most unpredictable.

Gemini – Gemini

A combination of these two unsteady people could be very exciting. However, Gemini frequently prefers three in a bed, which could make for a very large number once these two get together. Each likes new flesh and can, unfortunately, be mindlessly promiscuous. Sex is used mainly to relieve tension, rather than as a love tool. Even so, they will actually enjoy doing it with each other and long-term prospects are pretty good.

Gemini – Cancer

Gemini's sexual preferences for multiple partners and multiple experiences are likely to send the Crab into a frenzy of jealousy and anxiety. Unless Gemini is particularly moderate and Cancer particularly liberal, this affair could easily end in tears. However, the attraction is intense and physical contact pleasurable. If Cancerians keep their cool and Geminis curb their erratic behaviour, this could be a satisfying, albeit short-term, affair.

Gemini – Leo

Early on in this affair, the Lion will try to get on top and will, initially, find a fairly submissive partner in Gemini. However, as time goes on, Geminis learn how to manipulate the Lions and to cause them considerable insecurity, unless the latter can behave in the sexually reckless way that Geminis hanker after. Leos are, in truth, after a constant and loyal companion who will adore them and nurture them – so, Geminis are not really an ideal choice.

Gemini – Virgo

These two are likely to talk each other out of sex. Although Geminis find Virgos quite magnetic, they could find it difficult to respond to Virgos' needs for security and long-termism. Virgo is insatiable in bed and always wants more, whereas Gemini would prefer to move on to a new experience rather than risk spoiling the fun and getting bored. Virgo will not stand for this and will get rid of Gemini before they can say 'multiple orgasm'.

Gemini – Libra

This combination of two sophisticated and cultured signs is extremely satisfying. There will be so much to do and so much to talk about that sex will be a low priority. Although Geminis cannot help but flirt continuously, they meet their match in Libra, who will find Gemini's antics amusing, rather than threatening. Sex will be unadventurous and foreplay rather boring. Libra has little sense of the flesh, but will compensate for this by an endless stream of witty conversation, both in bed and out.

Gemini – Scorpio

The deep sexual urges of the Scorpion will not be fulfilled by the rather shallow desires of Gemini. Each will find the other quite fascinating, but when it comes to real sexual satisfaction, the affair will be lacking. Gemini can't get to grips with Scorpio's intensity and emotions. Scorpios can't understand why Geminis aren't looking for long-term soul mates and are likely to demand far more than they get. Gemini, on the other hand, could find Scorpio a rather gross and demanding lover.

Gemini – Sagittarius

An exciting attraction of opposites. Although both are into experimentation and wayward sexual activity, the Archer prefers one lover at a time. Even so, Geminis find Sagittarians to be adventurous and unpredictable partners, who keep them on tenterhooks much of the time. Neither is consistent in love and neither will give all his or her heart. However, when passion is released, both will experience the height of orgasmic and sensual delight.

Gemini – Capricorn

The passionate, earthy desires of the flesh-loving Goat could prove overwhelming for Gemini, who always hopes for an uncomplicated, light-hearted affair. Geminis are into self-gratification and, luckily, Capricorns give themselves completely. However, the Goats will expect something in return. If heavy sex isn't available, the least they'll expect is a long-term promise of security, or material comfort.

Gemini – Aquarius

On the face of it a pretty good match. Both Gemini and Aquarius are very free and open in their sexual expression and feel the need to get close to each other. Gemini will appreciate Aquarius's need for space and will, in turn, be granted as much freedom as he needs. This will foster good relations: if Geminis don't feel trapped, they are more likely to settle down and stick to one partner. They make each other feel wanted, but sex could be unexciting.

Gemini – Pisces

Two devious people together will either be tremendously exciting and unnerving, or totally boring and predictable. Whereas Gemini doesn't always understand the flesh, Pisces is a master of bodily matters and has a tendency to be sexually overactive. Pisceans believe themselves to be indispensable and could get a nasty shock when Gemini adopts a sexual policy of take it or leave it. Not a brilliant sexual partnership.

Cancer – Cancer

A very convincing sex coupling. Both understand the other's need for a lot of intimacy, closeness and intense sexual activity. Together they will explore every sexual angle and position available to mankind. The only drawback could be a tendency to get locked into this relationship to the exclusion of everything else. Lack of positive thinking could also be a problem, but on the whole these two watery creatures have the potential to go far.

Cancer – Leo

The Lion's need for adulation and nurturing will be met fully by the sensitive, selfless Crab. And the loyalty and consistency demanded by the Crab will be offered unreservedly by the Lion. Sexually, this could be an excellent match. Physical contact will be spine-tingling and it's possible that each will meet their sexual equal in the other. The Lion might appear to be a softie, but not in bed. Although some work is needed on a practical level, there is a lot going for these two.

Cancer – Virgo

Under pressure from the Crab, Virgo might be a little dishonest. Cancer's demands for absolute faithfulness could annoy

Virgo intensely. It's not that Virgo isn't into the same things as Cancer, but that he dislikes being reminded of his duty to the relationship. Duty is a big word here and could even crop up in bed. Even so, the sensuality of Virgo combined with the sexual prowess of the Crab is overwhelming and will be the biggest factor keeping these two together.

Cancer – Libra

The eroticism and sensuality of the Crab is largely wasted on Libra, who is more interested in going to a theatre or art gallery. As much as Cancer wants to get close, Libra feels a sense of being crowded and will pull away. Sex could be great, mainly because Cancer is highly motivated and skilful, but it may take some time to convince Libra just how good it can be. Overall, this could be a rewarding relationship, but it will take time.

Cancer – Scorpio

A fabulous match in every way. Both parties need a loyal, faithful and devoted partner who will not let them down. Both require absolute emotional security and will find it in each other. In bed, there is much fascinating territory to explore. Physical contact is mutually fulfilling and will get better and better as time passes. The Scorpions might annoy the Crabs with their independence and stubbornness, but will never ever betray them.

Cancer – Sagittarius

Not an easy match, but there is loads of potential for growth and intimacy. As long as Cancer can give Sagittarians the freedom they require and as long as Cancer doesn't feel threatened by the Archer's long absences, then there is definitely something to build on. The fiery unpredictability of Sagittarius combined with the intensity and passion of Cancer makes for a tantalising sexual recipe. The Crab will be an expert teacher and Sagittarius a receptive student!

Cancer – Capricorn

Two security-minded individuals together could be a bit boring. The Goat is primarily after material security, whilst the Crab hankers after emotional security. Even so, each understands the other's needs and will do their utmost to fulfil them. This applies in both practical and physical ways. Desires are strong and bodily contact is exciting – together they will make a very earthy, sensual couple.

Cancer – Aquarius

The more tightly the Crabs hang on to the Water Carriers, the more likely they are to lose them. Cancer will try desperately to make Aquarius feel loved and nurtured, when all the latter wants is to have unlimited space in which to explore new possibilities! In some ways Aquarius is astonishingly selfish, both in bed and out, whereas the Crab is too willing and too giving. In retrospect, Aquarians may realize that they have undervalued the Crab, but by then it may be too late.

Cancer – Pisces

A deep emotional relationship results from the combination of these two intense people. Sexually there will be no problems, since both understand the flesh entirely and feel at their most comfortable actually doing it. Pisces will tend to be the submissive partner, whilst the Crab will want to wield influence. However, the Crab should watch the Fish carefully, because he is a notoriously slippery customer, especially when it comes to long-term promises.

Leo – Leo

A match made in either heaven or hell! It depends, largely, on whether one Lion could relinquish a certain amount of control, back down and be a bit submissive. Brilliant sex could then result. If not, body contact could be violent, unsatisfactory and exhausting. On a brighter note, however, this combination brings out latent talents and skills, which can be put to very productive use, both in and out of bed.

Leo – Virgo

Whilst Virgo is nibbling the Lion's ear and not allowing physical contact to go too far, the Lion will want to bite Virgo's head off in frustration. Leos expect Virgos to be honoured by their sexual attention and find it humiliating in the extreme when they have to put their ardour on hold. In some cases, however, Virgo will act in the servile way that is expected, in which case the Lion will shower Virgo with gifts, grand gestures and big promises.

Leo – Libra

The Lions' desire for centre stage and their need for continual attention does not endear them to the Libran, whose needs tend to be quite different. Throwing Librans on to the bed passionately or grabbing their private parts is a total turn-off and the Lion must learn some restraint and some respect. Much as the Lions would like some heavy sex, they are unlikely to get it. Librans need to be treated nicely and are usually more at home with less egocentric signs.

Leo – Scorpio

No matter how much the Lions rant and roar, Scorpio will never give in to their orders. Scorpions demand respect and if

No matter how much the Lions rant and roar, Scorpio will never give in to their orders.

Leos don't offer it, then they will terminate the relationship. Stubbornness on both sides is a major stumbling block, but if the Lion can accept Scorpio as an equal, they can both look forward to incredible sex sessions and mutual gratification. Long term, the odds are against them, but it will be a worthwhile experience.

Leo – Sagittarius

Although well suited in superficial ways, at heart Leo prefers a more constant companion. The inconsistency and wanderlust of the Archer will be upsetting and the Lions won't understand why Sagittarius doesn't want to spend every waking moment in their fascinating company. The Archer, however, tires easily of Leo's incessant demands and although sex is pleasant enough, it's all too intense and serious for Sagittarius, who would prefer to go on a long hike.

Leo – Capricorn

Not traditionally a compatible match, but physically this combination has explosive potential. The earthy needs of the Goat can be met fully by the passionate fire of the Lion. It's a rare Capricorn who doesn't feel turned on and ready to submit totally. Because Capricorn is a quiet creature, Leo will be knocked out by the intensity of feeling and passion which the Goat engenders. On a practical level, there will be difficulties, but it's worth a try!

Leo – Aquarius

Aquarius is a talented flirt and cannot be pinned down. The Lion, however, can't bear to be ignored and could get very insecure as the affair progresses. Leos have a highly fertile mind and body, take sex very seriously and cannot wait to consummate their desires. Aquarius, however, is clever at love and can exercise incredible self-control at the pivotal moment. Even so, this is a magnetic combination and has terrific long-term potential.

Leo – Pisces

The devious Fish is too clever by half for the naive, trusting Lion. Pisces is agile and supple in bed and can adopt mind-blowingly absurd sexual positions. The Lion will squeal and squirm with delight at these games, but could in the process overlook the fundamental unreliability of the Fish. On the whole, Leo has strong morals and standards, which are unlikely to be duplicated in Pisces. Long-termism can, therefore, be counted out.

Virgo – Virgo

Uninterrupted sexual activity could result in a premature burn-out for either, or both, of these physical creatures. When it comes to sex, there is little self-control. Each is terrified by the thought that the other could find someone more satisfying and will go to extreme lengths to prove their desirability. Eventually, the first flush of sexual experience will fade and the durability of the affair will depend on overall compatibility (which is good).

Virgo – Libra

Virgo's boldness will initially put the Libran off. But at heart Virgo is a gentle person, who can slowly entice Libra down the path to wilder sexual adventures. However, Libra has a quiet strength which shouldn't be underestimated; if sex on the first night doesn't appeal, then Virgo will have to wait. When Virgo finally gets his way, sex will be an overwhelming experience which both of them will want to repeat and repeat and repeat . . .

Virgo – Scorpio

If Scorpios are interested in Virgo, then there is no stopping them. The Scorpion makes a deadly sexual enemy and Virgo is advised to submit early. After all, sex will be brilliant and Scorpio is an explosive and incredibly exciting lover. Virgo, too, will switch Scorpio on to new ideas and new positions, not to mention new places for doing it. As long as Virgo can stand up to Scorpio, this affair could turn into a long-term commitment.

Virgo – Sagittarius

Virgo is big on commitment and faithfulness, but Sagittarius tends to be big on adventure and multiple experience. However, in some cases the Archer is less fickle and Virgo is more into experimentation, in which case this could be the perfect match. In bed, Virgo will captivate the Archer's interest and it is this special talent which may hold the relationship together.

Virgo – Capricorn

Sexual urges are unrestrained, particularly on the part of Virgo, who hopes against hope that the Goat will fulfil all expectations. Virgo has little to worry about. Capricorn finds the stability and eroticism of Virgo enormously exciting and satisfying. Sex with Virgo is never threatening and the Goat gives in completely to insatiable desires.

Virgo – Aquarius

An unlikely combination, but Virgo has a knack of bringing out the best in the Water-bearer. Aquarius is not really into doing it as much as Virgo, but Virgo's obvious sexuality and mystery will be fascinating. Being one for adventure, Aquarius will find it hard to resist what Virgo has to offer – until, that is, it comes to more practical issues. Living together will be fraught with difficulty, unless Virgo is willing to let go a bit and Aquarius is able to toe the domestic line.

Virgo – Pisces

You might think that the earthiness of Virgo combined with the passion and depth of Pisces would make an ideal combination. And in many ways this is true, especially in the physical area. But fundamentally, they are coming from different places. Virgo needs to feel needed, wanted, nurtured and loved. Pisces also needs emotional security, but finds it impossible not to fish for other talent swimming around. This hurts Virgos, who will ultimately punish Pisceans in the way they deserve.

Libra – Libra

A mental rather than physical union. Cultural pursuits, the arts and extensive travelling are priorities for this sophisticated couple. Sex is low on the list and, although they both enjoy the occasional romp, it's really a matter of take it or leave it. In many ways, therefore, this is an ideal match. Problems could arise, however, when a Gemini or Aquarian sex-scientist floats on to the scene who appears to have just that little bit extra to offer.

Libra – Scorpio

The hot passions and emotions of the Scorpion are unlikely to find a receptive mate in Libra. To Scorpio, it is undying, eternal love that matters above all else, but Libra has more practical and material concerns to deal with. This will leave Scorpio feeling empty and dejected. Libra, in turn, will find the heavy intensity of Scorpio overwhelming. Sexually they will function adequately. But adequate is not a word in Scorpios' vocabulary and they'll soon be replacing Libra with a more responsive lover.

Libra – Sagittarius

The Archers like uninterrupted sex, with as many different partners as can be fitted into a 100-acre field, only when it suits them. Although Libra doesn't feel jealous or threatened by this behaviour, it's in very poor taste and will not do. Sagittarius must at least pretend to be faithful so that friends and acquaintances continue to hold them in high regard. If Sagittarius doesn't flout convention and Libra can learn to mellow out, this combination could work superbly.

Libra – Capricorn

Both have pretty conventional views on love and romance. Capricorn, although very much into sex, understands Libra's reluctance to plunge quickly into intense emotional relationships. However, there comes a point where the Goat wants to get sexual and may not hang around if Libra can't get similarly motivated and steamed up. Libra, however, finds Capricorn's earning abilities and career aspirations more of a turn on than his sexual prowess. Altogether a tricky match.

Libra – Aquarius

A stunning combination. Social events and superficial gloss mean a great deal. With or without sex, both know how to make the other feel wanted. Aquarius won't bore Libra with continual demands for physical contact and Libra respects the Aquarian's need for extensive socializing. Basic sexual drives are similar and they'll do it quietly together with no histrionics or loud noises. Neither sign will give all their heart to lovemaking but in this relationship it doesn't matter.

Libra – Pisces

The fertile Piscean mind is probably too much for straighttalking, honest Libra. With Libra, it's a case of what you see is what you get. With Pisces, it's a case of what you see is never what you get. Sexually, therefore, this could be an erotic and stimulating partnership. Pisceans are supple and lithe and will thrill Libra with their agile movements and devious manner. Sooner or later, however, mutual fascination will turn into mutual distrust, with Pisces (deservedly) taking most of the blame.

Scorpio – Scorpio

A meeting of heart, soul and body. An explosive sex life will hold things together for a reasonable length of time; but the Scorpion is ever distrustful and will pick up on the tiniest of incidents to prove disloyalty or betrayal. One Scorpio is bad enough, but two together could be enough to blow the relationship up in a cloud of jealousy, anger and bitterness. Alternatively, they will both recognize a soul mate and live happily ever after. But it's doubtful.

Scorpio – Sagittarius

Scorpio fantasizes about a lover who will take him away from dull routine and love him forever. Sagittarius will certainly take Scorpio to new and exotic places, but is unlikely to be the consistent lover that Scorpio demands. The Archers will pander to Scorpios' desires in the sack, but only for as long as Scorpio amuses and arouses them. Once the novelty of this sexual creature has worn off, Sagittarius is nowhere in sight and Scorpios are left licking their wounds.

Scorpio – Capricorn

Both are ruthless in the pursuit of their desires, but once they realize that they are both chasing the same dream, the situation rights itself. A mutually beneficial and pleasant relationship then develops. Sexually, these two are on the same wavelength and the affair will be consummated well before the practicalities are ironed out. Long, intimate sessions are what it's all about: Scorpio admires Capricorn's quiet strength. Capricorn, in turn, is intensely turned-on by Scorpio. An excellent match.

Scorpio – Aquarius

A stimulating match, but one in which the course of true love is unlikely to run smoothly. They are both coming from different places: Aquarius finds Scorpio's demands for absolute loyalty quite absurd. Scorpio can scarcely believe that Aquarius isn't turned on by the notion of deep and lasting love. Physical contact could be violent and once Aquarius becomes bored with the intensity of it all, Scorpio will be dispensable.

Scorpio – Pisces

Both of these watery, emotional people take love and romance seriously. Sexual interchange will be idyllic and mutually satisfying. Pisceans are into feet and legs and will calm Scorpio with their skilful massage and sensual moves. Scorpio will prove the dream lover that Pisces always yearned for. The Fish will meet his match in the Scorpion: Pisces deviousness is matched by Scorpio's manipulative abilities and together they will slide from one erotic experience to the next.

Sagittarius – Sagittarius

Restlessness and wanderlust will take this pair to far-away locations and adventurous settings. Together they revel in the exotic and the unusual. Provided there is enough material back-up for their trips, common interest will bind them together. Sex is not a priority and, although they both like the flesh, neither will mind the occasional infidelity or indiscretion. The real threat comes in the form of an equally reckless and impulsive outsider who promises even more in the way of fun and adventure.

Sagittarius – Capricorn

The Archer senses that the Goat is a good material bet and hopes earnestly that there will be plenty of money to fund wild projects and schemes. The Goats, however, have different ideas. Long-term security is important and they are looking for a supportive and loving mate. If they can get the physicalities right, then Capricorn will be far more inclined to submit to the Archer's whims. First, however, Sagittarius must prove his devotion.

Sagittarius – Aquarius

Neither partner is into long-termism or security. This means that they can give the other enough space as is needed to let the relationship blossom and grow. Sex will be brilliant because both partners understand that the experience can be enjoyed for its own sake, without the need for lasting emotional commitments. In this way, the affair is kept at its sparkling best. Over all, love-making is always an enjoyable experience. This relationship has enormous potential.

Sagittarius – Pisces

The honest Archer tends to believe everything that spurts out of the Fish's mouth and the latter is capable of taking Sagittarius for a very long ride indeed. Pisces wants heavy, hot sex. The Archer wants a lot of fun. There is common ground, but it will be hard to find it. Sooner or later Sagittarians realize that Piscean loyalty is a figment of their imagination. They will then have no compunction about indulging their fantasies when and where they choose.

Capricorn – Capricorn

Enormously skilful in bed, physical contact will be at a premium. For once, these two will forget the demands of everyday life and throw themselves headlong into weeks of continual sexual activity. Having emerged into the real world, they are capable of pulling together as a highly efficient and productive team. As time passes, material concerns could overtake them, but on the whole a truly superb match.

Capricorn – Aquarius

An odd couple, but it could work. Aquarian brilliance and intelligence can be used by the ever-practical and resourceful Goat in many lucrative ways, so a solid foundation to the relationship can be laid down early on. Capricorn's strong carnal desire for Aquarius may not be reciprocated initially, but as time passes, they will get closer and closer. Aquarius will be thrilled by the Goat's undoubted talent for sex and Capricorns will finally believe that Aquarians are returning their love.

Capricorn – Pisces

As much as the Fish tries to dupe the Goat, they won't succeed. Capricorn is too shrewd by half to believe the fairy-tales that the Fish spins. Once they have established the reality of their situation, they can get on with the serious business of making love. Both are experts in this field. Physical contact is so good that they'll both be utterly convinced that this time it's for real. And it might well be!

Aquarius – Aquarius

A quiet build-up from mutual regard and friendship into something more intimate will ensure the durability of this affair. Both want a friend first, a lover second – that's precisely what they'll get. Sexual matters tend to be downgraded in favour of social priorities – a good social life will ensure a great sex life, but not vice versa. These two are clever at love, have healthy sex-drives and are perfectly suited.

If the Fish let them down, Aquarians will throw them back into the sea.

Aquarius – Pisces

Pisceans pretend to hold Aquarians in high regard, but in truth are attempting to humour them and get their own way in the process. Aquarians are not the fools that Pisces imagines and will stop the Fish abruptly in their tracks. At heart, Aquarius has high moral standards and, although there will be enormous sexual spark and physical gratification, Aquarians never lose sight of what really matters. If the Fish let them down, Aquarians will throw them back into the sea.

Pisces – Pisces

What a combination! Each is aware of the motivations and intent of the other and it's clear that mind-games are out of the question. Their best bet is to concentrate on the emotional side of the relationship, always being aware that the nebulousness and vagueness of two Fish together could result in much confusion and little action. If they can get a grip and focus on reality, there's a lot to hope for. Sexually, there are few problems and the chances are that they'll get lost in a sea of passion and goodwill.

Chapter Four

HOW TO ENTRAP AND SEDUCE YOUR DREAM LOVER

In Chapter Two we gave you an in-depth description of the twelve signs of the zodiac. We told you all about their personalities and their approach to relationships. As you read about certain signs, you may have felt enchanted and intrigued. Other signs may have had a rather different effect on you. Perhaps you shuddered with revulsion at the very thought of sharing the same planet with them. As we explained in Chapter Three, these differences are often caused by astrological compatibility and incompatibility. So, we would expect a Sagittarian's zany sense of humour to fascinate an Aquarian but to revolt a Virgo.

Anyway, now that you've had a lick and a taste of the twelve signs, you are probably anxious to proceed to the next step: entrapping and seducing your dream lover. It's possible that, before you started reading this book, you already had someone special in mind and that you wanted some extra hints on how to ensnare him or her. This makes things easier, because at least you have a single target, which you can fire all your guns at. On the other hand, you may regard the last two chapters as being a consumer's guide. You flick through, choose the sign whose specification you like the best and then go out and find a lover, any lover, who was born under this sign. This approach is more difficult and rather puts you in the position of a hunter who is traipsing through a romantic jungle, looking for a particular animal.

You're not too sure where to look, but you reason that, if you carry on walking, you'll eventually strike lucky. However, you have to be careful. There is not only a possibility that you will never find your quarry, but there is also a danger that you will be pounced on by cannibals and eaten alive. So, to be on the safe side, you need the services of an expert guide, who can guide you to your prey and show you how to catch it. But have no fear – this chapter will act as your guide and will ensure that you come to no serious harm.

To give you an idea of how this chapter can help you, we print the following letter, which Barbara received a couple of years ago, from a girl called Samantha:

Dear Barbara,

Can you help me? I'm a Pisces (d.o.b. 11 March 1964) and there is a man at work who is a Leo. I've never talked to him, but I feel sure that he's the right man for me. A psychic told me that I would marry a Leo and he fits the description perfectly. He's a really powerful man and I don't know how to attract his attention. What do you think that I should do?

Yours sincerely,

Samantha

Samantha obviously believes that her Leo is the right man for her. She finds him attractive and he fits the description given to her by the psychic. However, first impressions can be deceptive and it may be that she's deluding herself. Perhaps they have nothing in common and if the two of them ever had a relationship, it would be a complete disaster. Matters are certainly not helped by the fact that he's a Leo and she's a Pisces, although there are cases on record of these signs having satisfactory relationships.

If Samantha had had a copy of this book at the time she wrote her letter, she may have gained some valuable insights. She could have turned to Chapter Two and discovered the true nature of the Leo personality, then moved on to Chapter Three and found out about the compatibility between Leos and Pisceans. At this stage, she may have decided that her man wasn't quite as desirable as she had first thought. At the end of the day, however, it is Samantha's decision. If she wants to entrap and seduce her Leo, then we're not going to question her wisdom. Indeed, we'll tell her how to do it and we'll wish her all the best. If things go wrong and she lives to regret entrapping and seducing him, that's not our problem – we take no responsibility for the consequences.

When you entrap and seduce people, it really is important to consider their Sun sign. The Sun sign tells you about the kinds of behaviour which they find attractive and the chat-up lines which turn them on. You may be surprised to know that the way you dress, as well as your colour scheme, can have a crucial impact. Some signs, for example Capricorn, are attracted to people who dress conservatively and who wear dark colours, like black or brown. Other signs, like Sagittarius, prefer bright colours and don't mind if their partners dress in a way which is daring and provocative. However, you won't find your ideal sign just by behaving, dressing and talking in the right way. This is because different signs hang out in different places. Virgos, for example, are often found in libraries and health clubs, while Pisceans tend to congregate in bars, pubs, churches and temples.

The rest of the chapter gives you the essential details about each Sun sign. We describe their natural habitat (e.g. health clubs, or churches) and we then give a star rating of how easy the signs are to seduce. We call this the 'seduceability' rating: signs given five stars are very easy to seduce, while those with one star are very difficult. After that, we tell you about the clothes and colours you should wear in order to attract the attention of the various signs. Hopefully, your wardrobe is sufficiently flexible to accommodate our suggestions, but don't burst a blood vessel trying to get hold of a pair of gold boxer shorts to impress a Leo, or a silver suspender belt to stun an Aquarian. Just do the best you can.

We then advise you on how to seduce each sign with your behaviour and your conversation. If you keep your nerve and follow this advice, you're almost certain to get what you want,

Hopefully your wardrobe is sufficiently flexible to accommodate our suggestions.

particularly if you attend to one final detail, namely food. By giving each of the signs their favourite food, you can raise their passions to a breathtaking climax. So make absolutely sure that you read our special tips on food and seduction. You can then move on to Chapter Five, where you will experience the full power of the zodiac's secret sexuality.

HOW TO TRAP ARIES

Their natural habitat

The Rams are versatile animals who can be found in a wide range of habitats. However, you must appreciate that they find it difficult to stay in one place for too long; they get itchy feet and start looking for fresh pastures. This means that the Rams spend a lot of time travelling, so it's always worth looking for them in their cars.

In general, Aries people are attracted to places where there is a lot of activity, like parties and clubs. You might also check out law courts and boxing rings, because Aries loves a good punch-up.

HOW TO SEDUCE ARIES

Seduceability rating: ★★★
Seducing an Aries isn't too difficult. If you're honest and direct and you're able to give as good as you get, then you'll eventually strike lucky.

Seducing with your clothes and your colour scheme

The Ram will notice what you wear and will have no hesitation in making cutting criticisms such as 'you forgot to iron your shirt' or 'that dress is a bit low cut'. You might then think that Aries really cares about clothes and that you have to wear exactly the right things if you want to successfully seduce them. Well, you'll be pleased to hear that this isn't the case. Rams like provoking people by criticizing their dress sense, in the hope that they can start an argument. But in their heart of hearts they don't care what you wear, particularly in romantic situations. So, if you're trying to seduce an Aries, wear whatever you feel comfortable in, even if that means wearing absolutely nothing except a few dabs of war paint to cover your modesty.

As far as colour is concerned, there is no doubt that the Ram is attracted to red and scarlet, so try to wear something which has one of these colours, even if it's only a hair-band.

Seducing with your behaviour

If you are someone who is aggressive and selfish and has no interest in other people's opinions, then you'll find it dead easy to seduce an Aries – the Ram respects strength and is intrigued by those who are prepared to take a stand against them.

You should also make an effort to show the Ram that you are capable of losing your temper, because anger really turns them on. So, if you are invited to their house, you can seduce them by throwing a hysterical tantrum, in which you smash a brick through the Louis-Quatorze mirror and empty a bottle of red wine over the Persian carpet.

Seducing with your conversation

When you're talking to Aries, say what you like and don't be afraid of getting into an argument. You should also make a real effort to be unreasonable and, if you possibly can, disagree with everything that the Ram says. This advice may seem rather harsh, but you have to remember that if you are not careful the Ram will start to dominate the conversation. They will become so excited by their own self-righteous garbage that they will forget about you and your attempts to seduce them.

By interrupting the Ram's flow and making them angry, you are taking control and forcing them into your web. The reason anger is important is that, for Aries, love and anger are similar emotions; once they're angry with you it's only a matter of time before they're in love with you.

One other thing about the Ram – swearing really turns them on; so the more four-letter words you use, the better your chances of seducing them.

Seducing with your food

Rams are quite choosy about food – if they don't like what you give them, they'll quite literally throw it back in your face. Aries people enjoy food which is of high quality and made from natural ingredients – so don't give them any canned rubbish. At the same time, they appreciate fairly strong flavours and are particularly fond of garlic. If you are entertaining Aries, try not to spend too long on the cooking, because they will quickly become impatient. To save time, it is often a good idea to get your wok out and to give them a stir fry.

HOW TO TRAP TAURUS

Their natural habitat

Taureans don't move around that much. They find a place that they like and they stick to it, which means once you have tracked a Bull down, you don't have to take immediate action. You can go away for a couple of years, come back, and still find the Bull chewing the cud in the same old spot.

Of course, Taureans do like their earthy pleasures and they tend to congregate in restaurants, bars and pubs. You might also try looking for them in clothes shops and at fashion shows. A large minority of Bulls like gardening, so you could have a scout round garden centres and horticultural exhibitions.

HOW TO SEDUCE TAURUS

Seduceability rating: *****

The Bulls are simple animals, with simple pleasures. They're fairly easy to please and, if you follow our advice, you shouldn't have any problems seducing them.

Seducing with your clothes and your colour scheme

Taureans judge things by their physical appearance so, if you're planning on seducing one of them, make sure that you pay careful attention to your clothes and your make-up. You should also check up on the personality of the Taurean you're after because there are two types of Taurus. One type is relatively civilized and has a veneer (only a veneer!) of sophisti-

Taureans LOVE good food.

cation. This Taurean is usually female and often claims to be an art lover. If you want to seduce this first type of Taurean, then you must wear expensive clothes and jewellery and saturate yourself with exotic perfumes and aftershaves. It is not necessary for you to be tasteful in your dress, but you must at least show that you've made a major effort.

The other type of Taurean is an animal and has no appreciation of the finer things of life. They are interested in the body and are not particularly concerned by fancy packaging. These Taureans can be quickly seduced by tight miniskirts and tight jeans, and by shirts and blouses that highlight hairy chests and ample cleavages.

The colour that is most likely to attract the attention of the Bull is green so, whatever you are wearing, make sure that this colour is strongly emphasized.

Seducing with your behaviour

When seducing a Taurus, you don't have to be very subtle. Be outrageously sexy and make sure that the Bull always has a good view of your body. You should also have as much physical contact with these people as possible. When talking to them, stroke their shoulder to emphasize a point. It is also worth hugging them and kissing them on the lips, at any opportunity, because Taureans find this kind of intimacy quite irresistible. It will then be a simple matter to move on to other kinds of intimacy.

If, despite your best efforts, you're still having difficulty seducing a Taurean, then it is often worth going for their stomachs. Buy them an expensive meal, or a huge box of chocolates. After that, they'll be quite literally eating out of your hand (at least!).

Seducing with your conversation

Conversation is not very important to Taureans, at least when it comes to love and romance. Provided that you look good and smile sweetly, they won't care what noises and grunts come out of your mouth.

If you're dealing with more intelligent Taureans, there's no harm in doing a bit of background reading on art: that way you'll be able to discuss with them the role of the nude in post-modern Slovenian sculpture. However, at the end of the day, it's not going to make much difference, because the Bull is far more interested in your body than your brain.

Seducing with your food

Taureans LOVE good food. If you remember this simple fact, you shouldn't go too far wrong. When giving them food you should make sure that it is always well-presented and always delicious. If you're a lousy cook, then you'll have no choice but to spend a fortune on restaurant bills. As far as content is concerned, Taureans expect every good meal to finish with a superb gâteau or trifle so rich and so creamy and so scrumptious that it gives them a cascade of super-ecstatic orgasms.

HOW TO TRAP GEMINI

Their natural habitat

The Twins are nervous animals, who find it difficult to settle down in any one habitat. Wherever they are, they feel that the environment isn't quite right or that their intellect isn't being sufficiently challenged so, like Aries, they move around a lot.

However, Geminis are obsessed by all forms of communication; before they leave anywhere, they usually insist on making a phone call so, if you're in a building and you want to bag a Gemini, you should wait by the telephone. Eventually, one of them will need to use it and you can make your move.

HOW TO SEDUCE GEMINI

Seduceability rating: **

Seducing Geminis isn't easy. They can be extremely insincere; even if you manage to seduce them there is a good chance that they will tire of your company after a few days or even hours.

Seducing with your clothes and your colour scheme

If you're planning on seducing the Twins, don't spend a fortune on expensive clothes. The Twins will at best be unimpressed and at worst will assume that you're going to a funeral. None the less, your clothes do matter, because Geminis will use them to categorize you. So, if you're wearing a dark blue suit and are carrying a golfing umbrella, Gemini may decide that you're a failed accountant, with a drink problem.

Now that we've told you that Geminis use appearance to judge other people's personalities (however incorrectly!), you can take appropriate action. This means dressing like an interesting and exciting person, the kind of person that Geminis find attractive. Wear clothes and jewellery that are unusual without being silly, and wear make-up which gives you an air of mystery.

As far as colour is concerned, it's not that important but, if you have the choice, go for yellows and oranges.

Seducing with your behaviour

When seducing Geminis, you must arouse their curiosity with your exciting and intriguing behaviour. You must also be fairly restrained in the early stages of your seduction attempt; if you behave in a way which is too over the top or too overtly sexual, Gemini will get bad vibes and run away. As you start seducing the Twins, be spontaneous and do something unusual: like dragging them off to see a Ukrainian science fiction film, which only a warped Gemini mind would understand.

When you feel confident that the Twins are responding to your charms, take them to sleazy parties and introduce them to some of your more unusual friends. That will reassure them that your interestingness is more than just skin deep.

The final stage of seduction is difficult. You have to force yourself on to the Twins, emotionally and sexually, and let them know about your real feelings towards them. If you act too early, they'll do a runner, if too late, they'll have lost interest in you and be looking for someone else. So get your timing right!

Seducing with your conversation

Conversation is essential to the seduction of a Gemini because they are not comfortable with emotions and find it easier to express themselves with words and ideas.

When you first start seducing a Gemini, keep the conversation interesting and avoid small talk. Talk about subjects which interest the Twins and, wherever possible, compliment them on their intelligence. Once you have gained their confidence, you can be more assertive. Start steering the conversation on to your own interests, and if necessary tell the Geminis that they're talking too much. If that doesn't scare the Twins off, you'll know that your seduction attempts are on the right track.

Seducing with your food

Geminis aren't too bothered by food, so if you want to seduce them, don't put yourself out. Many of the Twins actually enjoy eating pre-processed junk and are disappointed if they are given a meal which doesn't contain colourings, preservatives and a whiff of industrial pollution. However, to give them their due, Geminis are impressed by variety. If you serve them up marinated panda brains, with roast potatoes and chocolate sauce, they'll give you ten out of ten for originality. They will also go to bed with you, once they've washed the meal down with a glass of Amazonian Chardonnay.

HOW TO TRAP CANCER

Their natural habitat

Crabs are a domestically orientated group of animals, who are at their happiest when they are relaxing at home. If they're not at home, then they're likely to be shopping for food and drink in the nearest supermarket.

Crabs are, of course, sea-creatures, so it is always worth looking for them in or near water. You might then be able to track the Cancerians down in a swimming pool, or else on the beach. The male Crab often likes fishing, so if you know a river which has good trout, then have a wander down its bank and see if you can catch him unawares.

HOW TO SEDUCE CANCER

Seduceability rating: ★★★

If you try too hard to seduce Cancerians they will start questioning your motives. However, success is possible if you take things slowly, and give them plenty of space.

Seducing with your clothes and your colour scheme

When choosing a partner, Cancerians are in many respects looking for a parent. They want someone who is mature, who is reliable and who will hold their hand in a crisis. So if you wear a pair of torn jeans, a baseball cap and a T-shirt advertising a pop group that no one over the age of twenty has ever heard of, you are unlikely to be taken seriously.

No, the Cancerian is not interested in demented teenagers

The Cancerian is not interested in demented teenagers.

and is instead looking for someone who can dress like a mature adult. This means that if you're trying to seduce a Crab, your clothes should be conservative and, if possible, thirty years out of date. Therefore, tweed jackets, cavalry twill, morning coats, cocktail dresses and summer frocks will all catch the Cancerian's attention.

When it comes to colour, they are attracted to white and silver. You might then consider wearing white gloves and silver earrings, to help you seduce the Crab.

Seducing with your behaviour

Seducing a Cancerian needn't be too difficult, if you go about it the right way. The first thing you have to do is prove to the

Cancerian that you are a nice person who can be trusted. Let him or her see you perform an act of kindness, like helping an old lady across a road, or tending to a drunk who has passed out in a pool of vomit on the fast lane of the motorway. Once you know that the Crabs are taken in by your altruism, you can move on to the next phase of your seduction plan. This involves the principle that the best way of attracting and seducing someone is to let them help you. So start asking the Cancerian for small favours, such as 'can you help me move this table?', or 'can you help me translate this letter into Spanish?' This behaviour will make Cancerians feel that they are in control of the situation.

After a few more favours, you can intensify your efforts and start directly appealing to the Cancerians' sympathy. Make them think that you're helpless and that you really need someone to look after you. You might try having a fainting fit at work and telling the Crab that you're too ill to go home on your own. If the Crab falls for this ploy and agrees to take you home, then you can congratulate yourself on a successful seduction.

Seducing with your conversation

When seducing a Cancerian, try not to talk too much. This is because the more you say, the more rope you're giving to hang yourself. Or, to put it another way, a word out of place could blow your chances of getting hold of your favourite Cancerian. You must be particularly careful never to swear, to criticize them or to ask them why they're in such a foul mood. You should also avoid criticizing the Crabs' friends, family and workmates.

Seducing with your food

Although the Crabs will appreciate it if you take them out to a good restaurant, there is nothing they like better than old-fashioned home-cooked food, which reminds them of their idyllic childhoods. They are particularly fond of things like roast beef and Yorkshire pudding and bangers and mash. However, you should take into consideration national differences. If, for example, you are trying to seduce an American Crab on Thanksgiving day, it is essential that you provide turkey, pumpkin pie and a six-pack of Budweiser.

HOW TO TRAP LEO

Their natural habitat

The Lions love attention and are therefore magnetically attracted to places like theatres and television studios. If the Lions are unfortunate enough not to be celebrities, then they will make a real effort to at least brush with the rich and famous. That is why Leos can often be found gatecrashing society weddings; alternatively they may be at a concert, pining after back-stage passes so that they can meet, and sleep with, their rock idols.

One other thing about Leos is that they hate the cold. If the daytime temperature of their habitat falls below 25 °C, they head for sunnier climes.

HOW TO SEDUCE LEO

Seduceability rating: Males: **** Females: **

The male and female Leos are given different ratings. The male is relatively easy to seduce, because of his extreme vulnerability to flattery. The female, on the other hand, is difficult to impress and even more difficult to seduce.

Seducing with your clothes and your colour scheme

Clothes are important to Leos, so if you're planning on seducing them, pay careful attention to your wardrobe. When choosing the precise items of clothing to wear, you can take two different approaches. The safest is to show that you have made a real effort to look your best. You needn't be too extravagant, but you must remember that when Leos first clap eyes on you, they will immediately ask themselves, 'Can I be seen in public with this person, or will she embarrass me with her shoddy appearance and her total lack of style?'

The other approach to seducing a Leo is more risky and less honest. You buy one of those magazines which is full of glossy pictures of celebrities, in order to get an idea of how they dress. You then follow suit. So if you see three film stars and two politicians dressed up as giant pineapples, you too should dress up as a giant pineapple. When the Lions see you, they'll think that you must be someone famous, but they won't quite be able to put a name to a face. You can then brag about your next film and in no time the Leo will be on your casting couch – particularly if you can offer them a leading part. One other point about Leos is that they love gold, so include a flash of this colour in your attire.

Seducing with your behaviour

When seducing Leos, you should bear in mind that they believe in traditional gender roles. The Lioness is fiercely proud of her femininity and expects to be treated as a real woman. Her aspiring partner should open doors for her, stand up when she walks into a room and throw his cape over puddles in the road, so that she doesn't get her delicate feet wet. In restaurants the Lioness doesn't believe in going halves on the bill; if a man is to be taken seriously, he always pays the lot.

The male Lion is seduced by women who behave like women and who do what they're told. They should always be on hand to massage his ego and at the same time they should avoid doing unwomanly things, like ordering whole pints of beer, getting drunk and farting.

Seducing with your conversation

The conversational side of seducing Leos is dead easy. All you have to do is make them feel that you're someone who recognizes their brilliance. As we suggested in Chapter Two, you can gain considerable mileage by flattering the Lions and by always agreeing with them.

If you want to seduce a Lion who you have never met before, then you might like to try the following chat-up line, which can be very effective: 'My god! It's my hero! I've seen all your films and read all your books and I've been dying to have the honour of meeting you since I was fifteen.'

Seducing with your food

If you're using food to seduce a Leo, it is essential that it is extravagantly presented in lavish surroundings. If you want to give them lamb, it is not enough to take a lamb chop out of the freezer and then chuck it in the microwave. You'll have to get your private chef to roast a whole lamb, and then one of your servants will have to bring it into your banqueting hall on a silver platter.

Another thing about Leos is that they have a weakness for ice cream, so check out your local Italian delicatessen – you're bound to find a mouthwatering *gelato*, which will melt your favourite Leo's heart.

HOW TO TRAP VIRGO

Their natural habitat

Most Virgos are health-conscious animals who devote a lot of time, money and effort to their bodies. This means that you can often track them down in medical establishments, such as clinics and hospitals. You might also try health food shops, massage parlours, and the local gym. Another point to bear in mind is that Virgos are great researchers so they frequently hang out in libraries, trying to find out as much as they possibly can about their favourite subjects.

However, if you've tried hospitals and libraries and you've still drawn a blank, then go to a red light district, because many prostitutes are Virgos.

HOW TO SEDUCE VIRGO

Seduceability rating: ★★★
The Virgin's icy veil is usually skin-deep. If you are a careful and a caring person, who is capable of showing genuine love, you should have no difficulty penetrating it.

Seducing with your clothes and your colour scheme

When out seducing Virgos, your clothes must be neat, tidy and, above all, clean. Virgos will be appalled if they see congealed gravy on your sleeve or lipstick stains on your collar so, before seeing them, get your jackets dry cleaned and wash your shirts with extra-strength, super-biological, pesticidal, fungicidal washing powder. Another thing to watch out for is personal cleanliness. Always have a bath before seeing a Virgo, preferably in a mild disinfectant, and carefully check yourself for dandruff, body odour and lice. A few Virgos are totally obsessed with hygiene. If you want to seduce these people, then you should wear a face mask, rubber boots and surgical gloves.

For perfume, your best bet will be carbolic acid. As far as colour is concerned, Virgos respond best to grey and sky blue. We would recommend that you combine these colours: you might, for example, wear grey trousers and a sky blue jacket.

Seducing with your behaviour

Virgos seek partners who are stable, predictable and well organized so, when seducing Virgos, don't do anything unusual or unexpected. If you're a Sagittarian, be particularly careful. Virgos will be unimpressed by your sense of humour and if you carry out the same practical joke that you performed last year at John and Fiona's wedding, your favourite Virgo will never speak to you again (in case you'd forgotten, it was the stunt involving a strawberry trifle, a box of fireworks and a packet of condoms).

Another thing to remember is that Virgos are attracted to people who are good at tidying up. You can, therefore, seduce them by making a big show of hoovering and doing the washing up. However, make sure that you don't push the point too far, because the Virgo may become so effectively seduced that he or she marries you and then expects you to spend the rest of eternity keeping the matrimonial home spotlessly clean.

Seducing with your conversation

You should always make it clear to Virgos that you are completely healthy. So throw into a conversation lines such as 'only last month I had a medical check up. There was nothing wrong with me, and the doctor certified that I was free from every known infectious disease.' If you're lucky enough to be a doctor, say so, because Virgos fantasize about finding a partner who is always there to check their pulse and their blood pressure. More generally, we advise you to keep things simple when talking to Virgos. You must be especially careful not to change the topic of a conversation in mid-sentence: this upsets and confuses them and makes them think that you're a Gemini in disguise.

Seducing with your food

Don't use food to seduce a Virgo, unless you really know what you're doing. As we've already discussed, Virgos have exacting standards of hygiene and if you don't live up to them you're dead meat.

If you're cooking at home, it is probably best that the Virgo is with you when you buy the ingredients, just to check that you don't buy anything unhealthy or which has passed its sell-by date. As far as the actual cooking is concerned, you should probably get the Virgo to do it for you. That way you can't be blamed if later on he or she goes down with food poisoning.

HOW TO TRAP LIBRA

Their natural habitat

When you're hunting down Librans, bear in mind that they hate being alone and that they feel happiest when they are surrounded by other people. This means that you can often find them in places which are crowded, such as popular restaurants and clubs. You might also try theatres and opera houses, particularly on opening nights.

Another point about Librans is that they don't like living or working in basements or at ground level. So if you're in a block of flats or an office and you're desperate to find a Libran, any Libran, try the higher floors first.

HOW TO SEDUCE LIBRA

Seduceability rating: **

Librans are notorious flirts, who will get a real kick out of encouraging your romantic attentions. However, you will find them less forthcoming when you start asking them for firm commitments.

Seducing with your clothes and your colour scheme

If you are ever going to successfully seduce a Libran, you'll have to get everything right, including your clothes and your colour scheme. When it comes to clothes, Librans have good taste and appreciate quality. You should, therefore, make a real effort to dress elegantly and fashionably, even if this involves some extra expense. At the same time, your clothes should have a sophisticated sensuality and show off the sexiest parts of your anatomy without giving the whole game away.

Librans are also sensitive to colour. If you wear colours which blend well together, this will help the Libran to relax: he or she will then be much easier to seduce. However, if you decide to wear a yellow PVC miniskirt, bright purple moon boots and a Day-Glo orange tracksuit top, your prey is likely to die on the spot. As far as favourite colours are concerned, Librans are particularly partial to light green, provided that it doesn't clash with any other colour you might be wearing.

Seducing with your behaviour

Apart from clashing colours, there is nothing that upsets Librans more than bad behaviour, particularly when it takes place in a social setting. If you're planning on seducing one of these people, make sure that you are polite and that you aren't caught doing anything disgusting, like injecting heroin or urinating into the kitchen sink.

You should also appreciate that Librans love people and that they want a partner who can add something to their social life. This means that you must demonstrate excellent social skills and a natural ability to make new friends. Unfortunately, social skills alone won't guarantee the successful seduction of all Librans. You may also have to flirt openly, so that they can witness you being chatted up by many different people. If you do this, the Libran will eventually conclude that you are an extremely sexy and desirable person: they may then surrender to your charms.

Seducing with your conversation

You won't seduce many Librans unless you can make good conversation. You must be charming and amusing and, if possible, you should show that you are a cultured and knowledgeable person who can discuss a wide range of subjects.

One particular subject that you should swot up on is the latest gossip, because Librans find this fascinating. Indeed, they will listen with bated breath as you tell them about the bed-hopping antics of famous society names. You can often string them on indefinitely by saying things like 'if you wait five minutes, I'll tell you this incredible story about a bishop and a goat'. However, don't go too far: Librans' love of gossip never extends to dirty language.

Seducing with your food

Librans are not particularly sophisticated when it comes to food and you can often impress them by serving up romantic frivolities, such as heart-shaped cakes and sickly cocktails. On the subject of cocktails, you might like to give them a 'Venus Love Brew', which was specially designed by the authors of this book to seduce Librans. It consists of three parts Asti Spumante, two parts pineapple juice, one part vodka and a dash of Worcester sauce. Don't worry if the Libran hates it – he or she will be far too polite to say so.

HOW TO TRAP SCORPIO
Their natural habitat

Scorpios are secretive animals, who keep low profiles. They blend into their environments and are often difficult to spot. Scorpios are usually uncomfortable in direct sunlight and prefer habitats which are fairly dark, such as caves, crypts and basements.

If you are looking for these people, there is not much point in looking for them during the day: Scorpios are nocturnal creatures, who rarely engage in romantic activity during the daylight hours. In fact, probably the best time to catch Scorpios is soon after dusk, when they are waking up, but not fully on their guard.

Scorpios are nocturnal creatures; the best time to catch them is soon after dusk.

HOW TO SEDUCE SCORPIO

Seduceability rating: *

Seducing Scorpios is difficult. The moment they set eyes on you they decide whether or not they want you. After that, there's very little you can do to make them change their minds.

Seducing with your clothes and your colour scheme

When seducing Scorpios, it is important to realize that first appearances count, so try to look your best. However, you shouldn't try too hard, and under no circumstances should your dress be out of character. Scorpios are very intuitive and can immediately tell if you're wearing clothes which don't suit you. They will then become suspicious and wonder why you're making such an effort. This means that if you're used to wearing jeans and a donkey jacket, you should stick to this gear; a sudden switch to chiffon ball gowns would be unwise and would raise the Scorpio's defences.

Another point about Scorpios is that they are often attracted to people who look thin and emaciated. If you can't go on a starvation diet, then you should wear clothes which at least make you look thin. You could also use make-up to give yourself an unhealthy pallor. And, finally, there is the question of colour. We have done some research on this subject and discovered that Scorpios love red and black, particularly in combination.

Seducing with your behaviour

Many people are so terrified of seducing Scorpios that they never try and instead go for easier signs, such as Taurus or Sagittarius. However, you should remember that the best things in life are never given to us on a plate and that if you successfully seduce the Scorpion he or she will not disappoint you.

In order to be successful, it is vital that you get your behaviour right the first time, because you won't get another chance. You should be confident and assured, without being arrogant or pushy. It is important that you don't dither and that at an early stage you are direct and honest about your feelings and your intentions. At the same time, you must respect Scorpios' secretive nature: whatever you do, don't make extravagant romantic gestures to them in public.

Seducing with your conversation

Quite a few Scorpios, particularly the male ones, are uninterested in conversation; it is therefore possible to seduce them without saying very much. However, when dealing with Scorpios you shouldn't leave anything to chance, because otherwise you might get a nasty sting. If you do have to engage in a lengthy conversation, make sure that you take Scorpio seriously and that you listen to what is being said.

Don't be frivolous and don't laugh when they describe their worst nightmares. You should also be careful not to lie, because the Scorpios will always catch you out, and not to betray their confidences, because when they find out, they'll kill you (we're serious).

Seducing with your food

If you're having difficulty seducing a Scorpio, then it is always worth using food as a last resort. They like food which is well prepared and which has a touch of the exotic. Scorpios are especially fond of Chinese, Thai and Indonesian cuisine, so try taking them out to a restaurant which caters for these styles.

If you're entertaining at home and your target Scorpio is not a vegetarian, then give them something like duck or pheasant: the mere taste of a game bird will send their passions soaring. You could also give them foods which have general aphrodisiac properties, in particular oysters.

HOW TO TRAP SAGITTARIUS

Their natural habitat

When you're out looking for Sagittarians, you should appreciate that these animals love nature. They feel happiest when they are in the open country, and can often be found hill-walking and bird-watching. The Sagittarians tend to avoid cities; however, if they are forced to live in an urban environment, they will choose parts of town which have plenty of trees and parks. It's also worth noting that Sagittarians are great travellers, who enjoy moving across countries and continents. Good places to hunt them down are ports, railway stations and airports.

HOW TO SEDUCE SAGITTARIUS

Seduceability rating: ****
Sagittarians are always on the look out for excitement and adventure. If you can offer them an action-packed, romantic adventure, then they're unlikely to turn you down.

Seducing with your clothes and your colour scheme

Sagittarians appreciate clothes which are wild, outrageous and utterly tasteless, so let your fantasies rip! You can now wear with pride that pink caftan which you have been hiding under your bed for the last few decades; yes, the one with a two-foot-long green phallus embroidered on the front and a portrait of a smiling Robert Maxwell on the back.

If you are someone who enjoys wearing clothes which are at best erotic and at worst sordid, then don't hold back. Sagittarians are open-minded people and they won't bat an eyelid if your naked flesh is hanging out all over the place. Indeed, many of them will be grateful for the opportunity to have a stroke and a squeeze of your beautiful body. At this stage, you may be worried. What if you want to seduce a Sagittarian, but you're a tasteful dresser? Don't worry. Sagittarians are too big-hearted to hold it against you.

As far as colours are concerned, Sagittarians like them all, particularly if they are bright and they clash horribly. However, if you are forced to choose one colour to impress a Sagittarian, then go for purple.

Seducing with your behaviour

There can be little doubt that Sagittarians admire youthful spontaneity and are impressed by people who can motivate others with their energy and enthusiasm. You would have no trouble seducing a Sagittarian environmental activist if you organized and led a mass demonstration which prevented the building of a nuclear waste dump. However, to really seduce Sagittarians, you often have to show a softer side to your character as well. Sagittarians spend so much time zooming around from place to place, and from activity to activity, that they forget about their underlying emotional needs, yet, at some level they yearn for emotional security, an emotional security which can only be provided by a companion who is sympathetic, caring and understanding, as well as being exciting and spontaneous. If your behaviour demonstrates that you have these qualities, then you will have no difficulty seducing your dream Sagittarian.

Seducing with your conversation

Like Scorpios, Sagittarians put a high premium on both honesty and openness, so always tell them the truth. Your chances of seducing Sagittarians may be further improved if you tell them about the very worst aspects of both your character and past. They will respect your frankness and probably conclude that you are a person who can be trusted. One final point about Sagittarians is that they are great optimists who expect other people to have the same outlook. If you are a pessimist and you constantly tell the Sagittarians that there's no point in living, they'll soon confirm your worst fears and ditch you.

Seducing with your food

When seducing Sagittarians, you don't have to worry too much about food. If you have dressed, behaved and spoken in the right way, they'll be prepared to eat anything you give them, including jelly beans, frogs' legs and empty cardboard boxes. However, if you have botched up your seduction attempt and need to restore a Sagittarian's faith in you, then you have to be more discriminating. Sagittarians like food which is healthy and which contains plenty of garlic, olive oil and fresh vegetables, so it is not surprising that they are particularly fond of Italian and Spanish cuisine.

HOW TO TRAP CAPRICORN

Their natural habitat

The Goats don't suffer from idle curiosity. If they see a bomb lying on the pavement, they'll ignore it rather than pick it up and shake it. In the same way, the Goat won't visit a new restaurant, just to see what it's like; they will only go somewhere if they can benefit from the experience. This means that when Capricorns are not at a business meeting, they are either digging for buried treasure, or else trying to get elected to parliament or congress. If you see the Goat in a habitat where there are no obvious financial or political gains to be made, then they are almost certainly looking for sex.

HOW TO SEDUCE CAPRICORN

Seduceability rating: **

Capricorns are slow to express their feelings, so it may take a long time before you know whether or not you've successfully seduced them. You should be patient and not be put off if your early advances seem to hit a brick wall.

Seducing with your clothes and your colour scheme

Capricorns expect their partners to dress with decency and taste and to avoid wearing clothes which are either bizarre or provocative. In other words, you're not going to seduce a Goat if you dress up like a sex-mad Christmas tree, with tinsel round your waist, multi-coloured baubles dangling from your nipples and a naked sugar plum fairy perched on top of your head. Instead, dress as if you are going to a job interview. Wear a dark suit and sensible shoes and, if possible, carry a brief case.

At the same time, your clothes should have a quality that is unassuming. You should wear the kind of shoes that most people would regard as being boring and unexceptional but which, none the less, have been handmade by an expert craftsman out of the very finest leather. The same principle applies to your perfume or aftershave. Don't wear anything cheap and nasty, which makes you stink like a brothel. Instead, wear something with a subtle fragrance that tells Capricorn that you have breeding and class.

And, finally, there is the question of colour. The Goats dislike bright colours and are most attracted to black and dark green.

Seducing with your behaviour

You can seduce Capricorns by behaving in a mature and responsible manner and by showing that you are able to keep your cool in a difficult situation. If you want to seduce them as quickly as possible, then you should deliberately create a crisis, at a time when you know they will be watching you deal with it.

You might, for example, go to a dinner party and put rat poison in your favourite Capricorn's food. While he or she is rolling around in agony and the other guests are in a state of panic, you can be the one to administer first aid, to call for an ambulance and to ensure that the rice doesn't overcook. Once Capricorn has recovered from the poison, he or she will realize how marvellously efficient you are. It is then only a matter of time before your seduction attempts reach a successful conclusion.

Seducing with your conversation

It is a good idea to talk about money and politics, because these are subjects which Capricorns are very familiar with. However, you should remember that the Goat is a secretive animal, who trusts very few people. If you ask too many questions, particularly about their personal finances or political beliefs, they will suspect that you're an undercover journalist or policeman.

You should also bear in mind that Capricorns hate people who giggle too much, who talk mindless rubbish and who tell bad jokes. So if you're a moronic clown and you want to get inside the Goat's underwear, keep your mouth shut.

Seducing with your food

From a gastronomic point of view, Capricorn is probably the fussiest sign of the zodiac. There are many foods which the Goats don't like; if things aren't cooked in exactly the right way, they'll quickly throw a tantrum. So, if you're going to feed these people, you should first ask them about their likes and dislikes. In general, Capricorns like simple and unpretentious food and are often happiest with a hunk of oven-fresh bread and a wedge of mature Stilton. However, if you possibly can you should get the Goat to eat spinach – this vegetable has a marked aphrodisiac effect on them.

HOW TO TRAP AQUARIUS

Their natural habitat

The Water-carriers are at their happiest and healthiest in mountainous environments, where there is plenty of fresh air and very little pollution. It is therefore not surprising that ski resorts, particularly the less crowded ones, are a favourite haunt of Aquarians. If you're too lazy to seek them out in the Alps, the Rockies or the Himalayas, you might try the tops of skyscrapers (King Kong was probably an Aquarian), or else fairgrounds – Aquarians have a special fondness for the helter-skelter and the big dipper.

The Water-carriers can also be found in laboratories and workshops because of their fascination with science and technology.

HOW TO SEDUCE AQUARIUS

Seduceability rating: *

Aquarians are cool cucumbers, who have amazing powers of emotional self-control. This means that if you want to arouse their dormant passions, you'll have to do something very special.

Seducing with your clothes and your colour scheme

Aquarians do have a secret character trait, which you can take advantage of. They are all arrogant – as a result, they all believe that their taste in clothes and fashion is faultless. If you want to seduce Aquarians, you should adopt their style; this will show them that you share their cultural wavelength, and that you respect their excellent taste. However, you must be careful that you don't dress identically to your target Aquarians, otherwise they'll think that you're trying to upstage them.

To illustrate our recommended approach, let's say that you fall head over heels in love with an Aquarian punk who has a bright green Mohican haircut and eyelids which are pierced by a dozen safety pins. If you want to seduce this person, you should certainly adopt punk dress, but you should make sure that your hairstyle is slightly different (perhaps go for a dark blue Viking cut) and that the safety pins are piercing a slightly different part of your anatomy (such as your cheek, or your top lip).

Although the Water-carriers have few tastes in common, they have a common liking for metallic colours. They find silver to be particularly erotic, which is probably why so many Aquarians get seduced by space monsters.

Seducing with your behaviour

When you're out seducing Aquarians, it is essential that you keep your cool. If you allow your passions to get the better of you and act prematurely, then your efforts will come to nothing. We therefore advise readers who find it difficult to control their emotions to take a cold shower before approaching their favourite Aquarius.

Once you've established contact with the Water-carriers, you've got to excite their curiosity, while at the same time maintaining your detachment. You can do this by doing something interesting with your favourite piece of equipment. For example, you could play an exciting new tune on your electric guitar, or else start assembling a time bomb, using the latest computerized gadgetry. When you are sure that the

Water-carrier is fascinated by you, turn round to him or her, and say, 'If you come back to my place, I'll show you something really interesting.'

Seducing with your conversation

When you are talking to the Water-carriers, compliment them on their originality and tell them that you admire their creative courage. You should also compliment them on their dress sense, particularly if you're talking to an Aquarian who is known to be fashion conscious. However, don't go too far. If you tell the Water-carriers that they're stunningly attractive and that they've got the sex appeal of Marilyn Monroe and the body of Arnold Schwarzenegger, they'll soon smell a rat.

Seducing with your food

Aquarians are not particularly bothered by food; there is little point in using gastronomic means to seduce them. You might be interested to know that the Water-carriers hate variety in their diet and, left to their own devices, will eat the same thing, day in, day out. While it is difficult to be precise about their favourite food, there is some anecdotal evidence that they like pizza and pre-prepared supermarket salads. As far as dislikes are concerned, it seems that they are not very keen on mushrooms.

HOW TO TRAP PISCES

Their natural habitat

The Fish love water and all kinds of water sports. You should therefore look for them in swimming pools or else in the sea, where they will probably be surfing, water-skiing or scuba diving. Less energetic Pisceans can often be found wallowing away in hot baths.

If you can't find the Fish in their natural habitat of water, then you should turn your attentions to bars, pubs and breweries, because many of them are great drinkers. A fair few Pisceans have spiritual pretensions and believe that they can get in touch with higher states of consciousness. You can find them in churches, temples and meditation groups.

HOW TO SEDUCE PISCES

Seduceability rating: Males: ***   Females: *****

While it is possible to hook a male Fish, his inability to tell the truth makes him a slippery customer. Female Fish, on the other hand, are easy catches, who will fall for practically any bait, shrivelled maggots included.

Seducing with your clothes and your colour scheme

Seducing Pisceans with your clothes is easy. All you do is get the Fish drunk, ask them to describe their sexual fantasies and then dress accordingly. These fantasies usually involve meetings with exotic and bizarre lovers, who in ordinary circumstances are only encountered in early 1970s Scandinavian sex films. For example, you might find that you have to dress up as 'Sexy Erica, the Nymphomaniacal Traffic Cop', complete with a tight-fitting uniform, handcuffs and a rubber truncheon. Alternatively, you might assume the persona of 'Eric the Huge' (uncut).

If you remember the plot, he was a washing-machine repairman who had some interesting adventures while visiting bored housewives in a Stockholm suburb. He wore a pair of heavy jeans with a quick release zip and a lumberjack shirt with the top six buttons undone. And, of course, he always carried his trademark: a huge tool box.

More spiritual Pisceans fantasize about finding a partner who can save their souls and purify their bodies. You can impress them by dressing up as a monk, a priest or a guru (in case you don't know, gurus wear white robes, have very long hair, and have a dash of orange paint on their foreheads).

When it comes to colour, you can make the Piscean heart beat faster by wearing clothes or make-up which are either pink or light blue.

Seducing with your behaviour

If you can't find a fancy dress shop, all is not lost. The Fish are responsive animals and, if you get your behaviour right, there is a good chance that they'll come swimming into your arms. The first thing to do, when seducing Pisceans, is to make it quite clear to them that you recognize their sexuality. Make sure that they notice that you're eyeing up their every curve and sizing up their every bulge. Once you've got your message across, all you have to do is be boringly romantic. Ask the Pisceans for a slow dance and give them chocolates, flowers and champagne. If you're dealing with a male Piscean, don't worry about taking the initiative; he's certain to appreciate a domineering partner who can crack a whip.

Seducing with your conversation

Pisceans are not particularly verbal people, so don't worry if your conversation skills aren't up to scratch. None the less, if you're serious about seducing the Fish, it is worth speaking in a seductive voice full of erotic promise. You should pronounce your words slowly and meaningfully, and every now and then you should pause to seductively lick your lips. In this way the Pisceans will be able to admire the performance of your luscious tongue. If you carry on talking, they'll soon be asking you to perform something rather more intimate than mere conversation.

Seducing with your food

There are no prizes for guessing what Pisceans' favourite food is. Seafood. They like all kinds of seafood, even if they're allergic to it. The taste of fish, crabs, lobsters, crayfish, oysters and mussels makes the Pisceans feel secure and helps them to relax. Once they are relaxed, their passions start to flow. If you're dealing with Pisceans who are strict vegetarians, then you'll have to make use of particular kinds of fruit. Figs, grapes, pears and sometimes mangoes can have a powerful influence on their sex drive, so make sure that you force your favourite Fish to eat loads of them.

Chapter Five

....

UNLOCKING YOUR LOVER'S SECRET SEXUALITY

....

INTRODUCTION

So far, you have discovered an enormous amount about the astrology of relationships. You have found out what the twelve signs want from relationships, how they get on with, and how best to entrap and seduce, each other. Now for many people that may be enough, particularly if they believe in white weddings. However, as you look dreamily across the room, at that beautiful flesh standing demurely in the corner, your thoughts may wander. Once this miraculous apparition has fallen for your charms, what next? What will happen when your relationship becomes physical? How will your new lover behave sexually and what kind of sexual performance should you expect?

We appreciate how important these questions are, which is why we have written this chapter, which marks the culmination of a decade's research on astrology and sex and is, arguably, the climax of our book. Over the years, we have been uncovering the connection between the twelve signs of the zodiac and sex, by means of in-depth interviews with literally thousands of clients.

Slowly, but surely, a picture emerged, which confirmed that astrology is a vital key for unlocking people's sex secrets. To be more precise, it seems clear that a person's Sun sign can be used to build up an accurate sexual profile. This connection between astrology and sex is of earth-shattering significance and, in the long term, may revolutionize mankind's conception of human relationships.

It means that, if you see someone who looks interesting, perhaps at a party, or in your office, or even on TV, you can get a good idea of what it's like to sleep with him or her simply by knowing their sign. Indeed, if you can combine astrology with a fertile imagination, it should be possible to try someone out, without having to make a purchase.

In a few years' time, you won't even need a fertile imagination. Instead, you will be able to take advantage of the latest computer technology. For example, you might see a really attractive male Aquarius. He looks like the sort of person you'd like to have a relationship with, but you're not sure what having sex with him would be like. To satisfy your curiosity, you go down to your local computer shop and hire a 'Having sex with an Aquarius (male)' computer disk. You insert the disk, plus the Aquarian's photo (if you have it available), into your computer. You also tap into the computer his vital statistics, as well as your own. After that you put on the virtual reality headset, climb into the sex tank, then lie back and enjoy having computer-simulated sex with your target Aquarian. However, you mustn't forget to have your finger on the emergency cut-off button, just in case you find the experience unbearable. Once the simulation is finished, you will have a pretty good idea what it's like having sex with this particular Aquarian. You can then decide whether or not you want to take him out for an exploratory lunch-time drink.

When such technology becomes available, we will of course be producing a full set of computer disks, from Aries through to Pisces, which will simulate your wildest astrological fantasies in four-dimensional quadraphonic technicolour. In the meantime, in this chapter, we offer descriptions of each sign's sexual potential and sexual behaviour. Where appropriate, we have gone into considerable detail so, if you feel that you are not ready to discover your lover's secret sexuality, you should

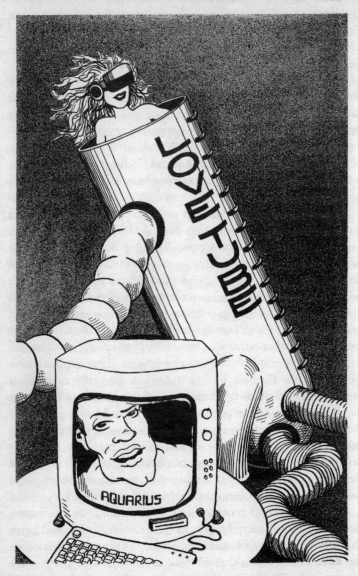

You lie back and enjoy having computer-simulated sex with your target Aquarian.

126

probably skip this chapter. It is, in fact, our policy to confront the issue of sex head on and not to beat about the bush. So don't expect any romantic euphemisms, such as 'Georgina the Gemini felt alternating waves of guilt and relief as she surrendered her virtue to the manly embrace of Lazlo the Scorpio'.

To give you an idea of the kind of questions people ask astrologers about sex and the kind of answers that astrologers can give, we would like to introduce you to Monica, one of Archie's regular clients who frequently rings him up for astrological advice. Monica is a stunning Aries in her late twenties who is, in many ways, very successful. She has a well-paid job, a beautiful flat in a prestigious part of London and also drives a fast and expensive car.

However, for a long time, she was unlucky in love. Although she had no difficulty attracting men, her relationships seldom lasted longer than a few weeks. In her first discussions with Archie, Monica claimed that the reason for this situation was that her men were unable to keep up with the breakneck pace of her action-packed life. Later on, she was more honest and conceded that the real problem was sex. Once she had slept with a man a few times, his novelty value wore off and she started looking elsewhere for sexual and emotional satisfaction.

Despite these problems, Monica remained an optimist. She believed that one day she would meet the perfect partner, someone who would have the versatility and the staying power to satisfy her many needs. After a while, it began to occur to her that before getting involved with a man, she should do a bit of research. This meant finding out his sign and then telephoning Archie to discover his hidden sexual potential. For the benefit of this book, Archie tape-recorded one of these telephone consultations and we now print it in full.

If you're worried about client confidentiality, we can assure you that Monica happily gave us permission to tape and print the following piece of dialogue. Before reading this dialogue, we have to warn you that Monica is an impulsive Aries, with strong likes and dislikes. There are certain signs that she can't stand and she makes no attempt to hide her feelings. If you are one of these signs, don't take it to heart and remember that Monica's views are not shared by the authors of this book.

ARCHIE: Hello.

MONICA: Hey, look, I've got to ask you a few questions. Are you busy?

ARCHIE: Yes.

MONICA: Anyway, I was at this party last night . . . Oh, by the way, did you get my cheque?

ARCHIE: Yes, thanks . . .

MONICA: Anyway, I was just about to leave. I've never tasted such bad champagne in all my life, and the people there were the absolute pits. They were all Pisceans and Virgos. God, don't you just hate Virgos?

ARCHIE: Well, some of my best friends . . .

MONICA: No, Virgos are the worst. Particularly Virgo men. Pisceans are nearly as bad. Once they've had a few drinks they're slobbering all over you. Like Joe. Yuk!

ARCHIE: Joe?

MONICA: Joe's an estate agent. He made loads of money in the eighties, ripping people off. Yeah, he was born on the 1st March. We call him Joe the Toad. He started groping my girlfriend Sandra. Disgusting.

ARCHIE: And what did she do about it?

MONICA: She stubbed a cigarette out on his wrist and told him to piss off. Typical Sagittarian, is our Sandra. That taught the Toad a lesson.

ARCHIE: But an enjoyable lesson.

MONICA: What?

ARCHIE: Pisceans often get a kick out of being beaten up and humiliated. It turns them on, and makes them feel special.

MONICA: Mmm. I hadn't thought of that. Mmm. Yeah, that's really amazing. That would explain Lawrence.

ARCHIE: Lawrence?

MONICA: Lawrence. Yeah, I think he's dead now. Some accident with an electric toaster. Yeah, I went out with him a couple of years ago. He was a Pisces. We went on holiday to Italy. Anyway, after a few days he was turning into a real pain. He wouldn't leave me alone, and he kept on wanting to have sex, even though he was useless at it. I was more interested in Mario. An incredible specimen of Italian manhood, with an amazing body. I think he was a Cancer. He cooked the most beautiful food. He was so upset when I told him that I wouldn't marry him. Where was I? Oh yes, the scorpions. Mario gave me this jam jar, with a couple of scorpions in it. They were really cute.

ARCHIE: What do you mean, scorpions?

MONICA: You know, scorpions. The things which sting. They're all over Italy. Anyway, I thought it would be a good idea to shut Lawrence up, so while he was in the shower I put the scorpions in his underpants.

ARCHIE: That was a bit irresponsible.

MONICA: Not really. Mario told me that they were harmless. Almost. Like hornets. Anyway, Lawrence got out of the shower and put his pants on, and got stung a couple of times. One fell out and got his foot. The other . . .

ARCHIE: Ouch!

MONICA: Actually, the injuries weren't very serious. But what was really amazing was his attitude. Once he'd been seen by the doctor, I told him what I thought of him and what I'd done to him. He was over the moon. He told me that I was exactly the woman he was looking for and he asked me to take a dozen scorpions home with me. He thought they might help the relationship. I think it was then that I realized that Lawrence was completely mad.

ARCHIE: You really pick them, don't you?

MONICA: It's just bad luck. It can't go on for ever. Anyway,

129

you told me that when Jupiter goes into Sagittarius, I'd do lots of travelling and my love life will pick up. By the way, when does Jupiter go into Sagittarius?

ARCHIE: Last week.

MONICA: Yes! That's why I rang you. Last night, just as that ghastly party was coming to an end, I saw Sandra talking to this guy who looked like a cross between Michelangelo's David and James Dean.

ARCHIE: Michelangelo's David? You mean he was seven feet tall and made out of marble?

MONICA: Well, almost. He had the same sculptured beauty, the same . . .

ARCHIE: So you wanted to be a Pygmalion, and bring David to life?

MONICA: Yes. And now I've found him. At last. He's called Mike. He's six foot three, athletic, sexy, intense, brooding, passionate. At least I think Mike's passionate. I hope he is.

ARCHIE: But didn't Sandra get to him first?

MONICA: Yeah, but there's no future there. She's a Sagittarian and Mike's a Libran. The two'll never get on.

ARCHIE: They might. It can be a very powerful combination.

MONICA: Are you sure?

ARCHIE: I said it can be a powerful combination. It doesn't always work out. It's usually better if the man's the Sagittarian and the woman is the Libran. If it's the other way round . . . well, Sagittarian women don't like indecisive partners.

MONICA: But Mike's not indecisive. Archie, can you hold on? There's someone trying to get through.

[There is a two-minute break in the tape.]

MONICA: It was him! It was him! It was him! He's asked

130

me out to dinner! Can you believe it? Just as we were talking about him. Mike must be telepathic. He was picking up on our conversation. Isn't that amazing?

ARCHIE: Yes.

MONICA: Anyway, look . . . Let me catch my breath. Anyway, this is it, I've found him, the perfect man. Adonis.

ARCHIE: I hate to say this, but he is probably the seventeenth perfect man you've met this year.

MONICA: Oh, don't spoil it. Anyway, this time nothing's going to go wrong.

ARCHIE: Yeah, but if he's a Libran he's going to be indecisive. And I know that you hate indecisive men.

MONICA: He's not indecisive. Look, he just rang me. Less than twenty-four hours after I gave him my card.

ARCHIE: We'll see.

MONICA: OK, what about sex? What are Librans like in bed?

ARCHIE: Wasn't that guy, what's his name, Tony, wasn't he a Libran?

MONICA: Oh no! So he was. That was hopeless.

ARCHIE: Maybe Mike's not a typical Libran. He does sound rather intense and brooding.

MONICA: Yeah, that's what I just said. Probably because he's a late Libran. 23rd October. Doesn't the Sun change into Scorpio on the 24th?

ARCHIE: No it's the 23rd. Which means that Mike's bound to be Scorpio, rather than a Libran.

MONICA: [after a few seconds of silence]: What, he's not a Libran? He's a Scorpio? Christ. [A few more seconds of silence.] I've never been out with a Scorpio. Never ever. Wasn't Charles Manson a Scorpio? Oh, God. Aries don't get on with Scorpios, do they?

ARCHIE: It can be difficult, but it's possible.

MONICA: Give an example.

ARCHIE: Of what?

MONICA: Of an Aries and a Scorpio who are happily married.

ARCHIE: Well, off hand, umm . . . what about your friends Mark and . . .?

MONICA: Mark and Trisha. They split up months ago. Any other examples?

ARCHIE: Look, if Mike desires you and wants to possess you, he won't care what sign you are.

MONICA: I suppose you're right. And what about sex? Will he give me what I want?

ARCHIE: What do you want?

MONICA: I want someone who can satisfy me, who can keep me interested, who can make me feel like a real woman.

ARCHIE: Well, Scorpio men have usually got a pretty powerful sex drive.

MONICA: I know. Rather, I could feel it when talking to Mike. I could imagine him controlling me, holding me, silently and passionately . . .

ARCHIE: Yes, Monica, I think you've got the idea. Scorpios have got good staying power and they tend to regard sex as being a near-religious experience. It's a way they can get in touch with a higher cosmic power, which allows them to transcend everyday reality.

MONICA: Wow!

ARCHIE: And they expect you to give them everything, to completely surrender to them. Mind, body and soul.

MONICA: How do you know?

ARCHIE: I'm an experienced astrologer.

MONICA: Of course you are. So anyway, you think Scorpios are good at sex?

ARCHIE: Yeah, I should think so.

MONICA: How good? I mean, how many marks out of ten?

ARCHIE: Oh, I should think eight or nine. Maybe even nine and a half on a good night.

MONICA: And he'll carry on . . . satisfying me?

ARCHIE: I can't guarantee that. After all, you are an Aries. However, I think you may find his intensity addictive. So maybe there's a chance.

MONICA: Thanks. And is there anything else I should know?

ARCHIE: No. Just go off and have fun.

MONICA: Mmm. But what about weird fetishes and perversions?

ARCHIE: Oh, come on, Monica . . .

MONICA: No, I'm serious. Look at Lawrence, and his Piscean kinks. And then there are Taureans. God, I'll never forget Dave. Hell on earth.

ARCHIE: And what did Dave do?

MONICA: Dave. Dave liked to eat and have sex at the same time. Can you believe it? Taureans are just so disgusting. I can still smell it. I never want to eat prawn curry again, never, ever. Yuk! Anyway, I forgot what I wanted to ask you.

ARCHIE: Umm . . .?

MONICA: Oh yeah. I don't know much about Scorpios. Are they kinky? Do they have any secret perversions? If it's anything to do with food or drink, I just don't want to know.

ARCHIE: Well, despite their reputation, they are really straightforward people. Particularly when it comes to sex. In fact, recent research has found that Scorpio is the least kinky sign of the zodiac. They don't need props.

MONICA: Props?

ARCHIE: Umm . . . you know, things like . . . umm . . . blue movies, whips, chains, strawberry ice-cream . . . live scorpions in their underwear . . .

MONICA: I got it. Yeah, that sounds great. And one other thing. Do Scorpios have any . . . what are they called? Erogenous zones? Is there any particular part of Mike's body I should work on? Some way of turning him on quickly?

ARCHIE: Umm . . .

MONICA: Hey, look, I've got a call coming through. I've got to go. I'll ring you tomorrow.

ARCHIE: Don't . . .

MONICA: Bye.

You will be pleased to know that Jupiter's entry into Sagittarius did indeed give a boost to Monica's love life. She and Mike quickly found that they couldn't keep their hands off each other. Indeed, they've just come back from a wonderful holiday on Tenerife, where they discovered new realms of passion. At least, that's what Monica told Archie. Now, at the time of writing, they have been together for six weeks, which for Monica is a world record.

As you read through the dialogue between Monica and Archie, you were no doubt impressed by their use of astrology to uncover people's sexual secrets. The mere fact that Mike was a Scorpio told Monica everything she needed to know about his sexual capabilities. She was even able to discover that he was straightforward and had no serious kinks. When describing Dave, one of her previous boyfriends, we could see that she was forming a connection between Taurus and food. While it would be a gross exaggeration to say that all Taureans like to have sex with their mouths full, we at least get a hint that they find food to be unusually erotic. As far as erogenous zones are concerned, Archie was prepared to tell Monica which parts of the Scorpio's anatomy are particularly sensitive. Unfortunately, she cut him off before he was able to give her an answer.

In the rest of the chapter, you can find out for yourself about the sex secrets of each sign of the zodiac. There are twelve sections, one for each sign. Each section is divided up as follows:

GENERAL INFORMATION ABOUT YOUR LOVER'S SEXUALITY

Here you will find out general information about your lover's sexuality, under the following sub-headings:

Turning them on

Every sign can be sexually turned on, if you know what their weak spots are.

Finding their erogenous zones

The erogenous zones are those parts of the body which cause sexual arousal when touched. Although there are some parts of the body which are universally erogenous, there are other parts which are uniquely erogenous for specific signs.

Locations where they most enjoy having sex

Different signs enjoy having sex in different places. Some like having sex in a four-poster bed, while others prefer it underwater.

Kinks and peculiarities you should watch out for

Every sign has special kinks and peculiarities. Some signs like to be dominated, others get turned on by three-in-a-bed sex, and so on.

HAVING SEX WITH THE MALE

The males and females of each sign will of course have different approaches to sex. The sub-section on the males will describe their specific sexual behaviour. It will include the following ratings, which give you the essential sexual information about each sign, at a glance: the **Stamina rating** describes a sign's staying power and general endurance. Five stars indicate a sign which can go on and on, while one star warns that a sign may start flagging halfway through. The **Promiscuity rating** gives you an indication of how promiscuous a sign is. If you are going out with signs which have a four- or five-star rating, you should always make sure that they wear a chastity belt – though make sure that you don't lose the key, or forget the combination! Signs which have one or two stars are usually faithful to their partners. The **Kinkiness rating** shows that some signs are kinkier than others. Those given five stars are super-kinky and they may require you to do some pretty strange things in bed. Those given one star will make no unusual demands on you; as a result you may find them a little boring, particularly if you've got a kinky streak yourself.

HAVING SEX WITH THE FEMALE

This sub-section is pretty much the same as the previous one, except that it covers the female of the species rather than the male. The only difference is that rather than giving women a **Stamina rating**, we have given them an **Insatiability rating**.

Signs which have a five-star Insatiability rating are extremely difficult to please sexually, because they keep on wanting more and more. Those of you who aren't complete studs (be honest!) should think very carefully before going to bed with a woman who has a five-star Insatiability rating. If your sexual performance isn't up to scratch, she'll make you feel very small indeed. On the other hand, signs with a one- or two-star Insatiability rating are fairly easy to satisfy. If you have any doubts about your sexual prowess, you'll probably find them to be the most satisfactory bed-mates.

Well, that's it. We've been through all the necessary formalities, and it is now up to you to unlock your lover's sexual secrets. If you dare . . .

GENERAL INFORMATION ABOUT YOUR ARIES LOVER'S SEXUALITY

Turning them on

When you first start to enter a relationship with the Ram, it is often a good idea to be cool and detached. Ignore their romantic signals and insist on treating them as a friend rather than a lover. This approach will drive their passions crazy and it won't be long before their sex drive goes nuclear. Once the explosion has happened and you've had full sex two or three times, it is important that you change your tack; otherwise there may not be a fourth time.

You should become increasingly assertive and you should avoid using pleasantries such as 'please', 'thank you' and 'do you mind?' If you want the Ram to do something special and intimate to you, make sure you demand it, rather than ask for it. That way he or she will continue to be turned on and aroused by your stunning body.

Finding their erogenous zones

Having sex with the Ram can be a furious experience and you may not get a chance to find their erogenous zones – except the obvious ones. However if you are dealing with a more laid-back Aries, you should concentrate on his or her face and head. Run your fingers over the face, and gently nibble the ears. Carry on doing this for a few minutes, and you will be pleasantly surprised by the response.

Locations where they most enjoy having sex

Once the Rams are aroused, they will want sex immediately. This can be very inconvenient, particularly if your Aries lover is engulfed by a wave of passion while you're both stuck inside a crowded lift.

On a different note, you should remember that the Rams are fire freaks. They will relish the experience of making love to you in the glow of a blazing log fire – though make sure that you don't get your toes burnt in the heat of the moment.

Kinks and peculiarities you should watch out for

If you've invited an Aries round for dinner and sex, then you need to bear in mind that the Rams make a lot of noise. As they get excited their soft moans will become animalistic grunts. These grunts will soon change into screams of ecstasy, which will reach a supersonic crescendo at the moment of final release. So, when you're sleeping with your Aries lover, always make sure that you practise safe sex – in other words, wear a pair of industrial-standard ear-protectors.

HAVING SEX WITH THE MALE ARIES

Stamina rating:****
Once your Aries lover gets into his stride, it is very difficult to interrupt his flow. You should therefore prepare yourself for a long and arduous night.

Promiscuity rating:*****
Aries men are always on the look out for new conquests with whom they can share their considerable sexual energy. So make sure that you keep your pet Ram on a short leash.

Kinkiness rating: **
The Aries male is a straightforward animal, who enjoys simple,

honest-to-god sex. He believes that toys and role-playing games are unnecessary distractions which have no place in the bedroom.

Once your Aries lover has decided that he wants to have sex with you, he'll just go for it. If you're lucky, you'll get a ten-second warning: you might become aware that he's breathing faster than usual, or he might finish his drink in one hurried gulp. However, very often there'll be no warning at all, and by the time you realize he's serious, he will have torn every last stitch of clothing from your body. From then on, your Aries lover will take complete command of the situation and all you have to do is passively respond.

There is no doubt that the Ram is a force to be reckoned with in bed; your first few sexual encounters with him will leave you deeply impressed. Indeed, you may come to the conclusion that you have found the perfect sex machine. Unfortunately, there is a down side. The Ram lacks imagination – once you have got used to his sexual style, you may find it rather boring and one-dimensional. This is particularly true if your own Sun sign has a four- or five-star kinkiness rating. In order to deal with this problem, it might be a good idea to buy him a fully illustrated copy of the *Kama Sutra* for his birthday.

HAVING SEX WITH THE FEMALE ARIES

Insatiability rating: *****
The female Aries is perhaps the most insatiable sexual animal in existence. She won't be satisfied until her partner has thrust her into a supernova of mind-disintegrating orgasmic bliss.

Promiscuity rating: ****
Your Aries partner is a lusty girl, so you'd better make sure

The sexuality of an Aries woman can be compared to an electric light bulb. It is either turned on or turned off.

that you can satisfy her needs, otherwise she'll look for someone else to bridge the gap.

Kinkiness rating: ★★★
The Aries woman is fairly open-minded when it comes to sex. If you want to try out an interesting idea, which doesn't involve bondage, she'll probably give it a whirl.

The sexuality of an Aries woman can be compared to an electric light bulb. It is either turned on or turned off. There is no middle ground, where it is half turned on. So, when you're trying to get an Aries into bed, you should appreciate that there is no warm-up period. One moment she'll be as cold as ice and the next moment she'll be like a furious Valkyrie, who'll want to ride you all the way to Valhalla. Once you have flicked her switch to the 'on' position, you will have an extremely demanding lover on your hands. The female Aries will expect you to take control of her and to give her maximum sexual pleasure. She has little patience with foreplay and she will want you to get to the point as soon as possible.

When you are having sex with a female Aries, try not to be too gentle or polite because otherwise she won't regard you as being a real man. You should be particularly careful to avoid saying things like 'please', 'thank you' or 'may I?'. If, horror of horrors, your performance is interrupted by a sudden mishap and you are forced to say 'sorry', then she will be most unamused, and it is unlikely your apology will be accepted.

GENERAL INFORMATION ABOUT YOUR TAURUS LOVER'S SEXUALITY

Turning them on

Taureans are extremely sensual people, so when turning them on you have to concentrate on their five senses – in particular their taste, touch and smell. It is usually worth whetting their sexual appetite with good food and good drink, although you do have to be careful. At the end of a five-course meal, you might find that your Taurus lover is too drunk and too bloated to move, let alone have sex with you.

Assuming that you've got the Bull as far as the bedroom, you can raise his or her passions by putting silk sheets on the bed and by placing a few red roses on each pillow. You should also have your sound system on, so that your lover's ears are caressed with soft and romantic music. The atmosphere can be further improved by lighting candles and by burning exotic and seductive incenses.

Finding their erogenous zones

If you want to make Taureans' sex drive go crazy, then touch and stroke their bodies. You don't have to worry too much which area of the body you start with, because every square inch of the Bull is erogenous. Including the nose, the tonsils and the big toe. However, if you're spoilt for choice, perhaps because your Taurean lover is lying naked before you, then get to work on his or her super-erogenous zones, which are the neck, the upper back and the nipples.

Locations where they most enjoy having sex

Most Taureans are fairly traditional, in the sense that they like having sex in a luxurious bed in sumptuous surroundings. Taurean farmers are not quite so insistent on beds; they are often at their most uninhibited best in haystacks and ploughed fields. However, it should be remembered that all Taureans, regardless of their profession, are nature-lovers, who have a special affinity with plants. As a result they perform very well in flower-beds and greenhouses.

Kinks and peculiarities you should watch out for

Taureans often believe that good food and good drink are the perfect complements to good sex. You should therefore not be surprised if your Taurean lover decides that your body is rather bland on its own and needs to be washed down with a plate of Turkish delight and a bottle of pink champagne. One other peculiarity to watch out for is drooling – after having sex with a Taurus, you may find yourself covered in saliva.

HAVING SEX WITH THE MALE TAURUS

Stamina rating: *****
When the Bull has finished eating, drinking and salivating over you and started having raw sex with you, you'll be pleasantly surprised by his concentration and staying power.

Promiscuity rating: *
The Bull is an uncomplicated animal who is easy to satisfy, so you shouldn't have to worry about him being unfaithful, provided that you treat him with decency and respect.

Kinkiness rating: *
Taurean men are prudes who are shocked by sexual experimentation. If you suggest anything which is too kinky, they'll call you a 'f— pervert' and then give you a good spanking.

Taurus will see you as a delicate creature who is as clean and unsullied as virgin snow. Indeed he will put you on a pedestal and worship you as the goddess of female virture. When it comes to having sex, the Bull regards it as a big step. He feels that he first has to prove his devotion to you, perhaps by beheading a workman who has wolf-whistled at you. So, when dating a Taurean, be patient and give him plenty of time to impress you. You should also watch your behaviour, particularly on the first few dates. If, for example, you were to stuff your knickers in his face and then make a lunge for his crotch, his illusions would be smashed and he'd start treating you as a worthless slut.

As far as sex is concerned, the Taurean probably enjoys foreplay more than the physical act. He will linger over your body and savour its texture and its taste. Once the Bull has explored your every nook and cranny, his passions will slowly but surely reach critical mass and you can then experience the slow but relentless tempo of his aroused virility. Unfortunately, he is not a particularly sensitive lover, so if you're stuck in an uncomfortable position you'll just have to groan and bear it.

HAVING SEX WITH THE FEMALE TAURUS

Insatiability rating: ★★★★
It is essential that you satisfy your Taurean partner's physical needs. If you are unable to satisfy her in the bedroom, then you'll have to do it in the kitchen – to gourmet standard.

Promiscuity rating: ★★★
Your partner will probably remain faithful, particularly if you give her regular sex. However, her loyalty to you will count for very little if a hunky millionaire makes her an attractive offer.

Kinkiness rating: ★★★
The Taurus woman has got nothing against kinky sex, particularly if it involves food and drink. Indeed, one of her fantasies is to be covered in golden syrup, and then licked clean by her partner.

Female Taureans enjoy sex; if you're just starting a relationship with one, you should find that it is fairly easy to get her into bed. However, you should remember that Taurus is a slow sign that doesn't like to do things in a hurry. Your partner will first want you to give her a thorough massage, to get her in the mood. After that, she'll enjoy sharing a long and scented bath with you. You can then rub her dry and take her to bed.

Once you start having sex with a female Taurean, you will find that she becomes more assertive. She will make it quite clear to you what manoeuvres she expects you to perform and what parts of her anatomy she wants you to stimulate. You shouldn't worry too much about the female's domineering approach to sex. After all, she is an expert on the subject, and if you follow her instructions you'll soon discover what the word 'pleasure' really means.

A final note: you might be interested to know that the experience of having sex with a female Taurus has been compared to 'eating a hot, buttered crumpet' and to 'sinking into a dark, chocolate mousse'.

GENERAL INFORMATION ABOUT YOUR GEMINI LOVER'S SEXUALITY

Turning them on

Geminis are turned on by anything which is unusual, weird and bizarre. So, if you're entertaining your Gemini lover and you want to activate his or her sex drive, make sure that you have some original ideas up your sleeve. At the very least you should suggest a game of after-dinner hide and seek, in the nude, with the lights off, with Kylie Minogue wailing out of your sound system at full blast.

However, once the Twins have found you hiding in the washing machine and given you a quick spin, they may get bored. In that case you'll have no choice but to re-enact the ancient mating ritual of the Mayan Indians, which involves your partner wearing a fake jaguar-skin loin-cloth and dancing the samba, and you donning a parrot-feather robe and beating the rainbow spirit's cosmic passion drums.

Finding their erogenous zones

Many Geminis are seriously out of touch with their bodies and, as a result, it can be very difficult to find their erogenous zones. None the less, it is possible, provided that you are patient. The first point of contact is the hands. If you softly stroke their hands, you will eventually evoke some kind of erotic response. You can then kiss the Gemini and so make contact with his or her other erogenous zones: the lips, the mouth and the tongue.

Locations where they most enjoy having sex

Geminis have a claustrophobic streak and don't like having sex in tight spaces, such as broom cupboards, coffins and the back seat of sports cars. They are happiest when they have plenty of room to move around in, so if you've got a triple bed to hand, they're unlikely to turn you down. However, if your home is fitted with thick and luxuriant carpets, then the Twins would take great pleasure in making love to you on the floor.

Kinks and peculiarities you should watch out for

Geminis are capable of displaying every kink and peculiarity known to mankind. One of the most famous Geminis was the Marquis de Sade, who was turned on by eating omelettes off naked women's buttocks. Other Geminis find the concept of having sex with one person rather boring and wherever possible they share beds with two or more people. A few Geminis are more interested in sex as a fantasy, rather than as reality. They usually get their kicks from pornography, blue videos and sex toys.

HAVING SEX WITH THE MALE GEMINI

Stamina rating: **
Your Gemini lover may find it difficult to concentrate on the sexual act for longer than a few seconds and as a result his staying power is frequently disappointing.

Promiscuity rating: ****
The Gemini man is promiscuous, in the sense that he likes to have two of everything. So, in an ideal world, he will have four women at his disposal – namely, his two wives and his two mistresses.

Kinkiness rating: *****
The Gemini man's kinkiness is legendary, hence the five-star rating. He loves sexual experimentation and often treats his women as laboratory rats rather than as human beings.

There are two approaches to having sex with a Gemini. The

first approach is to pander to his fantasies. You begin by watching an adult video with him; this helps him to relax and stimulates his powerful imagination. The Gemini will soon start discussing his current fantasies with you. If at this stage you want to tell him about your own fantasies, then feel free. After that, he might suggest that you dress up as a customs officer, while he pretends to be a drugs smuggler who you have just caught. You will, of course, be expected to give him a full body search. Unfortunately by the time you progress to having sex, your lover's enthusiasm will have wilted and you'll be back to watching videos.

The second approach to having sex with a Gemini is to switch his brain off. That way his fantasies will lose their hold over him. To do this, you must force him to use his body, preferably by taking him out on a twenty-mile run, followed by a hundred lengths in a swimming pool. You then give him a long massage, during which he is not allowed to speak. When you finally get to having sex, be patient, and do nothing to encourage his fantasies. This approach, if repeated daily, will massively improve the Gemini's sexual performance.

HAVING SEX WITH THE FEMALE GEMINI

Insatiability rating: ****
It can be difficult to satisfy a Gemini. She has read far too many glossy women's magazines and as a result she over-estimates her capacity for having multiple orgasms.

Promiscuity rating: ****
The Gemini woman regards her sex life as being one big research project. So, like every good researcher, she will inter-view and sleep with as many subjects as possible.

Kinkiness rating: ****
Compared with the male Gemini, the female Gemini is rather conventional in her sexual tastes. However by most

standards she's a wacky girl, who will try everything once, except monogamy.

Your Gemini girlfriend was the ideal partner. She had amazing versatility and was able to combine intellectual brilliance with gymnastic excellence. When your relationship became sexual, she did her best to please you, and if you had any unusual requests, she was happy to comply. The first time you made love to her was glorious; she was just so responsive, and within minutes you had her moaning with sheer delight. So why did she dump you two weeks into the relationship?

First, you made the mistake of thinking that your Gemini girlfriend was only interested in pleasing you. The reason she was so co-operative was because she wanted to give you every possible chance of satisfying her. She tried it your way for a couple of weeks and it didn't work.

'Ah,' you might say, 'but my girlfriend was so obviously satisfied by my sexual technique.' That was your second mistake – Geminis are notorious liars and fakers. If you want to genuinely satisfy a Gemini in bed, you'll have to make a real effort to keep her excited. You must not only be inventive in your sexual style, but you must also show a relentless vigour, which carries on and on and on, until you know for sure that she's totally exhausted.

GENERAL INFORMATION ABOUT YOUR CANCERIAN LOVER'S SEXUALITY

Turning them on

If you want to turn on a Crab, you have to create a secure and reassuring environment for them. In terms of décor, have soft lighting and make sure that there are plenty of cushions, sofas and armchairs around the place. You should also hang up a tacky, framed embroidery, with 'Home Sweet Home' written on it. Once you have cultivated the Cancerian's trust, you can be more direct. This may mean petting and stroking him or her on the sofa, though you have to be careful – if you come on too strong, your lover might get frightened and make a sideways exit. No, it is better that you take a more subtle approach. Late in the evening, when you are both feeling tired, you should put on a pair of pyjamas and suggest that your lover does the same. You can then coax him or her into bed, with the promise of a mug of hot cocoa.

Finding their erogenous zones

At the beginning of a relationship the Cancerian's erogenous zones are not particularly important; so, in the first instance, don't feel obliged to get your hands on them. However, as the relationship progresses, you should slowly explore them. Begin by running your fingers across the Crab's stomach and then move on to the most important erogenous zones, which are the breasts and the chest. If you're dealing with a male Cancerian, don't forget the hair on his chest – he'll love your gentle tugs.

Locations where they most enjoy having sex

Boring as it may sound, the majority of Cancerians like to have sex at home, in the comfort of their own beds. However, there are a few Crabs who have a keen sense of history: they enjoy making love in castles and museums. They would get a massive kick out of going to bed with you in the same room that Mary Queen of Scots bonked Lord Darnley and conceived King James I of England (for your interest, that was back in 1565).

Kinks and peculiarities you should watch out for

The Crab is a fairly straightforward animal, who doesn't have any major kinks or peculiarities. The only thing that you might notice is a slight masochistic streak. You may find that your

Some Cancerians enjoy making love in museums.

lover enjoys being ordered around and can tolerate a very high level of verbal abuse. So, if you ever have difficulty arousing the Crabs' sexual passions, you might, as a last resort, force them to do the housework.

HAVING SEX WITH THE MALE CANCERIAN

Stamina rating: ★★★
Like his mood, the Cancerian's stamina varies enormously. On good nights he can qualify for five stars, while on bad ones his performance can crash to a zero-rated wash-out.

Promiscuity rating: ★
The Cancerian is good at convincing himself that his partner is

150

the perfect lover; even if she's useless in bed. As a result of this delusion, the Crab doesn't feel any need to be promiscuous.

Kinkiness rating: **
Some people think that the Cancerian's obsession with female breasts borders on the kinky. It is as if he wants to regress back to his childhood and be breast-fed all over again by a strong mother-figure.

Cancerian men are sensitive to the lunar cycle and they perform best soon after the New Moon. At the time of the Full Moon, they are extremely tense and, as a result, their sex-drive is often non-functional.

When you do go to bed with your Cancerian lover, assuming that it's not on the night of a Full Moon, you will find that he is not very aggressive and he will be prepared to follow your lead. However, if you want to make the Crab feel really happy, you should comfort and mother him, before and after having sex. Tell him that you don't mind about his performance and that as far as you're concerned love is more important than sex. As far as the sexual act is concerned, your lover will be very considerate and he won't do anything new without giving you plenty of warning.

If you are an assertive and dynamic woman, who likes to get on top of things, then feel free to let your Cancerian lover know about your preferences. You should, none the less, be careful that you don't over-dominate the Crab. Otherwise he will end up as a half-emasculated teddy bear, who is only good for cuddling and for making babies.

HAVING SEX WITH THE FEMALE CANCERIAN

Insatiability rating: **
From a sexual point of view, the female Crab is not very demanding. She simply wants to share her bed with a tender

and affectionate man, who knows how to make her feel special.

Promiscuity rating: *
The Cancerian woman is completely unpromiscuous and once she has fallen in love with you, she'll stick to you through thick and thin. Make sure that you show her the same loyalty.

Kinkiness rating: *
If you've got a five-star kinkiness rating, then you may find the female Crab rather boring in bed. We would therefore recommend that you either find someone else, or that you get her drunk.

Although the Cancerian has a low insatiability rating, she will insist on having regular sex with you. The reason for this is that she is a jealous and possessive woman, who is worried that you might fall into the arms of a rival lover. By draining off your surplus sexual energy, she ensures that you won't be able to satisfy anyone else.

The experience of having sex with a Cancerian is very pleasant. She will treat you with tenderness and affection and she will cuddle up to you like a giant Persian cat. When it comes to the physical act, you will find that she is responsive and appreciative. You shouldn't worry if she doesn't make any noise during sex – the Crab is, after all, a silent creature who hates waking up the neighbours.

However, we must warn you that what we have said so far about your Cancerian woman assumes that she hasn't been drinking. If you get her drunk, she goes absolutely berserk and her insatiability, promiscuity and kinkiness ratings soar into the five-star zones. She will tear your clothes off (or the clothes of any man or woman who's within five yards of her) and then expect you to make continuous love to her until she finally falls off the bed, or the table, or the park bench, in a drunken stupor.

GENERAL INFORMATION ABOUT YOUR LEO LOVER'S SEXUALITY

Turning them on

If you want to turn your Leo lover on, then you should take advantage of the fact that the Lions, of both sexes, enjoy strip shows. So if you are going out for a date, make sure that your clothes can be easily removed and that the zips, catches and padlocks are all in perfect working order.

As your evening with the Lion progresses, take your clothes off, one item at a time. If you get your timing right, this should mean that your coat goes by 7.30 p.m., your shoes by 8.00 p.m., your trousers or skirt by 10.00 p.m., and your G-string by midnight. Don't worry if you are in a public place, such as a restaurant, club or theatre. Your Leo lover will not only enjoy all the attention, but he or she will also get a real kick out of watching other people jealously ogle your beautiful, naked physique.

Finding their erogenous zones

The Leos are very proud of their hair and you can usually rouse them sexually by stroking and brushing it. If you're lucky enough to be sharing a bath or a shower with them, then you could go further and give them a long and sensual shampoo. Once you've finished with the hair, you can turn to other erogenous zones. These include the upper arms, in particular the pectoral muscles, and the area of the torso around the rib cage.

Locations where they most enjoy having sex

If possible, Leos like to have sex in places which ooze money and wealth. If you can afford it, you should whisk your lover off to Las Vegas and book the bridal suite in the best and most

153

opulent hotel in town. If you're absolutely desperate for sex when you first arrive at Las Vegas, then the generous Lion will be quite happy to make love to you in the back of the stretch-limousine which is ferrying you from the airport to the hotel.

Kinks and peculiarities you should watch out for

The one kink that nearly all Leos possess is narcissism. In other words, they are in love with themselves. This means that you can usually get the Leo's passions racing by having his or her photograph in every room of your house or flat. If you want to make the very most of this narcissism, it might also be worth visiting a tattoo artist, and getting a giant-sized portrait of your favourite Leo tattooed on your back (we take no responsibility for the consequences).

HAVING SEX WITH THE MALE LEO

Stamina rating: **
Before making love to you, the Leo will boast about his superb staying power. Afterwards, he will tell you that the only thing that spoilt his performance was your complete lack of appreciation.

Promiscuity rating: ***
The Lion enjoys describing his exploits, in particular the time when he satisfied half of Amsterdam's prostitutes, in a non-stop, one-month sex marathon. As usual, he's exaggerating.

Kinkiness rating: **
Despite his claims, the male Leo has very few kinks. The only thing you might notice is that his bedroom has ceiling-to-floor mirrors, so that he can watch himself in action.

As far as the Leo is concerned, he is doing you a favour by having sex with you. After all, it is not very often that you are

154

given the opportunity to sleep with god's personal gift to women. So when he makes that first advance, be humble, and be thankful. If possible, kiss his feet and tell him that you are a mere mortal and that you are not worthy of such an enormous honour.

Your Leo lover will then lead you into his bedroom and show you his magnificent body. As he lies naked on his bed, admiring his own reflection in the overhanging mirror, you should display a sense of profound awe, as if Apollo the Sun God has revealed his blinding brilliance to you. You can then climb into the light and have sex with your Leo lover. When you are actually having sex with him, it is important that you pay attention and that you savour every glorious second of this wonderful experience. You must be particularly careful not to blink, because otherwise you might miss a spectacular event. Once the Leo has reached the breathtaking summit of his passion, he will roll off you and immediately fall into a deep and well-deserved slumber.

HAVING SEX WITH THE FEMALE LEO

Insatiability rating: *****
It will be extremely difficult to satisfy your Leo partner's ravenous sexual appetite. However, your task will be made easier if you are rich, famous and well-endowed.

Promiscuity rating: ***
Your Leo partner will be loyal to you, particularly if you're married to her. None the less, she may have the occasional affair, just to prove to herself that she is as sexy and attractive as ever.

Kinkiness rating: **
Leos are proud of their agility and expertise. As a result, they often make video recordings of their sexual exploits, which go on to become smash hits with the viewing public.

If you're up to the challenge, then you will find that sex with a Lioness is an exciting and exhilarating experience. When your Leo partner's sex drive starts roaring into life, she will have an immediate need to show off. She will dance and strut around the place, so as to give you an idea of what it might be like to have sex with her.

After that, your Leo woman will take her clothes off, climb on top of you and then bounce up and down as hard as she can. All the while, the Lioness is trying to provoke you into showing that you are not only able to take the initiative, but that you are also able to tame her. This is no easy feat, as you will discover when you move on to the actual sex act. She will squeeze you, stretch you, bend you, bomb you, twist you, ride you, hurl you, blitz you, suck you, throw you and finally, if you've got the magic touch, surrender to you, in a virtuoso performance which will make the Vietnam War seem like a walk in the woods.

Once you have proved to your Lioness that you are strong enough for her, you should find that your encounters with her become less frantic: you will be given the time and the space to savour the amazing grace and elegance of her sexual manoeuvres.

GENERAL INFORMATION ABOUT YOUR VIRGO LOVER'S SEXUALITY

Turning them on

Your Virgo lover is a down-to-earth person who is unimpressed by flattery and show. You should, therefore, make no special effort to turn him or her on. However, there are a number of things you can do to improve your chances of getting Virgo into bed. One thing you can do is be honest, because Virgos are turned on by honesty. You might, for example, say that you're not very good at sex and that you prefer trading rubber futures on the London and New York commodity markets. Alternatively, you could try arousing the Virgos' interest by being brutally critical of their appearance and their attractiveness. So, if your Virgo lover is being stubbornly unresponsive, turn to them and say, 'Who in their right mind would want to sleep with someone who has the sex appeal of an Albanian tractor factory and the deportment of a trussed-up baby elephant?'

Finding their erogenous zones

Virgos are very aware of their bodies; if you want to activate their sex drive, it's essential that you stimulate their erogenous zones. So, as soon as your Virgo lover is within range, start massaging his or her lower back. After a while, shift your attention to the buttocks and the upper thighs. Once your lover is showing definite signs of arousal, concentrate on the navel, which is of special erotic significance to every Virgo.

Locations where they most enjoy having sex

Most Virgos are fond of trees and shrubs and enjoy having sex in places like woods, forests, jungles and hedges. If it is too cold to have sex outdoors, or your Virgoan lover has come down with flu, then he or she will be happy to sleep with you in a cupboard or an oxygen tent. Other locations that you might consider are libraries, hospitals and doctors' surgeries.

Kinks and peculiarities you should watch out for

The kinks and peculiarities associated with Virgo are rather strange and somewhat contradictory. On one hand, Virgos are obsessed by cleanliness: sex with them may involve lengthy decontamination procedures such as being scrubbed down, checked for radiation, and so on. However, several of our informants have reported lapses in the Virgins' own personal

157

hygiene – dirty fingernails are a particularly common complaint. There is also some evidence that Virgos get a kick out of urinating on their partners.

HAVING SEX WITH THE MALE VIRGO

Stamina rating: ★★★★
Virgos are always on the look out for ways of improving their performance. So, when your lover manages to keep going for three solid hours, it's a sure sign that's he's been reading the right books.

Promiscuity rating: ★★★
When it comes to promiscuity, you do have to watch the Virgo man. He enjoys hunting a woman down, but once he has had his way with her, he gets bored and starts looking for a new quarry.

Kinkiness rating: ★★★
Although the Virgo has some weird fantasies in his head, he is too self-conscious to act them out. However, if you give him some encouragement, you might be given an interesting surprise.

Having sex with a male Virgo is, generally speaking, a rewarding experience. Eight times out of ten you will find that your Virgo lover is extremely considerate and does his best to satisfy you. If there is anything you don't like about his performance, then don't be afraid of telling him. Your lover will go back to his sex manuals, or to his sex therapist, and sort the problem out.

One aspect of Virgo's sexual technique you might like to criticize is his foreplay. He doesn't take it particularly seriously and is anxious to get on to the physical sex as soon as he possibly can. So next time you have sex with a Virgo, insist that he lies back and allows you to play with his all-important erogenous zones. This kind of foreplay will further improve his sexual performance.

When it comes to making physical love to the Virgo, it is unlikely that you will be disappointed, either by his staying power or his creativity. You are, after all, dealing with a well-read man, who has an expert knowledge of the ins and outs of the female anatomy. The only thing that might upset you is Virgo's occasional habit of verbally insulting his partners during sex. However if you insult him back, that should shut him up.

HAVING SEX WITH THE FEMALE VIRGO

Insatiability rating: ****
The female Virgo has ridiculously high sexual standards, which few of her lovers are able to satisfy. So if she criticizes your performance, don't take it personally.

Promiscuity rating: Either * or ****
There are two types of Virgo. One is a paragon of virtue, who loses her virginity on her wedding night. The other is a maneater, who changes her lover as often as she changes her knickers.

Kinkiness rating: **
On the whole Virgos like their sex to be straight and uncomplicated, with no extra frills. However, a small minority of the Virgins enjoy being paid for their sexual services.

We recently asked a female Virgo what it was like having sex with her. She replied, 'It's as romantic as having a cold bath.' When having sex with a Virgo, you may indeed find that she is detached and, if you are observant, you may catch her looking at her watch. On second thoughts you might not, because Virgos like to have sex with the lights off.

When it comes to foreplay, you'll find her fairly unresponsive

159

and unco-operative, though if you want to help her with the washing up, that's fine. If your lover is in a bad mood, or is upset with you for some reason, she may start undermining your confidence at the foreplay stage. So when you start massaging her inner thigh, she might yawn, and say, 'I'm bored. Let's turn on the TV, and watch England trying to play cricket.'

When you start having sex with a female Virgo, she'll just lie there, and expect you to do all the work. Once you've finished with her, she will cut your manhood down with a few barbed and sarcastic comments and then head straight for the bathroom in order to clean herself up.

GENERAL INFORMATION ABOUT YOUR LIBRAN LOVER'S SEXUALITY

Turning them on

Librans are obsessed about aesthetics, so if you want to turn them on, you must make sure that everything is in perfect order. Your underwear should be spotlessly clean and your body should look and feel good.

Librans are often turned on by physical fitness, even if they're complete slobs themselves. You can therefore impress them by doing press ups, or weightlifting, in front of them, particularly if you wear as few clothes as possible. However, don't work out for too long, because once your Libran lover catches a whiff of your body odour, he or she will run a mile.

Finding their erogenous zones

Once you are in physical contact with the Libran, it is important that you focus your attention on their erogenous zones. In the first place, this means stroking your lover's chin and cheek, either with your finger, your tongue or your nose. You will soon hear sighs of delight, after which you should work your

160

way down the Libran's body. Concentrate your effort on the small of the back, and the area around the kidneys, before moving on to the buttocks.

Locations where they most enjoy having sex

As far as location is concerned, Librans are very refined, so don't expect them to make love to you in a back alley, up against a pile of dustbins. Instead, Librans fantasize about having sex in beautiful surroundings, such as on a secluded Caribbean beach, at sunrise, or else in an art gallery. However, in practice, these people are too damn lazy to get their fantasies together and, as a result, end up having sex under a clean duvet.

Kinks and peculiarities you should watch out for

There are few kinks or peculiarities which are specifically associated with Librans. None the less, you may be interested to know that most Librans have a special psychic gift, which enables them to telepathically tune into their lover's pet kinks and fetishes. So your Libran lover will happily treat you to your favourite sexual delicacies, usually without having to be asked beforehand. However, you shouldn't expect him or her to do anything which is too disgusting or perverted.

HAVING SEX WITH THE MALE LIBRAN

Stamina rating: **
Male Librans don't feel any great motivation to impress their partners in bed. Your Libran lover will therefore do next to nothing to improve his sub-standard staying power.

Promiscuity rating: *****
The Libran man loves pulling new women. So have your lover

followed around by a private detective and regularly check his underpants for blonde hairs and lipstick stains.

Kinkiness Rating: Look up your own Kinkiness Rating

Your lover's kinkiness rating is the same as yours because Libran men are mirrors, who reflect their bed-mates' kinks back at them. That means that if you're into bondage, he'll be into it as well. If you and your lover are both gay, male Librans, then you both have a two-star kinkiness rating.

The Libran sees sex as a romantic fantasy, which is completely divorced from the real world. It is an act which is smooth and beautiful, and unspoilt by messy biological details. He will, likewise, regard you as being an icon of perfection, as someone who has just walked out of a fashion magazine. He would be horrified to discover that you urinate, have periods, have excess fat around your tummy and have a mole just below your navel. Given these circumstances, you should turn the lights low, so that your lover can't focus on your bodily imperfections.

Once the actual sex starts, you'll find that the Libran is completely indecisive. He will expect you to supervise and direct him, and to show him where all your special hot spots are. If you are not prepared to give this kind of guidance, then you may eventually conclude that you're having sex with a vegetarian snake. He will slip, slide and curl all over you, without making any effort to locate and strike his prey. Occasionally, he will hiss a few compliments, such as 'you're absolutely divine', or 'your breasts are simply gorgeous', but these are unlikely to satisfy you, unless you're a Leo on tranquillizers.

HAVING SEX WITH THE FEMALE LIBRAN

Insatiability rating: ★★★

If your partner finds you stunningly sexy, then you'll have to take time off work in order to satisfy her. However, if she sees you as being just another stale lunch-time snack, then she'll have had her fill by the time she's finished her cigarette.

Promiscuity rating: *****
The Libran loves being chatted up by a complete stranger, because it reminds her of how irresistibly attractive she is. And if she's got a moment spare, she'll quite happily sleep with him.

Kinkiness rating: ***
Your partner uses sex to manipulate and control her men. Once she discovers your secret kinks, she will adjust her behaviour accordingly and then wait for you to become sexually addicted to her.

On the surface the Libran woman seems soft, gentle and accommodating and you would have expected sex with her to be a complete breeze. However, appearances can be deceptive. Behind the sweet and smiling mask is a ruthless operator who lives by her own selfish agenda. If she agrees to have sex with you, it will not be out of weakness, but because she wants something from you.

You can sometimes tell what she's looking for by listening to her pillow talk. If she tells you how poor she is, then it's a fair bet that she's sleeping with you for your money. If she talks about politics, then you're probably a politician and she's hoping that you'll use your influence to help her get elected. However, if your partner talks dirty, then she wants you for your body and, in the ensuing sex session, she'll be extremely aggressive and won't hesitate to use physical force on you. While you're actually having sex with her, she'll drag you round the bed, all the while imploring you to try harder and to thrust deeper. Indeed, you will find that your lover is a slave-driver and that she only lets go of you when you have completely satisfied her.

GENERAL INFORMATION ABOUT YOUR SCORPIO LOVER'S SEXUALITY

Turning them on

When Scorpios talk about sex, they often refer to the mind and the brain. They say things like 'I want to f— your brains out', and 'You're a real mind-f—.' This underlines the fact that Scorpios regard sex as taking place on a mental, as well as a physical, level. Indeed, if you want to go to bed with them, you usually have to turn them on mentally before you turn them on physically. You should therefore show your lover that you are an intellectual challenge, perhaps by beating him or her at chess, or by demonstrating that you have a superior knowledge of Cartesian dualism. By doing this you are engaging in an act of mental sex, and the moment you say 'checkmate', or 'I think you've completely misunderstood Descartes's penultimate thesis', Scorpio will have a spontaneous mental orgasm.

Finding their erogenous zones

Once Scorpios allow you to touch them, start by massaging their temples. This action not only soothes their restless brains, but it also breaks down their inhibitions. You should then move down to the neck. This part of the Scorpios' anatomy is extremely erogenous, and if you massage it for long enough, you'll find that their passions hit the roof. After that, go straight for your lover's super-erogenous zone: the genital area.

Locations where they most enjoy having sex

Scorpios like being in control of their immediate environment, so it is not surprising that most of them prefer having sex in their own homes. A few Scorpios are more adventurous and more degenerate. They enjoy having sexual experiences in places which ooze sleaze, such as seedy nightclubs, brothels and government offices. Other possible venues for making love to Scorpios include caves, cellars and torture chambers.

Kinks and peculiarities you should watch out for

Eighty per cent of Scorpios are straightforward in their sexual tastes and find kinky practices somewhat distasteful. If they do have a peculiarity, it is a certain tendency to dominate their partners in bed. However, there are a small minority of Scorpios who are totally weird – even weirder than Gemini men. Their fantasies are quite horrific and the actual experience of making love to them is comparable to being crushed and impaled by the iron maiden.

HAVING SEX WITH THE MALE SCORPIO

Stamina rating: *****
Your Scorpio lover is not someone to trifle with in bed. He has complete control of his body and once he starts having sex with you, he can keep going for weeks.

Promiscuity rating: ***
If your lover sees you as being the perfect partner, he'll be utterly loyal to you. However, if he regards you as being a temporary fixture, then he'll have a couple of other mares hidden in his stable.

Kinkiness rating: **
Scorpio men like to be in control in bed and they will expect you to be compliant. If you try too hard to resist them, they will have no hesitation in tying you up and blindfolding you.

Whatever he says in public, your Scorpio lover doesn't believe in sexual equality, particularly in the bedroom. He regards himself as being the master and you as being his slave. As far as he is concerned, this unequal relationship is ordained by nature and it is not for us mortals to interfere with it. None the less, the Scorpio likes a struggle. When he sees you boasting about your intellectual brilliance and how you're as good as any man, he shudders with anticipation, particularly if he's less educated than you are.

When the relationship moves from the mental to the physical level, you soon feel his devastating sting. He uses his immense physical and emotional power to tear away your verbal and academic finery, and then breaks and possesses you. While he is actually having sex with you, you will feel your identity and your independence disintegrating. Your lover's unbeatable, rock-solid ego will penetrate into the depths of your soul and it won't be long before you are desperate to surrender your entire being to him. After a few hours, if you're lucky, he'll agree to accept your surrender.

HAVING SEX WITH THE FEMALE SCORPIO

Insatiability rating: ****
The Scorpio regards sex as being a spiritual encounter, which is on a par with birth and death. She therefore expects you to use your manhood to initiate her into new realms of cosmic experience.

Promiscuity rating: *
Your partner will never stab you in the back. So, if she meets someone who is better endowed than you are, she will tell you to your face that the relationship is over, before sleeping with him.

Kinkiness rating: **
Overall, your Scorpio partner is not very kinky. However, once she's made love to you, she does like to leave her calling card. This consists of a series of deep scratch marks across your face and back.

Although Scorpio is a tantalizingly beautiful woman, you may think that it's impossible to penetrate her icy exterior and actually have sex with her. Well, it's certainly true that she's a difficult catch, but once you turn her on you'll discover that she's an intensely sexual animal who has an inner core of red-hot passion.

This woman is not someone who takes sex lightly and you shouldn't go to bed with her unless you've got plenty of spare time and spare energy. Once you start engaging in foreplay with the Scorpio, you will soon realize that you are dealing with an expert, who can perform some quite amazing feats. It will indeed seem that she has six hands and that her tongue has the magical ability to lick two different parts of your anatomy simultaneously.

When the Scorpio starts having sex with you, she'll give you everything that she's got and somehow her will-power and enthusiasm will help sustain your stamina and staying power. As your rhythm starts to synchronize with hers, your respective minds, bodies and spirits will merge with each other and, after that, you will both be able to transcend time and space and discover the true meaning of orgasmic immortality.

GENERAL INFORMATION ABOUT YOUR SAGITTARIAN LOVER'S SEXUALITY

Turning them on

If you want to turn on Sagittarians, it is essential that you are as crude and as unsubtle as possible. You should begin by getting them outrageously drunk. The alcohol will not only give their sex drives a powerful boost, but it will also make them more susceptible to your charm and charisma. After that, you should let the Sagittarians know that you're well and truly on their wavelength. You can do this by telling them a string of disgusting jokes that are full of explicit references to condoms, tampons, sexual organs and bodily fluids.

Once your Sagittarian lover is ready and willing to have sex with you, make sure that you don't give in too easily because he or she is a keen hunter who will be turned on to bursting point by the thrill of the chase.

Finding their erogenous zones

Sagittarians' erogenous zones cover a wide area of their bodies, so if you're drunk there's no danger of you missing your target. Broadly speaking, these zones consist of the thighs, the hips and the buttocks. The arms, the wrists and the hands also have erogenous properties. However, we have noticed that Sagittarians born up until the 5th December have incredibly erogenous inner thighs, while those born after this date have the greatest sensitivity around their lower buttocks.

Locations where they most enjoy having sex

Sagittarians love outdoor pursuits and their greatest pleasure is having sex in the open countryside. If there's a thunderstorm going on at the same time, so much the better. Sagittarians are also great explorers and like to boast of the exotic locations in which they've made love, so, if you want to make your lover really happy, grab a sleeping bag and treat him or her to a sex tour of the Australian outback.

Kinks and peculiarities you should watch out for

Although Sagittarians love talking about other people's kinks and peculiarities, they are themselves pretty straightforward. The only thing that you might notice is that their sexual behaviour is rather clumsy and ham-fisted. In their attempts to get hold of you, Sagittarius will often knock things over and if you hear glass breaking while you're making love to them, it

168

probably means that they've accidentally thrown you through a window.

HAVING SEX WITH THE MALE SAGITTARIAN

Stamina rating: ***
Sagittarian men are confident lovers, who hardly ever suffer from performance anxiety – once they are aroused, it is very difficult to blunt their sexual enthusiasm.

Promiscuity rating: **
You know those adverts that tell you to take handfuls of condoms with you when you go abroad? Well, they're specifically aimed at Sagittarian men, who enjoy travelling the world in search of new sex partners.

Kinkiness rating: *
Your lover is extremely unkinky and he will never initiate unusual sexual practices. However, you may find this hard to believe after he's made love to you for five solid hours in a snake-infested swamp.

Once your lover has decided that he wants to have sex with you, he'll be anxious to get down to it as soon as possible. So don't spend too long in the bathroom making last-minute preparations, because otherwise he'll kick the door down and take you there and then. However, before getting too physical with him, you must at least give yourself time to change out of your expensive silk lingerie – whatever you're wearing will soon be torn, splattered and wrecked by the Sagittarian's relentless lust.

When it comes to foreplay, you can expect utter chaos, particularly if you're having sex indoors. Bedclothes, furniture and assorted parts of your anatomy will go flying around the room and your lover may at the same time hurl numerous insults at you. Such as 'Guess what, love? Yer tits are sagging!'

Despite its frantic nature, the foreplay won't last long and you'll soon be on to the actual sex. This is an incredibly dramatic experience. Your legs will be thrown up in the air and the Sagittarian will leap up and down on you, with natural and unaffected gusto and vigour. By the time he has finished with you, you'll be completely shattered and completely satisfied.

HAVING SEX WITH THE FEMALE SAGITTARIAN

Insatiability rating: ★★★★
Your Sagittarian partner sees sex not just as a pleasurable activity, but also as aerobic exercise. She therefore expects you to keep her heart rate at 150 beats a minute for at least half an hour.

Promiscuity rating: ★★★★★
The Sagittarian woman is very promiscuous and she indulges in frequent one-night stands. If you're at a party, she'll be the one having sex on top of everyone's coats.

Kinkiness rating: ★★
Like the male of the species, the female is not particularly kinky. The only odd thing you'll notice about her is that she enjoys making love with the radio on at full volume.

One problem about having sex with the Sagittarian is that she refuses to keep still. She will run around all over the place and if you're in the open country you may need a motorbike in order to keep up with her. Once you've managed to pin her down, you'll discover that your partner is a fun-loving animal who has few hang-ups. She is very relaxed about her body and doesn't mind who sees her naked, so she'll happily have sex with all the lights on and with the bedroom curtains wide open.

Sexual foreplay with the Sagittarian is a mock-battle, in which she expects you to establish your supremacy. This can be exhausting, particularly if she's physically stronger than you. When you move on to having actual sex, it is essential that you give her value for money. Adopt an imaginative approach to your love-making and make sure that you frequently change your sexual position.

The Sagittarian will take it for granted that you've got plenty of staying power and that you won't run out of steam in mid-session. If, when all is said and done, she feels let down by your performance, she won't keep her feelings to herself. No, this woman's got a cruel streak and she'll tell the whole world what a terrible lover you are.

GENERAL INFORMATION ABOUT YOUR CAPRICORN LOVER'S SEXUALITY

Turning them on

Most Capricorns are sexually stimulated by money. If you stuff a thousand pounds down their cleavage, or down the front of their jeans, their sex drive will go ballistic, and within seconds they'll be making passionate love to you.

If you are not financially well-endowed, then you'll have to turn Capricorns on with your body. Your bodily movements should be intensely erotic and you should leave as little as possible to their imagination. You might, for example, eat a stick of celery very slowly, showing sensual delight as you suck and nibble its moist and fibrous flesh. Alternatively, you could run your hands over your body and every now and then moan with affected sexual pleasure. However, while you're doing all this, you should avoid touching the Goats, unless invited, because otherwise they might accuse you of being pushy.

Finding their erogenous zones

Once you've turned the Goats on, their whole body becomes erogenous. So, if you give any part of their anatomy a squeeze,

171

there is a good chance that you will elicit a favourable response. However, we have found that the Goat's teeth are particularly erogenous. You can check this out for yourself, by massaging your Capricorn lover's front teeth with either your fingers or your tongue: after a few minutes, you will have driven him or her into a sexual frenzy.

Locations where they most enjoy having sex

Your Capricorn lover regards sex as an animalistic experience, which shouldn't be dressed up with satin sheets and champagne. To emphasize this, he or she likes making love in places which are absolutely basic. A favourite location is up against the brick wall of a railway bridge, on a grey Sunday morning, while walking you back from an all-night party. Your lover will also enjoy having sex with you in the snow, provided that you're both completely naked.

Kinks and peculiarities you should watch out for

If you get to know your Capricorn lover well, you'll probably notice that he or she gets a real kick out of tickling your erogenous zones. Apart from that, there is some anecdotal evidence that Capricorns get turned on by uniforms, so if you're finding it difficult to stimulate your lover, try dressing up as a schoolmistress or a soldier.

HAVING SEX WITH THE MALE CAPRICORN

Stamina rating: *****
If you're looking for pure, undiluted sex, then you've found your man. The male Capricorn is, after all, the zodiac's greatest stud and you'll find his staying power nothing short of magnificent.

172

There is some anecdotal evidence that Capricorns get turned on by uniforms.

Promiscuity rating: ★★
Capricorns regard chatting up women as a boring and time-consuming exercise, which can easily end in failure and humiliation. So once the Goat finds a partner, he counts his blessings and remains faithful to her.

Kinkiness rating: ★
Your lover is concerned about his reputation and he secretly fears that you are working for a tabloid newspaper. He will never risk having kinky sex with you.

When you first start flirting with a Capricorn, you will find that he is reserved and keeps his feelings to himself. You may then decide that either he is not interested in you or he is sexually repressed. However, before you jump to conclusions, you must appreciate that it takes time for the Goat's passions to reach critical mass. Once critical mass is reached, his personality transforms and he becomes a caveman. We mean this literally. His glands start producing a sex chemical, which causes an evolutionary regression to a Neanderthal state. The Capricorn will then drag you to the nearest wall, snowdrift or cave and show you why his virility is so legendary.

The experience of making love to a Capricorn is unforgettable. His five-star stamina will keep him, and you, going for as long as he likes; as he pumps away, you will feel your own animal nature exploding into life. You will then reach the stage where the more he satisfies you, the more you want to be satisfied. However, all good things have to come to an end and immediately the Goat has finished with you, he will revert to his normal self and ring up his stockbroker for a market update.

HAVING SEX WITH THE FEMALE CAPRICORN

Insatiability rating: ★★★★
The sexual metabolism of female Capricorns is rather slow so it takes a long time for them to reach orgasm. If your staying power isn't up to scratch, some practice may be required.

Promiscuity rating: ★★
Your lover will remain absolutely loyal to you, provided that you carry on making good money and carry on giving her an enormous allowance, which rises by thirty per cent per annum.

Kinkiness rating: ★★
On the whole your Capricorn lover is not very kinky. However, if you consistently misbehave, she will eventually tie you up and give your rump a taste of her horse whip.

If you want to get a female Capricorn into bed, it is important that you are patient. She first has to decide whether or not it's in her best interests to make love to you. This can take months, if not years. Once the Capricorn has decided in principle to open her legs and let you into her life, she has to get herself into the right mood. Again, this can take time.

However the moment that the Capricorn's sex drive becomes operational, you'll find that you're dealing with an assertive and uninhibited woman. She will order you around, and she'll have no hesitation in shouting at you if you handle her in the wrong way. One thing that Capricorn women have a particular hatred of is indecisiveness, so if you want to caress her thighs, don't just gently run your fingers over the surface hair. Instead, throw your weight into them and give them a vigorous, in-depth massage.

As far as the physical sex is concerned, the Capricorn woman is very selfish and she will expect you to provide complete, and lasting, satisfaction. If you are unable to do this, she will assume that you have a medical problem and force you to consult a doctor or a sex counsellor.

GENERAL INFORMATION ABOUT YOUR AQUARIAN LOVER'S SEXUALITY

Turning them on

Aquarians are turned on by unpredictability, so make sure that you keep them guessing about your sexual intentions. You might, for example, enjoy a romantic dinner with your Aquarian lover that is full of sexual promise. When it's finished, complain of a headache and rush home, leaving him or her to pay the bill. After a decent interval, ring your lover up and say that you're feeling better and that you're desperate for sex. When the Aquarian finally turns up on your door step, say that your lawnmower's broken and that you can't have sex until it's fixed.

Aquarians are also turned on by body paint. When they see your multicoloured flesh, with Salvador Dali's indelible signature across your gluteus maximus, they will be overcome by sheer lust and it won't be long before they're giving your body a good smudging.

Finding their erogenous zones

The Aquarians' main erogenous zones are found on the legs, between the knee and the ankle. So if you're trying to arouse them, it is always worth giving this area a gentle massage. However, you must be careful not to stray below the ankle line, because most Aquarians hate their feet. One other thing to remember when dealing with Aquarians is that they dislike being licked or sucked, so keep your mouth and tongue to yourself.

Locations where they most enjoy having sex

Aquarians are unconventional people who enjoy having sex in unusual locations. This was borne out by a recent sex survey, which found that the three locations most frequently chosen by Aquarians were nuclear power stations, wardrobes and confession boxes. There is, however, a small group of Aquarians who have more conservative tastes. They like having sex either on river banks, or at masked balls, with anonymous partners.

Kinks and peculiarities you should watch out for

One of the problems about having sex with Aquarians is that they don't have any sense of limitation. So once they start doing something to you, they don't know when to stop. You should therefore avoid being tied up by them, because you might not be released for weeks.

Another peculiarity that you will notice in some Aquarians

is that they are voyeuristic. In other words, they get a kick out of watching other people have sex.

HAVING SEX WITH THE MALE AQUARIAN

Stamina rating: ★★★
The Aquarian is obsessed with himself and he seldom makes allowances for his partner's sexual needs. So we'll give him six out of ten for performance and nought out of ten for effort.

Promiscuity rating: ★ or ★★★★★
There are two kinds of Aquarian men. One kind is devoted to his partner and would never betray her. The other type is utterly promiscuous and prefers not to sleep with the same woman twice.

Kinkiness rating: ★★★★
Aquarian men have few moral hang-ups and they are happy to engage in most kinds of sexual activity. However, they don't like being dominated or flagellated, which is why they fail to get a five-star kinkiness rating.

The Aquarian man likes to be in control of his women, so if you want to go to bed with him, it is important that you know your place and that you avoid being assertive. At the beginning of a sex session, the Aquarian will tell you what to do and will describe the position he wants you to assume. He will have probably got this position out of a science fiction or black magic book that he's just finished reading and he'll be curious to know whether or not it's feasible.

Once the Aquarian is ready to have sex with you, he'll put on some music. If you're lucky this will be either Ravi Shankar or some stirring classical symphony. Unfortunately, there's a good chance that it'll be a piece of anodyne New Age garbage, such as 'Meditations on the healing properties of brain death', played by a quartet of didgeridoos, to the accompaniment of a meat cleaver.

When your lover finally gets down to having sex with you, he will become engrossed in himself and at times you may feel that he's not aware of your existence. However, the Aquarian will always keep one eye on you, because he will want to watch the expression on your face change as you come to a sexual climax.

HAVING SEX WITH THE FEMALE AQUARIAN

Insatiability rating: ★★★★
Your partner loves sex and if you turn her on in the right way, she'll be insatiable. If you doubt your ability to keep up with her, then get her drunk: that will reduce her insatiability to a three-star rating.

Promiscuity rating: ★★★
If you have got either a good body, or a good mind, then there is an excellent chance that your partner will remain faithful to you. However, if you're a flabby idiot, then its only a matter of time before she finds someone else.

Kinkiness rating: ★★
This woman is not very kinky and it is unlikely that you'll be shocked by her antics. She, is, none the less, not a prude; if you want to play weird bedroom games, she'll happily join in.

The Aquarian woman has a clinical approach to sex, in the sense that she regards it as a method for giving her maximum pleasure with minimum cost. If a pill was invented, which provided a chemical substitute for the sexual experience, she would be the first to subscribe to it.

In the run up to sex, the Aquarian will be very fussy and you'll find there are a number of things which you're not allowed to do to her. Banned activities include kissing, cuddling and stroking her hair. However, if you're an artist, she won't mind if you give her body a lick of paint. And if you're an acupuncturist, she'll squirm with pleasure as you stick pre-sterilized acupuncture needles into her erogenous zones.

Once you start making love to the Aquarian, she won't be particularly co-operative. She'll just expect you to get on with the job and see it through to satisfaction. At this stage we should point out that the Aquarian woman prefers not to look at her partner during sex, so if possible you should manoeuvre yourself into such a position where she can't see you. By and large, the female Aquarian comes to a climax quickly, and once she's finished with you she'll be rather detached.

GENERAL INFORMATION ABOUT YOUR PISCES LOVER'S SEXUALITY

Turning them on

Pisceans are chaotic and undisciplined people, who are looking for a strong partner who can give them a sense of purpose and direction. When you start trying to turn them on, it is there-fore essential that you are bossy and arrogant. You should also make it clear to them, at a very early stage, that you are ready and willing to take over and organize their sex lives. Make sure that you tell the Fish what you want from them in bed and don't think twice about making unreasonable demands.

However, it would be wrong to think that Pisceans are complete masochists; if you want to successfully turn them on, you should show frequent displays of romantic affection. You might, for example, buy your lover a pair of gold handcuffs for his or her birthday, on which have been engraved words such as SADIE AND MALCOLM — BOUND TOGETHER IN ETERNAL BLISS.

Finding their erogenous zones

When you first get your hands on your Piscean lover's body, you should start work on the ear lobes, because these have marked erogenous properties. After that, move straight to the feet. Pisceans' feet are super-erogenous and if you tickle the soles of your lover's feet with your fingers, or with a make-up brush, you will send him or her into an immediate rapture of delight.

Locations where they most enjoy having sex

Pisceans find water irresistible and, as a result, they enjoy having sex in the sea and in swimming pools. The more adventurous Pisceans will go so far as to take their partners scuba diving and make love to them a hundred feet down. Other favoured places include boats, submarines and oil rigs. However, if such dream locations are not available, the Pisces will be happy to have sex in the bath, on a water-bed or in an aquarium.

Kinks and peculiarities you should watch out for

There is some argument among astrologers as to whether Gemini or Pisces is the kinkiest sign of the zodiac. On balance it's probably Gemini, but it's a close-run thing. Pisceans exhibit a variety of kinks and peculiarities, many of which involve being dominated by tyrannical partners. The Fish will sometime indulge in religious fantasies as well and decide that their partner is either the Whore of Babylon, or the Antichrist.

HAVING SEX WITH THE MALE PISCES

Stamina rating: * (variable)**
The Pisces man's staying power is variable. If you don't give him any sympathy or support, it can be counted in seconds. If,

on the other hand, you give him plenty of encouragement, then he'll have no difficulty staying the course.

Promiscuity rating: ** (variable)
It's rather up to you how promiscuous your Pisces lover is. If you allow him complete freedom of movement, then he'll almost certainly sleep around. However, if you're very strict with him, his loyalty can be guaranteed.

Kinkiness rating: ***
Your lover adores exotic footwear. So carry on wearing your shiny, thigh-length patent leather boots, though make sure that you sharpen the stiletto heels and that you fit steel toecaps.

When it comes to sex, the male Pisces expects his partner to be assertive and to tell him exactly what to do. So if you're planning on going to bed with him, it is important to have a clear idea of what you want, because otherwise you'll get very little out of him.

At the foreplay stage, the Pisces will be afraid to move, so it will be up to you to initiate physical contact. He is unlikely to make any surprise manoeuvres, though if he's feeling brave he'll give your feet, or your shoes, a quick grope. After a while, you'll get bored with foreplay and you'll either take a sleeping pill, or suggest to the Fish that he makes love to you. If you choose the second alternative, you'll find his initial strokes rather hesitant and unsatisfying. However, once you've given the Pisces a bit of encouragement and reassured him that he's on the right track, his performance will slowly improve. Eventually, he'll get into a steady rhythm and you'll realize that you're dealing with a competent lover, who has above-average staying power.

HAVING SEX WITH THE FEMALE PISCES

Insatiability Rating: * (variable)**
Your Pisces partner has a variable insatiability rating. This

means that whatever you do to her, and however long you go on for, she'll always be satisfied.

Promiscuity rating: ★★★★
The Pisces woman is never deliberately unfaithful to her partner. However, when someone new and exciting propositions her, she finds it impossible to say no.

Kinkiness rating: ★★★ (variable)
Your partner is a generous and adaptable woman, who will do everything in her power to keep you happy. So if you've got a high kinkiness rating, you've probably found yourself the perfect bed-mate.

The Pisces is an old-school romantic who wants to make herself look stunningly beautiful, and infinitely desirable, before making love to her partner. So she'll anoint herself with rare and exotic perfumes, before slipping into a nightgown made of the finest white silk. She will then lie on her bed with the innocent and virginal expectancy that the bride of Dracula must have felt on her wedding night.

Once you make physical contact with the Pisces, she will arouse your passions with care and sensitivity and if you allow her, she'll oil and massage the most erogenous and private parts of your anatomy. If you want to do anything special to her anatomy, you'll find that she is completely co-operative and that she never utters a word of complaint. We would, none the less, urge you to exercise a modicum of decency and self-discipline, particularly if your sign is Gemini, Scorpio or Aquarius.

When it comes to having sex with the Pisces, she is very responsive and her body movements will automatically adjust to your own. She will at the same time do her best to convince you that she's enjoying herself, though if your staying power isn't up to scratch, you may find that she fakes the occasional orgasm.

Chapter Six

THE BEST DAYS FOR HAVING SEX WITH YOUR LOVER

INTRODUCTION

As you are no doubt aware, one of the keys to romantic success is good timing. You need to plan your moves carefully and make sure that you don't act too early or too late. In most cases you can trust your intuition, but sometimes you need a bit of extra help, which is where astrology comes in. If you can harmonize your love life with the stars, then you'll be able to make the most out of the romantic opportunities that come your way. You will also increase your chances of finding sexual fulfilment.

To illustrate how astrology can be used to help plan our love lives, we print the following letter, which Barbara received a few years ago.

Dear Barbara,

I am writing to you because I'm going on holiday to Ibiza in July and I wanted to know about my romantic prospects. I'm going for a month. I've just split up from my boyfriend. Will I meet anyone? What about sex? I'm a Pisces, born at the beginning of March. Thank you.

Yours sincerely,
Karen

Barbara's reply to Karen read as follows:

Dear Karen,

Sorry I've taken so long to reply to your letter, but I've been really busy recently. It's great you're going to Ibiza and I feel sure that astrology can help you make the most of your holiday.

However, you can't expect the stars to do all the work for you: if you want to see an improvement in your love life, it is important that you make an effort and that you lead an active, high-profile social life. So make sure that you go to plenty of late-night parties.

Now, as far as July is concerned, things look a bit slow up until the 11th of the month. The people you meet could be boring and, if you do have any sexual encounters, they're unlikely to be very satisfying, so it might be best to hold back and enjoy Ibiza's historical sights. However, on the 11th, Venus, the planet of love, dances into Virgo, your opposite sign, giving your sex life a major boost, and by the 15th there is no reason why you can't be involved in a steamy, uninhibited relationship. In this light, the 15th and 16th are both great days for sex, particularly if your partner is a Virgo or a fellow Pisces.

So, in general terms, the last half of July looks very passionate and I'm confident that at a sexual level you'll find total fulfilment. Good luck, and have fun.

Best wishes,

Barbara

You can see that Barbara was advising Karen to get her timing right. Karen had to accept that the first ten days of July were not very good for sex and that she should therefore avoid physical relationships. However, from the 11th of July onwards the situation completely changed. Karen's sex appeal and sex drive went into top gear and this was clearly a time when she would find overnight sexual satisfaction.

In order to give Karen this advice, Barbara had looked at the planetary positions in July 1991 and used her astrological skills to work out how they would affect Pisceans' sex lives.

For the purposes of this chapter, Barbara and Archie have combined their astrological skills and have written a month-by-month account of how these positions affect the twelve signs' sex lives from January 1996 through to December 1997. If you want to use astrology to plan your sex life, turn to the section of this chapter which covers your Sun sign, look up the month and year that you're interested in and let the cosmos do the rest.

Oh, one final point. These descriptions are written for your benefit, not for anyone else's. So there's no need to feel obliged to look up your lover's best days for sex, unless you've got plenty of spare time.

ARIES

Best days in 1996 for sex

January: A brilliant month for having sex with Capricorns or Aquarians, but you'll have to adapt to their whims and demands. The 8th onwards is best for devising love strategies. Don't expect instant results. Restrain yourself sexually on the 20th. Monday afternoons are lucky.

February: Until the 19th, Aquarians give you a hard time, so switch your attentions to Pisceans. They can be devious, canny and manipulative. Beat them at their own game. Approach in a group situation, attack from underneath and you'll get what you want.

March: A bumper month: aim high (or low). The 20th to the 31st is a fast-moving phase with a huge hint of sexual promise. Taureans and Leos fall instant victim to Aries charm. Corniest chat-up lines work splendidly. More than one over-sexed sign will come steaming your way.

185

April: Early April is sub-ruled by the love planet Venus and the lust planet Mars: a hot wind blows through your sex life. Seek out fellow Ariens. Arrange evening dates – very late evening. Physical contact is unavoidable: get stuck in speedily. Sex is terrific.

May: Live up to your reputation: a trip down the Zambezi on an Icelandic fishing vessel, or a deep-sea wreck-finding vacation gets it moving (your sex-life, that is). Engineer disaster, then grab your victim by the feet. Such courage will engender big rewards and indebtedness.

June: The 12th to the 20th is the time to strike. Make your mark, insist on a date and don't listen to anything negative. Taureans submit quickly. Scorpios hold out for longer, but Sagittarians will beat you to it. Be discreet, but be ready for uninterrupted sex at the first signal.

July: You won't be taken seriously. Geminis are having pedicures, Librans are distracted and Leos are dreaming up the fiftieth big scheme of the month. Demand what you like, but don't bank on results. Be patient and concentrate energies on Aquarians from the 23rd.

August: If the bold approach cuts no ice with sex partners, copy someone else. Be a Pisces. Talk your way into their pants. Tell lies, be unreliable and laugh in a vulgar way. Librans will despise you. But Scorpios or Virgos will be queuing up for your sex adventures.

September: Ingratiate yourself with Librans. Be polite, reasoned and arrange leisurely walks to places of cultural interest. Late mornings/early afternoons work best. Mid-September is most fruitful. The 14th and 18th are star days. If you don't get lucky at these times, move on.

October: Sign up for the next space programme. Let everyone know about it. Sagittarians are the biggest suckers and will sign up too! Amazement at your audacity ignites interest. Leos

May 1996 (Aries): On your fishing trip down the Zambezi engineer disaster, then grab your victim by the feet.

want to jump on your bandwagon. A quick date with sex to follow is the asking price.

November: A sexy, smouldering month. Scorpios have it all. Leap quickly in pursuit of one. The 3rd to the 12th is peak time. The stronger you come on, the more they like it. More delicacy is required with Aquarians. Keep it light, even if intentions are dishonourable.

December: You're spoilt for choice: Christmas is your bumper season. Work hard, play hard and get hard. If you're turned down, turn up anyway. Best lovers are Leos, Libras and Scorpios. Concentrate on the run-up to the 25th, when mind and body are most fertile.

Best days in 1997 for sex

January: Saturn in Aries makes for delays, so approach romance and sex from a new and different angle in this brand New Year. Amorous encounters won't be dull, but they might be demanding. Best dates: the 1st, 2nd, 28th and 29th. Resist that urge to be domineering or arrogant!

February: A lover urges you to explore further afield sexually. If things go too easily there's a danger of smugness and complacency. Mars in your love sector could wipe that smile off your face. But equally, Mars will bring an attractive person into your life – be prepared.

March: You'll profit from a stunning lunar eclipse: dig deep for answers to relationship queries and look ahead to a phase of emotional enrichment. There seem to be a lot of genuinely sexy people around. Sort the sheep from the goats and focus on the longer term.

April: The love planet thunders through Aries. Things fall into place, you'll be approached by all the right people and your sexual horizons will widen drastically. Physically you're looking radiant, so attack on the 6th, 7th, 13th and 14th.

May: Helpful trends continue. Be absurd. Pretend you're a Capricorn – steady, ambitious and reserved. You'll get Virgos and Taureans into bed with your material attitude and security-minded talk. Curb your sexual recklessness. Lovers are into tame sex and gentle manners.

June: Sex in a boat is indicated: be a member of the 'mile low' club – the lower the better. Sex is grippingly exciting and, for those inclined towards uninterrupted intercourse, make sure your mate is a Scorpio or Taurus. Cancer will do nicely but might fall in love on the way.

July: A hot, fiery month: sexual energies will be greatly enhanced under the influence of Venus and Mars. Speedy progress is expected, especially from the 1st to the 24th and especially with Leos and Librans. Wider sexual relations are spotlighted – what could be better?

August: A low patch. There's a shift in relationships and things are up in the air. Perhaps you should be too: book a long-distance flight to Surinam, Brazil or similar: check out local talent and screw around (using condoms). Take a copy of our book *Life, Love and Destiny*.

September: Expansive planets will expand your area of conquest, but generally you'll prefer one sex partner this month. Providence is a guiding force through the sexual minefield. Concentrate on fellow Ariens and Librans between the 1st and the 12th. Ignore promiscuous Sagittarians.

October: There's a real danger of falling in love. But are you ready for commitment? If not, abandon unrealistic visions and focus on abandonment and wild times. A pragmatic Taurus may surprise you in bed with one or two incredible positions from the 4th to the 20th.

November: Capricorns and Sagittarians are the sexiest around. Be prepared to disrupt existing arrangements to accommodate one or more of these raging beasts. If your style is being cramped by a Cancer or Pisces, your last chance to change direction arrives on the 8th.

December: A rank outsider in the sexual stakes romps home a winner in mid-month – probably an Aquarian. A favourable New Moon on the 14th points to a new beginning in love/sex for adventurous Rams. Christmas holds loads of promise, but be ready for sweeping changes.

TAURUS

Best days in 1996 for sex

January: Go for warm Earth signs in this cold month: Virgos and Capricorns will respond quickly to your warm suggestions. Early month is best. Results are slow in coming, but you'll plant seeds for the future. Confine sex to the first week. Keep it intense and erotic.

February: Be ridiculous, especially with Geminis. Do it in the dead of night and appeal to their humour: take a packed lunch, a strong drink and be open to suggestion. Confirm future sex dates, but don't insist on good time-keeping, especially with Pisceans and Sagittarians.

March: Mid-March is lucky. Emotions are hot, libido high and a frisky Leo would be perfect. Be prepared to play, to have fun and to let go of inhibitions. In late March, expect less: wise Bulls will go for it sooner rather than later. Put yourself out to pasture from the 24th.

April: A brilliant month. Indulge freely in the flesh. Lovers are in plentiful supply and Taurean charms on sparkling form. Don't give all your heart: be choosy. Arrange sex close to weekends and line up three lovers. By the 21st, be clear on each one's pros and cons.

May: Material concerns creep in. But you are only having sex!

You're not getting married (yet)! The 7th, 9th and 17th are superstar days. Be open to more spiritual partners. You'll be surprised how deep emotions can be. An absurd Aquarian will show the way.

June: A month to re-evaluate and plan. Early June is the luckiest. Geminis and Cancers get in the mood. Keep them at a distance until the third week. String them along. Geminis adore you, but the Crab sulks. The 15th and 18th stand out: use these dates to get results.

July: Take an unusual holiday in mid-July. It's the wackiest time of the month. Avoid the 26th to the 31st. Be receptive to foreigners, especially Librans. Arrange heavy sex on the 17th and 20th – preferably all day long. If you're at home, go for Virgos. Be frivolous and be loose.

August: Not a brilliant month, but progress can be made, especially with stubborn Scorpios and Capricorns. Forget about Leos. Coaxing and teasing work best in early August. Feed them a line, preferably a sex line. It always works. You'll get a one-night stand at least.

September: A mellow month for mellow people. Security issues are on your mind. Unless you're aiming for Scorpios, Cancers or Capricorns, hide your real intentions. The 1st, 3rd, 9th, 19th and 23rd are great for building up a new relationship. Be patient and flexible.

October: Aggressive types are on your trail. The autumn chill increases their sex drive. Early month is best for hot dates. The love planet, Venus, helps on the 6th, 8th, 10th and 25th. Don't give too much away. Be mysterious, alluring and sensual.

November: Definitely a month to hook up with Scorpios and Sagittarians. Your physicality is overwhelming at this time. Be clever: be precise in your timing and you'll pull in exactly who you want. Strike well before the 22nd, preferably on the 7th, 9th, 12th or 16th.

December: Eat, drink and be moderate! Taurus excesses are your downfall. Dating on a full stomach is bad enough; sex on one is impossible! Capricorns are open to your vivacity and charm. If you are thinking long term, get hold of a Goat by the 24th and hold tight!

Best days in 1997 for sex

January: Opportunities arise at the right time and right place. But you've got to be more broad-minded and more open to adventure. Materialism is one thing, but what about tempestuous romance and absurd sex? Your New Year's resolution is to let rip. Best sex dates: the 9th to the 31st.

February: A new sexual experience will leave you gasping. Insatiable desires force you to demand more than you could realistically get. Mindless promiscuity is not usually your thing, but between the 8th and the 14th you'll verge on it. By the 22nd, your sexual drive decreases slightly.

March: Pisceans are all the rage and they could certainly teach you a thing or two – not so much about sex, but about how to get more of it. Venus resides in lucky Pisces from the 1st to the 22nd, making this a thrilling, erotic and fantasy-ridden patch for sex-mad Bulls.

April: A calmer month, when rational Mercury in Taurus urges you to slow down, take a breather and reassess certain romantic and sexual objectives. A lover is highly convincing during sex, but you want more. Wider social relations will bring success from the 1st to the 15th.

May: Venus is in Taurus and her benevolent vibrations are triggered by a New Moon on the 6th. The sexual landscape will be fruitful and fertile up until the 11th. A stroke of sex luck on the 22nd will set the tone for the summer months.

June: Cancerians are most attractive and alluring. You've got big incentives for pushing forward with one romantic objective, which should turn sexual by the 3rd or 4th. Key dates are the 2nd, 3rd, 16th, 17th, 29th and 30th. Expect emotional trauma on the 27th.

July: An admirer you thought boring and sexless is greatly sought after: more fool you if you've missed the boat! You've some serious backtracking to do: if you're clever, you'll strike on the 14th, 15th, 26th or 27th. Alternatives arise on the 16th and 17th.

August: You tend to use sex as a means to an end – usually a material end. Recently you've discovered how brilliant it can be. But security issues are creeping in again. Resist such considerations when choosing a lover. Best sex is on the 10th, 11th, 23rd and 24th.

September: Two big eclipses dominate the month. If you're involved with a Virgo or Pisces, tread carefully. Stick to one partner, and avoid taking sexual risks. Romantic good luck is indicated from the 1st to the 12th. If you're searching for new love, go for Libra or Scorpio.

October: Don't try to force issues – be content with small successes and gains, whether emotional or sexual. It's not a month for major achievement. Avoid new sexual adventures, they'll be more trouble than they're worth. If you have to do it, go for the 3rd or 4th.

November: Traditionally a fulfilling month for the Bull, especially with randy Scorpios or Sagittarians. Be ready to meet fate head-on in the form of a new partner. A Taurus full Moon on the 14th will help you make the best use of planetary sex trends. Expect stunning results.

December: Your susceptibility to well-endowed lovers makes you a big sucker. Don't believe all you're told, especially by Virgos/Pisceans. Check the facts and don't give your body on the strength of one bank statement. Opt for fellow Bulls in the fortnight before Christmas.

GEMINI

Best days in 1996 for sex

January: Christmas socializing leaves your sexual batteries drained. Early January is the time for recuperation: to recharge batteries and inject new life into your libido. Concentrate on the 15th to the 25th for light sex; the 25th to the 30th for heavier stuff. You need to release tension. Use your body fully, with a willing Leo.

February: You want a mate to talk to. Forget earthy people (Taurus and Capricorn): they want to marry you. An Aquarian is best. Go for later days: specifically the 21st and 22nd. Talk incessantly about what you want – 'the squeakiest wheel gets the most oil'!

March: Try and act materially. Latch on to Taureans and talk big money. It fires their sexuality. They fall immediately. Their bodies follow shortly. By the 24th, you'll be a financial advisor. When you get bored, chase Leos. The most propitious time is from the 27th onwards.

April: Be yourself. Arrogance, selfishness and monotonous chatter drives away all but the super-keen (Pisceans who can't tell the difference between talk and action). Bore them on the 13th, 18th and 20th. Fill their heads with emotionally meaningful material, then dump them.

May: A month when you fascinate Sagittarians. They find you intelligent, reckless, entertaining and want to get close. The 21st to the 31st works best for Geminis with ulterior motives. If you get serious about someone, go for earlier days, preferably the 1st, 3rd or 6th.

June: A super month. Get into some serious sex, especially from the 1st to the 7th. Fellow Twins are your best bet, but Libra comes a close second. Don't expect everyone to fall for your garbage. If you want results, act like a serious, intensely emotional Scorpio.

July: A month when Cancerians and Leos rule. If you manage to get lucky with one, expect entertainment, extravagance and over-indulgence. Opt for the Crab up until the 23rd; the Lion thereafter. Be humble: the Crab loves to help and the Lion loves to grant favours.

August: A time when you can find the perfect lover. Virgos can be more than a match. Not only can they out-talk you, but they can also out-sex you. This is a fine challenge for the Gemini ego. The first and third week are smoothest. Late month is difficult.

September: Ariens arrive in large numbers. They are usually keen. But you frighten them with your sarcastic wit. Go for mid-month sex and go gently if you want lasting results. Keep opinions to yourself, opt for bright, loud restaurants and loud music. It'll keep you awake.

October: A month when Geminis can get confused. You get the settling-down urge but, on a deeper level, the idea is abhorrent. Go for someone of like mind and your problem is solved. Avoid Scorpios, Cancers and Taureans. Join up with Leos, Aquarians or fellow Twins.

November: With the end of the year come recriminations and regrets. What if ... what if ...? Be more positive. Screw a Sagittarius. Be gregarious. Don't let winter blues cool the Gemini ardour. By the 23rd you are back to your wittiest best. Date heavily on the 28th.

December: So much happens so quickly in December. What is a Gemini to do? Which invitations are to be taken up? ALL of them. Even if you have to fit them in on the same night. All days are stunningly brilliant. Choose whoever you want and chase them unremittingly!

Best days in 1997 for sex

January: A changeable month. You can't decide between various courses of action and various lovers. Capricorn or Libra would be best. They take sex seriously. But do practise it safely. The post-Christmas period could be fraught with danger. Best days: the 6th, 7th and 18th.

February: You're being dishonest. By withholding your true feelings you'll go backwards. Spine-tingling experiences await you, so go for it: indulge yourself and fulfil long-held fantasies. Super-star sex days are the 15th and 16th with Aquarians, Aries or fellow Twins.

March: A lunar eclipse in the pleasure zone of your Solar Chart presages tantalizing things to come. Rearrange routines if you are seeking a more erotic companion. A new method fires up desires and makes you sexually over-active, particularly in mid-month.

April: You'll frighten off certain lovers, but thrill others, with the prospect of three or more in a bed. You're entering a phase (beginning on the 16th) when your sexual drive is heightened drastically and only selected lovers can satisfy your rather basic desires.

May: Venus enters Gemini on the 11th. Lovers you're bored with will re-emerge revamped! Foreplay will be fresh and stimulating and you'll want to wield a lot of influence. So get on top quickly, take what's on offer and immerse yourself in sexual bliss.

June: A Gemini New Moon on the 5th should coincide with your best efforts at enticing new talent. You need plenty of sex to release tension: romantic love is not necessary and if it takes more than one quickie every day, so be it. The 1st to the 20th is the most auspicious period.

July: No one could say that you don't try! In fact, you are trying people's patience to the limit! If you don't get what you want early on, let things lie for a while. Leos are this month's sexual prize, but they won't be hurried – not by you or anyone else!

April 1997 (Gemini): You'll frighten off certain lovers, but thrill others, with the prospect of three or more in a bed.

August: Book a biking holiday to the Swiss Alps. Cycling shorts will show off your thighs, buttocks and lower parts. You'll pull within minutes and get things off to a speedy start. Virgos are big suckers for a health freak, but in reality you're just a sex freak.

September: Your sexuality knows no limits: you think about it hourly. Lustful Mars, currently in Scorpio, indicates Scorpios are a good bet. But don't give them 'multiple partner' talk – they're often monogamous. Any hint of sexual deviance will send them packing.

October: Don't push your luck, unless your lover is a Sagittarian – you can push them as far as you like: they have no sexual limits known to man or woman. Your prowess for the act is at a peak, so use it wisely and think long term. All month is terrific for whatever grabs you.

November: Late November is a time of endings/new beginnings. A deep quest could finally be realized, especially if it concerns a Scorpio or Taurus. But don't make big promises or big commitments. Keep them dangling and keep your options open, especially from the 8th to the 30th.

December: If you thought you had conquered all frontiers, think again. One or two particularly stubborn outposts are about to fall. Jump in quickly and seize what you can, rounding off 1997 with an armful of victories. By Christmas itself you'll sink into sexual oblivion.

CANCER

Best days in 1996 for sex

January: A contradictory month for the Crab. Post-Christmas after-effects tend to be heavy: you need a light, stimulating mate. You're strongly attracted to Capricorns, but their irritating habits leave you cold. Sex only would be OK. Opt for Geminis in mid-month.

February: Don't take yourself too seriously. Life is fun: even more so with the right partner. You've got an eye for attractive adolescents. Female Crabs want to respond to a virile male and vice versa. Scorpios fit the bill, but avoid late February. Star sex date: the 23rd.

March: You want to be desired and to give love. Mutual lust rears its head, but forget about heavy commitment. Be content with what relationships bring and don't try to pin lovers down. The 1st to the 7th is an astro-passion period, the 9th to the 15th less sexy. Late month dull.

April: Cold winds freeze your sex drive. Your conformity to traditional concepts of love is outdated: when the sun comes out you'll see it all differently. Sagittarian/Aquarian lovers drive you mad with talk: concentrate on the 20th to the 28th to seek out sexy Taureans and Virgos.

May: Confusion, unreal affairs and fantasies are what May brings. 'We're just good friends' are dirty words in the Cancerian vocabulary. But you'll have to make do. The first nine days are revealing but not shocking, the last nine are progressive but flat.

June: What sort of love can you give and what sort will you attract? Ask yourself before you steam into a new relationship. Planetary emphasis shifts into your sign in late June. Use this auspicious time to make plans with a new lover or to upgrade an existing affair.

July: Excellence is within your reach. This is a prize month for the Crab. Any day up to the 23rd is fabulous for serious sex and getting where you want to be. Enjoy all the attention you receive, but keep an eye on the main chance. Star dates are the 27th and the 28th.

August: Pretend you are a Gemini. Talk others into a coma, be shallow, be flirtatious and take nothing to heart. The planets put you in touch with a Scorpio who is good for you. It's just a matter of deciding how to play your hand. Awareness of your physical desires leads the way.

September: You know that happiness doesn't derive from wealth or social status, but a Taurus or Capricorn admirer thinks otherwise. True love, support and strong moral values are what matter to you, so stick to your principles. This is a month for meeting your soul mate.

October: You have a long memory: as the nights draw in, you dwell on past trauma, broken promises and other set-backs. This could thwart your quest for personal happiness. In late month, bad memories will be behind you and new sexual conquests before you.

November: Get friendly with Virgos who can help you in the fight against junk food. If you have to screw one, get on with it – you might even enjoy the experience. November as a whole is marvellous. Dry Cancerian wit and attractive temperament pull a dream lover.

December: You come into your own this month. As one of the most tactile signs of the zodiac, your reputation as a brilliant lover grows. Christmas gossip will support your sexual aims. Aim high between the 6th and 19th. Date frequently from the 20th to the 23rd.

Best days in 1997 for sex

January: Your opposite sign of Capricorn holds most promise. Demanding, sensual and earthy, they've loads to give and you've loads on offer. Venus enters the zone of relationships on the 10th, giving all your sexual desires free rein until early February.

February: Free-ranging Aquarians are on your case. You can have as many as you want, but act as they act if you want a lot of sex. Don't scare them with words like 'commitment' or 'living-in'. Be gregarious and open, in bed and out. Best days are the 4th, 5th, 17th and 18th.

March: A potentially negative event is the backward movement of the lust planet Mars. But it simply means you'll have to take a backward or devious approach. Nothing is upfront or straightforward. Sexual susceptibility to Librans is obvious, especially from the 1st to the 8th.

April: A barren patch in an otherwise fertile period. The combination of loving Venus with stern Saturn bodes ill for new relationships or sexual experiences. Wait until the 16th before trying your luck. An affair with an Aries/Leo could develop into something serious.

May: A volatile month. Domestic improvements are vital: a new and sparkling interior will fascinate and impress Taurus, Capricorn and Pisces. A wider social orbit is the key to sexual success for singles. Avoid the 1st to the 8th. Concentrate best efforts on the 24th and 25th.

June: Opportunities to express latent talents loom ahead. When Venus enters Cancer on the 4th, there's no limit to your achievements. Spine-tingling developments in one special romance continue until the 29th. Extra luck comes through liaising with a Gemini.

July: You excel in the water, whether it's deep-sea diving or deep-sea sex. Your body is at its rippling and supple best. A Cancer New Moon on the 4th signals a wet and wonderful time for bold Crabs. Entrap watery Scorpio and Pisces for out-of-this-world intercourse.

August: Close co-operation with a Leo or Sagittarius will prove rewarding in more ways than one. They like the heat and they like you. Book a tropical holiday in a deserted location. There'll be only one thing to do – and between the 1st and the 25th you'll do it expertly.

September: You need a submissive partner in this cooler month. A Virgo will do adequately, but don't expect too much too soon. A sudden turn of events on the 1st or the 16th could be very unsettling for Crabs trying to get their pincers into new flesh. Proceed slowly and gracefully.

October: Developments may be overwhelming. Certain lovers prove too costly in emotional terms. Get rid of dead wood and be open to the new. A sex-starved Gemini is ready to be consumed. If that's not to your taste, opt for Scorpio or Aquarius on the 8th, 9th, 21st or 22nd.

November: Your erogenous zones are strongly stimulated. Lucky breaks are on the agenda. Avoid the temptation for quick conquests – go for more difficult, but more worthwhile, prey. What you lose in pride you'll make up for in better sex. Strike on the 17th and the 18th.

December: You're seeing a brighter future as one close relationship gathers momentum. Crabs wanting to dive in should do it on the 15th or the 16th. The Moon in your sign gives you the luck and the know-how. A clandestine relationship just before Christmas should be avoided.

LEO

Best days in 1996 for sex

January: The planets come to your rescue: either extricate yourself from a lover who is unworthy, or get it together with someone who is. The lions/lionesses are luckiest in late month, when the Sun boosts their sex lives. A streak of creativity and fire attracts similar types.

February: You yearn for complete union, but it's unlikely. However, lines of communication are wide open for a Gemini, Libra or Aquarian to tune into. Early month is unproductive, but sex games played from the 8th to the 24th will spark a new relationship. Let rip and be indulgent.

March: An inflated ego is a problem. Get real, Leo, and get yourself into perspective. Pisceans rule this month. Their apparent humility fools you. As you contrast yourself favourably, they play patronizing mind-games with you. Screw Aquarians in late March.

April: Plans need revising; it'll be easy to take things the wrong way. An ongoing relationship is stuck in a rut. Book a long-distance one-way cruise to Tonga. Get into the scene, have sex with the most attractive locals on the island and get married if need be.

May: You're running out of steam. Get new ideas from *Life, Love and Destiny*, our first book. The sexual merry-go-round beckons again by the 23rd. There is no mistaking the eagerness in your eyes, so keep them shut if you are trying to play it cool.

June: Your antennae are up and running. Signals come thick and fast, but whom should you choose? A sensual Taurus, provocative Aries or adventurous Sagittarian? If you're clever, you can have them all. It'll be hazardous around the 15th, but no one will ever know.

July: Until the 22nd, pretend to be a Virgo: humble, conscientious, finicky and servile. Squeezing your ego into this minuscule role is most difficult. You'll enjoy the challenge but not the response. Next time, you'll treat a Virgo lover more reasonably.

August: Do your own thing in your own way. Take no heed of others. Any time from the 12th to the 25th is fabulous, because your luck is of a special kind. Avoid unpromising emotional situations from the 2nd to the 11th. Plan an unusual date on the 30th.

September: The Nile crocodile starts sex very gently but ends up in a thrashing frenzy of desire. One special admirer will respond similarly if you use the right approach. A predominance of planets in fiery, passionate signs will point you in this direction from the 7th onwards.

October: A camel ride through deepest Africa provides the perfect setting for a new love affair – as long as you can put up with the humps. After twenty-four hours, your lover will beg for mercy and be the malleable, submissive sex partner that you always wanted. Long may it last.

November: The sign of Scorpio dominates the month. It's a time of commitment and setting dates to tie the knot. Other gratifying developments will get off the ground from the 3rd to the 17th. Popularity increases, compatibility ratings soar and the Lion has a lot to be happy about.

December: It's green lights all the way for enterprising Leos. It's your favourite time of year: generosity and magnanimity are qualities that shine through. And you'll be rewarded from the 4th to the 10th. Unexpected sex offers crop up. One in particular you can't refuse.

Best days in 1997 for sex

January: Uranus in your relationship zone may be disruptive, but this planet will surely bring an array of romantic opportunities. Your sexual energies are greatly enhanced under these erratic vibrations: the 10th, 11th, 23rd and 24th will bring sudden and novel experiences.

February: Your mating habits resemble those of the grey seal. You insist on dominating a certain territory and of coupling with anyone on it. This gives you a certain reputation, which less amorous partners might find hard to deal with. Be choosy and avoid late-month sex.

March: A brilliantly lucky cycle is underway: Jupiter is influencing your love zone throughout 1997. You'll be in great demand and most things (including lovers) will fall quickly into place. The 23rd to the 31st are optimum days for intimate soirées and slow sex.

April: Security conscious you are not, but you don't mind humouring the odd Virgo or Taurus who is hovering. Developments could be positively thrilling around the 16th, 17th and 24th. But make sure that expectations are carefully spelled out by the 29th.

May: An unremarkable month. Taureans are getting in your way and there's little you can do about it – cross your legs and bear it! By the 22nd the situation eases up and you'll be back on shining Leo form. You'll be indispensable to a loyal Scorpio, so take advantage of it.

June: Cast aside dull cares and get into party mood. Sexual pastures are waiting to be explored. The entrance of Venus into Leo on the 29th guarantees total success. If you can't have sex with the one you want, do it with the nearest Aries. Bumper days are the 9th and the 10th.

July: Geminis are becoming a distinct pain in the genitals. It's vital to deal with them by the 24th. Until then, brilliant Venus dominates your love and sex zones. Being in Leo, a fixed sign, Venus makes your desires equally fixed, so aim unremittingly for what you want.

August: Doubts about your attractiveness will be resolved by the 3rd. Virgos come on so strong that you lose your breath. They're amusing enough, but not to be taken seriously. Aquarians/fellow Lions are where the real action is and you'll snare one between the 14th and the 23rd.

September: An unpredictable set-back turns into an unmissable opportunity for one-off saturating sex with a water sign (Scorpio, Pisces, Cancer). It's just what you need and will restore and recharge vital energies: the 6th, 7th, 14th, 26th and 27th are when it all happens.

October: Single-mindedness is required for a result. It's no good dithering over the pros and cons of Capricorns, Ariens or Librans. Be decisive, choose your target and shoot. Give freely in sex and demand the same back. By the 23rd, Scorpios will be the main dish.

November: Higher than average sexual temperatures predominate until the 21st. It's a question of how to squeeze everybody in (not at the same time) and how to give a stunning performance every time. Memorize lovers' names and faces. Carelessness is most unbecoming for a Lion.

December: Impulsive actions get you into cold water. Keep things at a festive heat of 100 °F by being constantly attentive, especially from the 12th onwards. Don't be influenced by staid Taurus/boring Aries. Experience it with the mother of all experiences: slippery Pisces.

VIRGO

Best days in 1996 for sex

January: The year ahead has loads to offer. The planets in January bring new fascinations and occasional upheavals. You may not feel secure, but exciting Ariens, Leos and Sagittarians get you out of a rut. Don't make wise choices: make absurd ones on the 16th, 19th and 30th.

February: Revamp your image, enhance your appearance and pull lovers who are unusual and unlikely. Celestial forces emphasize differences between you. You learn a lot about yourself and your relationships. The 24th, 25th and 28th are super-stellar sex days.

March: Act totally out of character: be careless, untidy, super-tolerant and disorganized. You'll attract lovers who want to help you straighten up! Book a long-distance break from the 4th to the 18th; don't check the tour details and choose an erotic Piscean as a travelling companion.

April: Treat yourself to flying lessons. Your instructor wants sex in mid-air. It'll have a liberating effect on you, but don't plan a follow-up. From the 16th, the month takes on a peaceful note. Taureans and Leos are in pursuit. There's a change for the better.

May: Geminis are everywhere and are coming on strong. Make a sex date on the 13th or 16th. If it's exciting, carry on. If not, terminate the affair in a detached way – it'll blow Gemini's head off. Concentrate on Cancerians from the 23rd. They are super compatible with you!

June: Energies are at a peak. A major hindrance in your love life eases off. Restructure goals, re-evaluate strategies and put them to work on different lovers: a cool approach for Librans, a sentimental one for Pisceans, a total blank for Leos and heavy sex for Scorpios.

July: A hot month. Play lovers hard and don't feel guilty: the meaner you treat them, the keener they get, especially Leos, who'll be desperate for approval. Middle month is best for sex: people who appreciate your special talents will burst on to your scene and into your bed.

August: You're in an artistic, impressionable and imaginative mood. Seek out similar mates. Pisces will do, but don't expect much. If you want to get rid of one, take up an interest in higher mathematics or advanced computing. Leos and fellow Virgos are a great bet.

September: Be wild, passionate and daring. Hook up with a Scorpio. Defy your destiny and keep a clear vision. By the 25th, you'll feel elated and ready for new sexual adventures. Take a married lover on a secret journey in the last week of the month. Have a pleasant trip.

October: Beneficial planetary activity propels you forward. Plan ahead, but don't be too conservative. What really matters is that you enjoy life, you enjoy your body and you let others enjoy it too. If you're into more than one lover, go for Geminis; if not, go for Taurus.

November: Life takes on a new meaning. Enjoy the attention. One special person does wonders for your confidence and ego. A time to accept changes and to come to terms with your sexuality. Joint efforts are most successful from the 14th to the 19th. On the 27th screw in the morning.

December: New friends/new scenery are part of the Christmas package. If a Leo or Libran doesn't spoil you, then spoil yourself. Erotic dates are lined up for the 17th, 19th and 23rd. Reserve the big day for old lovers. An intensely personal issue looms. Solve it with sex.

Best days in 1997 for sex

January: A fabulous start to what promises to be a fabulous year. A time to concentrate on people who support and motivate you and to avoid those who undermine you. Intriguing and enticing developments are afoot from the 10th to the 27th. Sexual dealings will bring fringe benefits.

February: Use your sensors to find new prey. Gather information secretly and use it to captivate or befuddle a new lover. Very lucky days are the 8th, 9th, 10th, 22nd and 23rd. Keep a low profile, but come to the surface on these days – PATIENTLY PERSISTENT is your new motto.

March: A solar eclipse on the 9th signals new beginnings. You'll be better placed to make headway in love, but specifically in sex. Venus adds to the pleasurable movements of bodies entwined together. Indulge as much as you can.

April: Demanding Mars thunders through Virgo every day in April. You'll get who and what you desire, but feelings may get hurt in the process. Like the Bengal tiger, spring is a great time to mate but gently does it! Gentle Librans/Taureans don't want to be eaten alive.

May: Exquisite grace and dynamic power characterize all Virgos all month. Follow your sexual inclinations closely and you can't go wrong. The 11th to the 31st are most propitious days, with the 15th, 16th and 30th standing out. Singles should go on the prowl at this time.

June: Any time, anywhere, with anyone are thoughts crossing your mind. This is poor form. Live up to your reputation as a finicky, fussy Virgo. It's not quantity that counts. Feed on top-quality prey; lovers who fall into this category expand and enrich your life.

July: You feel at home with fellow Earth signs (Taurus/Capricorn), so don't refuse a date with one in mid-July. While you're out on the town, you can swipe surreptitiously at passing talent, particularly Aries, Leo or Aquarius – signs that are always into clandestine arrangements.

August: No less than three planets in Virgo denotes a vivacious and upbeat month. You can hunt and court all at the same time – just like the blue whale. By the 18th, you'll see excellent results for effort expended and can focus on the 19th and 20th for further successes.

September: A brilliant month. A Virgo solar eclipse on the 1st is enormously important and augurs well for Virgos wanting something a bit serious. Allow personal plans to brew gently behind the scenes. Sex is not a priority: talk your way into a lover's affections.

October: The realization of ideals and dreams lifts the tone of the month. Lingering love-making and lingering memories both hang in the autumn air. Desires and drives are strong and steady, especially from the 7th. The 26th and the 27th are excellent days for cementing a special plan.

November: Get away. A trekking holiday through cowboy country puts you in touch with pioneers – probably Ariens. They're not slow in coming forward. A subtle hint and you've got sex on a plate for the duration. You'll return inspired, contented and glowing.

December: Capricorns or Aquarians are your best bet sexually. Heightened charm gets you to the centre of the action, which will be between the sheets. Christmas festivities boost luck even further. An unexpected party could be the source of erotic new interests!

LIBRA

Best days in 1996 for sex

January: Don't be in a position where you have regrets, especially about Christmas. Make sure you've given it your best – you've been outrageous and can now capitalize on promising opportunities. Mid-month is peak time. You look sexy, inviting and utterly irresistible.

February: Being a conventional person at heart, try to loosen up. Look at life and love with more gusto and enthusiasm. The Sun, natural ruler of lust, makes a brilliant aspect to your sign. So go for it between the 6th and the 18th. Aquarians and Geminis are in; Virgos and Pisceans are out!

March: Urges are strong in March. New lovers are waiting for singles. Grab opportunity when it comes. Believe in your dreams and keep going. Late month is most auspicious. Your passions are strongly activated. Be daring and wicked.

April: Make dates from the 1st to the 20th. Forget gentility and refinement: choose lovers who are bold and rough, preferably Ariens or Sagittarians. Romantic evenings hold enormous potential. The melody lingers for a long time. Emotional appeal is soaring.

May: Spur-of-the-moment encounters take you on a wild trip. Shark-fishing, bungie-jumping and wind-surfing are brilliant pursuits to catch a new mate. Emotions run high, romantic vibes are strong. The 23rd, 24th and 28th are spectacular sexual days for all.

June: Important changes take place in the pattern of your life.

It takes a lot for you to be deflated. Gossipy bits of news lighten your spirit and make you inclined to hook up with a Gemini or Aquarian. Your love life takes off like a rocket from the 12th to the 24th.

July: Avoid Cancerians in early July. Aim for Leos and aim high. If you've fancied one for ages, steam in. Your're highly energized and highly sexed. The less said the better. Don't keep emotions under control - give them free rein, especially from the 15th to the 30th.

August: A mellow time of year for Librans. You bask in popularity in early month. Long hot evenings bring loads of potential, as long as you're adaptable and willing to take a risk. Lofty aspirations show signs of becoming true. Pisceans and Virgos are ideal lovers.

September: Early month is discouraging. Love affairs are slow moving or slow in starting,. The 14th to the 29th is altogether more rewarding. Short trips are productive if you're looking for sex, but boring if you aren't. Read *Life, Love and Destiny,* our first book.

October: The Sun's movement through your birth sign puts you in the mood for making love. Fresh contacts and ideas boost weary Librans. The memory of last month's indulgences gets the better of you. But be restrained, especially if you're dealing with a suspicious Taurus or Cancer.

November: Scorpios are everywhere and trying hard to get you into bed. That's fine if they're attractive. Arrange dates from the 2nd to the 8th for fastest results. Late November favours hot-blooded Sagittarians or earthy Capricorns. But play hard to get if you want wild sex.

December: You're at a loose end in the first week, but an old lover boosts your ego and gives good advice. By the festive season itself, a stunning array of opportunities crops up. The only questions are: which way to go and whom to go with? Leos have the answer.

Best days in 1997 for sex

January: A slow start to the New Year in sexual terms, but emotionally you're getting your act together. Mars in Libra makes you feel sexy and receptive to the new. Fantasies are coming true and a host of fresh ideas pertaining to image and appeal are about to come flooding in.

February: If you're keen to get involved with a new lover, be patient. Adopt a low profile as you lie in deadly wait for your prey. Iridescent Libran beauty belies your lethal objectives, but you'll get what you want. Sex will be mind-blowing on the 10th, 11th, 25th and 26th.

March: Until the 8th you have powerful Mars as an ally. Thereafter, be clever and accept your lot: simply sail along the surface of events until the time is right for attack – namely the 24th or 25th. Stroke a lover into submission, pretend to be in love and lie back!

April: Three planets reside in your partnership zone, so you can now take your pick of what's available. Take a passive, subdued approach and you'll fool more gentle types (Cancer, Taurus and Virgo) into thinking it's safe to come close. All dates are good from the 2nd.

May: Spread your tentacles far and wide – like a Portuguese man-of-war. Your ruler, Venus, is positioned in a sensual, appealing position. This is great news for all Librans. Self-gratification is top of your agenda, so get in the sex-mood. Best days are from the 1st to the 10th.

June: An on-off affair is finally consummated (about time, too)! But your lover wants promises and commitment. If it doesn't appeal, you've only one recourse. Be hopeless in the sack: be clumsy, inept and stupid. Do it on unlucky days – the 9th, 19th, 20th, 29th and 30th.

July: Leos and Cancerians top the list of sexually active and attractive people. They generally have huge talent for the sex act. With a surprising burst of speed and energy they'll approach you directly and forcefully. Respond similarly from the 1st to the 23rd and be bold.

August: Venus enters Libra on the 18th, giving added charm, tact and diplomacy. You'll attract admiration, respect and devotion. But don't waste energies on too many sex partners. Choose one or two – preferably Virgo or Aries from the 18th to the 31st – they'll give unreservedly.

September: Extricate yourself from sticky situations. Piscean partners could be a lot of aggravation. Displays of strength and loud bluster won't hide their innate weakness. Sex could be disappointing: lovers are astonishingly selfish. Look for new flesh from the 4th.

October: Good vibrations abound. But curb excessive optimism about one sex objective, particularly if you're after a Scorpio: it'll take more than flattery and charm; sincerity and depth are also required. Go for fellow Librans on the 1st, Aries on the 16th, Scorpios on the 31st.

November: You're in a rut. Grab a Sagittarian and fly away. Soft-pedal the differences between you but hard-pedal the sex. Stir up some action from the 1st to the 9th and be ready for anything. Sex in a pot-hole or sand-dune would be interesting and guaranteed to keep you amused.

December: Double-check arrangements, especially new dates. There's an awful lot going on and you mustn't miss out. Important personal plans are brewing and it's vital you keep one step ahead, especially from the 12th to the 23rd. Lots of Christmas sex is coming and so will you!

SCORPIO

Best days in 1996 for sex

January: No one can tell Scorpios how to strike and how to do it: it comes naturally. Post-Christmas is chaotic. So many dates, so much sex – where is it all leading? Everywhere and nowhere: it depends on you and your drive (what's left of it). Reserve new sex for late month.

February: The Scorpio Moon on the 10th, 11th and 12th highlights an erotic affair. But be subtle. Don't give clues and don't capitulate to unexpected demands – in bed or out. On the 23rd and 24th, the Moon travels through your partnership zone: make decisions at this time.

March: A fabulous month if you're looking for sex, or a serious affair. The love planet enters the love sign on the 6th. Love and sex will rejuvenate you, especially on the 21st, 22nd and 23rd. Sexual favours will be returned in full, especially by Taureans and Leos.

April: Two eclipses on the 4th and 17th put you in a bonding mood. Learn to consult the stars and find out who sticks together best. Ariens and Librans fit perfectly this month. A different kind of love experience is in store from the 20th. Be prepared and be smart.

May: The best month in 1996. Relationships are positively emphasized. Erotic attractions gather momentum, sparkling encounters lead somewhere quickly. The periods around the 3rd and the 17th are brilliantly auspicious. Strong desires will get steady responses.

June: Act out of character if you want some eccentric or unusual sex: talk frivolously and carelessly, give away your secrets and use a loud, vulgar approach. Leos will feel a magnetic attraction, but Aquarians will patronize you mercilessly. It all adds to the fun!

July: Enrol on a short psychology course. It'll help you find your psyche and hopefully a new sex partner. Be picky: avoid professor types or those who are seeking enlightenment. Jump on those who are looking for something deeper if you get our drift. Cancer is a sure bet.

August: The locality is teeming with Sagittarians and Geminis. They'll give good sex on the 7th, 8th, 9th, 22nd and 23rd. Avoid these two signs on all other dates. Venus and Mars reside in Cancer and it's this sign which is hot, heavy and sexually primed all month. Get one quickly.

September: Teach the secrets of sexual attraction to Virgos by giving them a free lesson. Lovers who are much older or younger will be most exciting. But the emphasis is on Leos. They'll pull you in from the 7th onwards. You can be desired and loved all at the same time.

December 1996 (Scorpio): If Sagittarians get too big for their pants, bury them in the sand and hook up elsewhere.

October: An innovative slant to your sexual technique makes this a memorable month. Your reputation and love life get a welcome boost and so does your sex life. The 26th and the 27th bring one outstanding matter to a climax. Don't let emotions rule your genitals.

November: Your mood is all love, sex and indulgence. An affair that's beginning to waver requires vigorous boosting in the way you know best. The Scorpio New Moon on the 11th heralds a brand new phase in your sex life. Set high goals.

December: Extricate yourself from family get-togethers: fly to a tropical location, dig a hole on the beach and have a long love-in. Sagittarians will be willing partners. If they get too big for their pants, bury them in the sand and hook up elsewhere.

Best days in 1997 for sex

January: The two planetary giants – Jupiter and Saturn – will make this a year to remember. Marital affairs, love affairs and sex affairs will be a source of satisfaction and pleasure. Early month is best for sex, mid-month for love and late month for new strategies. Be daring.

February: Your in-built magnetic compass locates the best sex-mates. And they'll be Aquarians, Librans or Ariens. The New Moon on the 7th stirs up powerful Scorpionic emotions and feelings. From that date onwards, love matters will pan out in precisely the way you want.

March: A highly energized phase: romantic/sexual vibes seep through the fabric of your underwear. Well-built, fair-headed types hold your interest up until the 23rd. But you'll get bored and need a sexual hike in late month. Get immersed with a Pisces, but don't drown.

April: In your heart of hearts you're looking for a soul mate, but no one matches up. Make do with what's available. You're keenly aware of Taureans, but scan the horizon for other signs.

A frisky start to the month will raise hopes, but brazen Leos won't fulfil expectations.

May: Customary routines bring biggest rewards. A potential partner has been under your nose for months! You're itching to experiment sexually. Deep thoughts blind you to others. Emotions are running high from the 6th, but make sure you take it slowly and gently.

June: You're a deadly predator – some might say the largest land flesh-eater alive. You don't care: you seek to conquer and always succeed. Fortuitous trends propel you forwards up until the 23rd. Leos and Taureans are mesmerized by your enormous sexual appetite.

July: In the heat of the summer, you dominate the environment with a special heat of your own (sexual heat). Most are in awe of it (Scorpio/Cancer), some dislike it (refined Libran/ Aquarius). But you'll pull fiery types effortlessly (Leo, Aries and Sagittarius).

August: You respond instinctively to a pass in mid-month. But you're highly suspicious: it's all too easy. You may get your wires crossed. Have some fun and don't take it too seriously. Play-ful Sagittarians and Geminis are just what the therapist ordered.

September: Mars in Scorpio is a fearsome combination. You're unstoppable, unbeatable and generally unbearable. Sexually receptive every hour, the urge is irresistible and only fellow Scorpios can respond adequately. Active copulation and pleasure lasts from the 1st to the 28th.

October: The emphasis shifts to courtship and foreplay. Venus in Scorpio makes you naturally attractive and helps delude those naturally repulsed by your basic desires. Intruders may muscle in on your patch from the 8th: ignore them – you've plenty to be getting on with.

November: Avoid sexually immature partners. Focus on those your own age. Be gentle and sociable: you don't have to fight to establish territory. Whether or not a lover will be faithful, there's little you can do. A Full Moon on the 14th signals an end and a beginning.

December: Your sexual apparatus is highly sensitive and you can do without lovers who are rough and clumsy. Amid the festive euphoria, you'll attract the odd bad apple. From the 12th, things pick up substantially. Mobility, speed and sexual glint give you the edge.

SAGITTARIUS

Best days in 1996 for sex

January: The type of love you give and the type of love you receive are highlighted by the stars. The 16th, 17th and 18th are dazzling days. A love interest from pre-Christmas will turn into a sex interest by late month. Take it easy: a rocky start is predicted.

February: Sexual developments are subtle, but enlightening. Scorpios and Cancers give nothing away. If you want open-ended eroticism, opt for Geminis and fellow Saggies. The love planet enters steamy Aries on the 9th, when you can adopt a more blatant and fiery approach.

March: Continual flirting does nothing for your self-image. If you want a constant supply of sex, at least PRETEND to be faithful: you can be more than convincing if you try. If you want the odd quickie, reserve the 11th, 12th and 25th for first-time sex with new lovers.

April: Venus's erotic influence is stunningly helpful for Saggies with faltering sex lives. Basic drives heat up, passions increase and one or two bold admirers will try their luck. A sexually adventurous Leo will take you by surprise and give you a big lift.

218

May: You want a change, so turn into a Cancer – clingy, possessive and security-mad. You'll pull in Taureans and Capricorns with serious long-term plans. You'll also get your way in bed on the 16th, 17th and 25th. An agile, supple Scorpio will crop up on the 30th.

June: A reputation as a selfish lover is building, unless you take quick remedial action. Yes, occasionally a lover bores you to sleep, but is dull sex better than no sex at all? Think about it. Excitement comes from Leos, Aquarians and Geminis on the 2nd, 6th and 19th.

July: Capricorns are incredibly lucky for you – they have bountiful Jupiter going through their sign. Whatever they touch turns to gold, so get touching with them. Their bodies turn on your desires: by the time of the New Moon on the 15th, they'll give themselves completely.

August: If on holiday, beware of throbbing Romeos and juicy Juliets with unsettling sexual tastes. Important planets are in weak positions – it's no time for fooling around: opt for intelligent chat with Librans. Avoid those who've got more sex cells than brain cells.

September: You're in a sexual mood but can't do anything until Venus enters Leo on the 7th. Productive sex trends will then continue, but concentrate major efforts on Leos and Aquarians. For new sex, use condoms: make sure they're made of extra-strong, long-lasting polyurethane if you're with Scorpios.

October: Pitch in early and grab the best of the bunch – a sensual Cancer or smooth-talking Pisces. Not that talk is what you're after. You'll accomplish goals in fits and starts from the 4th to the 29th. Beware of an over-zealous approach: it could hamper one important relationship.

November: Your second best month of the year. Planetary activity in Sagittarius gets to boiling point. Big events and developments around the 25th will determine the course of your love and sex life for the next three months. Luck on the 12th and the 13th boosts sex prospects in a big way.

December: Your best month. Venus in Sagittarius from the 17th gets the pre-Christmas period off to a rip-roaring start. You'll be basking in sexual warmth and bliss up until the 24th. On top is the best position. Take a break until the 28th, then back to business.

Best days in 1997 for sex

January: An expert and streamlined lover, you're graceful in seduction and even better in bed. The New Year brings challenges and conquests. In mid-month move in on a lover who eluded you in 1996. You dislike intimate attachments, but you want intimate sex. You'll get it.

February: You're a prime target for every restless sex-fiend around. Be choosy or you'll never survive the pace. Submit to a security-loving Taurus or steady Cancerian. They'll be after your money before your body. Stunning sexual times feature on the 6th, 7th and 18th.

March: You have a special talent for ensnaring quality lovers. Ruthless hunting always brings results. But you tire quickly in the first week and may flag out before the sexual act is completed. Late March sees a revival of energy: you'll catch prey in unusual places.   ·

April: The chase usually thrills you, but in mid-April you'll fade away silently and get distinctly bored. Like a wild cat, there is a limit to your interest when a lover plays hard-to-get. By the 16th, you're back on the case and this time you'll score!

May: As it gets hotter, so do you. But your heat can be

inconstant. Fellow fire signs (Aries/Leo) understand your moodiness, but earthy people find it infuriating (Taurus/Capricorn/Virgo). Use stealth to trap your victims: once you've caught them, hold on tight.

June: This long and busy month will be rewarded by unexpected sex in the later days. A New Moon early month makes relationships more palatable, but the Full Moon on the 20th will give you a new way out – if you need it. You're more likely to want a new way in!

July: You're a large, powerful being with desires that equal your size. In the sexual pecking order you're close to the top. Sexual aspirations are frequently fulfilled and July is no exception – providing you opt for suitable mates in mid-month (Aries and Leo).

August: You're in a playful and fun-loving mood. Book an adventure holiday in a travelling circus. You could perform acrobatic feats and tricks in return for sex. Daytime sex will bring the best orgasm. Night-time sex will bring an unexpected cash reward.

September: Back to earth and back to base. Recent activities hover in your mind. Choose an off-beat partner and indulge your wickedest fantasies. Mixed-sex group activities provide the most erotic experiences. Mars in Scorpio all month boosts carnal desire.

October: Match your mating cycle to the number of rainy days. You'll be at it continually. Effortless propulsion into unknown waters speeds up the sexual pace. You'll be panting furiously to get rid of excess sexual heat. The 8th to the 31st is particularly riveting and orgasmic.

November: A shy and rare type of lover enters your scene. What do you do? Drop usual assertive tactics in favour of a more Scorpio-type approach. Cunning and devious, you'll get a result around the 8th/9th. A Sagittarian New Moon on the 30th sets the tone one way or another.

December: An extremely agile performer, you'll come into your own between the 14th and the 31st. Just lie down wherever you happen to be and take what's offered, twisting and turning with natural grace. Fellow Sagittarians/Scorpios will offer the most.

CAPRICORN

Best days in 1996 for sex

January: Of all the zodiacal signs, 1996 is luckiest for you. Brilliant Jupiter resides in Capricorn all year. And Jupiter will give you what you want: whether it's a lasting relationship, numerous love affairs or a plentiful supply of sex. In January, it's new sex from the 3rd.

February: Even if you are a gross, demanding lover, others are magnetically drawn to you. From the 1st to the 14th you are utterly irresistible. Don't let the momentum fizzle. Be organized and make lists of dates: for outings, sex and new encounters. An Aries will make your month!

March: Be adaptable to change. A long-term affair may not be right. Take a Taurus for a ride. Allow flesh to be penetrated, but keep your emotions intact. Social life takes off from the 20th and you'll be going somewhere fast. Anticipate something promiscuous from the 25th.

April: Two eclipses energize and propel you forwards around the 4th and the 17th. Your performance in bed shoots into the red-hot zone. Put lovers on top, but be ready for quick reversals. Your prowess and reputation go before you. Leos are dying for a piece of the action.

May: Our first book, *Life, Love and Destiny*, gives vital clues about your love life. A sex dream or related fantasy has every chance of coming true, but do your homework! A clever idea, plus charm and initiative, will pull the pants off the most stubborn lover.

June: Jupiter moves backwards and so might your sex life. An old lover will make the month more palatable, but don't be too encouraging: a short-term fling is all that's on offer. A bit of luck from the 16th to the 18th perks you up, but wait longer for bigger/better fish.

July: A Capricorn Full Moon on the 1st forces you to leave the past behind: get on with the new and indulge in some experimentation. A Cancer or Pisces will do nicely. A new chapter in your sex life takes off beautifully. Excellent sex is within your reach.

August: Yielding Venus and thrusting Mars aspect your Sun sign, bringing vigorous sexual encounters in unusual positions. A kinky lover pushes your body to the very limits, but it all adds to the fun and makes for strong and memorable climaxes. Avoid screwing heavy objects on the 8th/9th, because otherwise you'll strain your back.

September: The memory of one particular liaison lingers on. Sentiment won't do much good. Privately you may think you're in love, but be reluctant to let on. There are two options: put yourself around unremittingly, or pursue one challenge, but whatever happens, be prepared for delayed orgasms from the 4th to the 27th.

October: Time to change: be a Leo. Capricorn ambition, love of security and steadfastness can be dropped in favour of a more flamboyant, conceited and upfront approach. It'll thrill Geminis, Sagittarians and Leos. An unusual sexual fantasy will go down brilliantly.

November: Background developments hold the key to new

sexual conquests: you may think you're getting nowhere, but Jupiter boosts your sex appeal and makes for a frisky period mid-month. A minor snag may hinder plans, but the period from the 1st to the 22nd could be one of your luckiest yet!

December: In the sack and out you're a star – shining brightly throughout the festive season. Physical contact will be an explosion of passion. You fascinate almost everybody (especially those whose desires run as hot as yours). Aim directly on the 21st, 23rd and 30th.

Best days in 1997 for sex

January: Jupiter in your sign up until the 22nd makes for a pretty expansive, exciting and auspicious introduction to the New Year. You'll get who you want with effortless grace and speed. From the 23rd, be extra sensitive to sex vibrations and offers, especially from Leos.

February: Divide your time between resting and planning (until the 9th) and actively hunting (after the 9th). You're not a predatory type, but this month you'll have to exert more energy if you want to achieve at least one sex-aim. Be less tolerant of competition and push in at the front.

March: You've learnt how to survive in barren sexual conditions: this experience is useful now. The planet Saturn mitigates against indulgent pleasure and wild abandonment. Keep cool, concentrate on material aims and wait patiently for the blossoming of sexual promise.

April: On the 16th, sensual Venus enters lucky Taurus, marking the start of a new phase and a significant penetration of the ranks. You'll attract and devour as never before. Taureans/Scorpios in particular will lunge amorously forwards. You can finally pick and choose.

May: There are large numbers in pursuit of one exceptionally attractive human being. Be canny and cunning. Stay well camouflaged and keep desires and motives to yourself. That way you'll be victorious through a surprise attack. The most auspicious period is the 1st to the 10th.

June: Teach a Gemini/Libra how to unlock frozen desires and frozen organs: crack the surface with a masterful sexual act and clear the clogging once and for all. They'll be utterly grateful and reward you with their bodies on demand. Venus in your love zone from the 4th to the 28th is brilliant.

July: Adapt to the environment and you'll survive on a diet of low-grade sex (temporarily)! The summer heat appears to have produced desert-like, arid conditions. If you score in mid-month, don't cling on to your prey for too long: fresher, juicier talent is on the way.

August: You'll need to tune in sensitively and pick up low-frequency sex signals – specifically from Cancer/Scorpio. You'll soon pinpoint the sender and home in dramatically, with no warning. Later in the month there are exceptional sexual results, especially on the 27th/28th.

September: A solitary animal is what you'll be in early month. Sex is in plentiful supply, but you're not interested. The new autumn season finds you re-evaluating objectives and plans. You prefer to blend into your habitat and lie low. You'll perk up later – much later.

October: You're back on fighting form and in hot pursuit of a Leo, Libra or Aries. You're in the mood for a variety of different mates. Once you've pounced, don't waste time with words. Sink your claws into their privates and drag them back to your den on the 8th, 9th and 21st.

November: Keen senses keep you on top of the situation, especially where sex is concerned. You can't be fooled and are seldom taken for a ride. But Scorpios can get the better of you. They'll promise loads, but won't deliver: avoid them on the 1st, 2nd and 14th (especially the 14th)!

December: Fertility and sex appeal radiate outwards like a beacon. A minor sexual skirmish on the 12th and the 13th leads to something meaningful just before Christmas day. An unusual encounter on the 26th and the 27th may lead to an out-of-body experience.

AQUARIUS

Best days in 1996 for sex

January: Lustful Mars in your Sun sign means its time to go the whole hog over romantic and emotional matters. Don't let old ties get in the way of new conquests. From the 21st to the 31st the pleasure pace speeds up dramatically. Leos, Taureans and Capricorns are good sex bets.

February: The Aquarian New Moon on the 18th puts heavy emphasis on close relationships. Unexpected encounters lead to sudden and unexpected sex. Fellow Aquarians want to get closer and give as much as they demand: bold and promiscuous they might be, but boring – never!

March: You're overextending yourself sexually: by spreading yourself thinly, you don't satisfy anyone, least of all yourself. Erratic Uranus, currently in Aquarius, makes it hard for you to relax and get a perspective. Streamline affairs and get on top of things quickly.

April: A low point. Insubstantial lovers come into your life. They need security, but it's not on offer. Physical contact is sparse. Concentrate on the 20th to the 30th for livelier lovers, specifically Cancer and Leo. They have a natural understanding of the flesh.

May: If you want your way you'll have to be selfish. You fascinate Taureans and together you make a sensual couple. Be demanding, domineering and indispensable. Mid-May is tricky. Avoid heavy sex and concentrate on light chat. By the 23rd it's back to normal.

June: Power struggles loom. You're no match for Capricorns and Scorpios: be submissive and allow them the dominance they crave. But you'll get one over Geminis and Librans. You are obsessed with sex in late month, and may need electronic gadgetry to fill in a gap.

July: Existing relationships need spicing up, with leather, PVC and bull-whips. If your lover's of a conventional type, then break the ice first with blue movies and red satin. The 8th to the 15th are good days to be tied up. Flagellation is best from the 25th onwards.

August: Your capabilities in bed are about to be tested. The period around the 14th is critical. But you'll pass with flying colours and emerge with a new lover in your grasp. Super-star sex dates are the 5th, 6th, 8th, 26th, 27th and 28th. Keep emotions under control.

September: Dynamic and lusty lovers are now hovering in the wings. You'll accomplish a lot where quick affairs are concerned. Brilliant ideas and Aquarian imagination boost sexual credibility. An illicit meeting around the 23rd and the 24th will be gratifying.

October: The eclipse on the 12th coincides with puzzling developments. As the month unfolds, you'll get a handle on a difficult situation and could be in luck – if a new lover is a priority. Sagittarians will be super-receptive to any and every idea. Oral sex is the key to lasting love after the 21st.

November: The planets shift into critical positions. Short- and long-term arrangements will be accepted unreservedly. Reckless enthusiasm on your part will go down well between the 2nd and 17th. Provocative gestures get a great response, especially from Aries and Gemini.

December: Most of the month will find you busy organizing, entertaining and partying. But there will be time for the odd one-night stand. If you play your cards right, you'll be knee-deep in writhing lovers. Pre-Christmas orgies are OK, provided you're well stocked with champagne-flavoured condoms.

Best days in 1997 for sex

January: You like sex at any time, but it's important to start off the New Year as you mean to carry on – do it as much as possible, thereby setting the tone for the months ahead. Your sex scent is alluring and magnetic, so use it to take advantage of unsuspecting Virgos.

February: Remarkably agile, you catch prey by pursuing them, cornering them and attacking from the side. Fire signs (Leo/Aries/Sagittarius) are particularly delighted by this fearless approach and will succumb immediately. The Aquarian who dares wins. The 7th to the 22nd are super sex dates.

March: Don't fall into the trap of chasing anything that moves. March is a month for discretion and discrimination. Many planets in seductive Pisces make this sign a must for sleeping with. Be quietly open and responsive and one will come swimming your way between the 1st and the 22nd.

April: At least three admirers are queuing up for your favours. Mate with them intermittently. Cuddly-looking and innocent, each will believe you're monogamous. Keep up the act unremittingly – have sex on any pretext, in weird locations (geographically and anatomically), especially from the 10th onwards.

May: Jupiter in Aquarius is really fortunate for all of you. Fulfilling relationships, satisfying sex and a generally happy time is ahead. The only danger is in overdoing the physicalities. Take daytime naps, get a substantial recharge and prepare for new conquests.

June: Be secretive in your movements and don't be seen on open ground. Do your mating in private, secluded places. Ariens accompany sex with assorted grunts and screams: it's embarrassing. Get fierce and aggressive if you want to get rid of them. Good sex days: 9th, 10th, 23rd.

July: Be blatant in your sex signals: follow lovers around, nibble their necks and generally be a pain. They'll give in and will enjoy the experience more than they ever dreamt possible. Once hooked, manipulate them unmercifully. The 23rd to the 31st is highly productive.

August: A retrograde Jupiter makes for a dry month. Preserve sanity by devising sexual strategies that can be implemented

July 1997 (Aquarius): If you nibble your lover's neck, he will enjoy the experience more than he ever dreamt possible.

after the 29th. Avoid futile pursuits or wasteful telephone calls: accept the situation and renew attempts on the 30th and the 31st. A Leo will provide what you need.

September: Although you glide from lover to lover with exceptional grace, you're still vulnerable to a sincere Cancer, Scorpio or Capricorn. Face up to your feelings: if it's real love you're after, admit it and act. But pre-love sex can come first, on the 13th, the 14th and the 26th.

October: Time to gather in lovers and hoard them, in time for the lean winter months ahead. A short exploratory outing will make it clear who's available and willing and who's not. Chances are that Librans and Scorpios are quickest on the uptake. Avoid mid-month intercourse.

November: A month to be super-active in the sack: sharp turns, spirals and corkscrews thrill partners, especially Geminis and Sagittarians, who will join in and improve on your performance. Intense coupling and post-sex games are great fun between the 8th and the 30th.

December: A lethargic start wears off on the 9th. You'll emerge in hungry mood, well prepared for a dazzling round of festivities and encounters. Highly developed intuition and long, sensitive fingers are your basic erotic weapons: use them to locate your ideal mate.

PISCES

Best days in 1996 for sex

January: The love planet, Venus, enters Pisces on the 15th. A totally magical month: unbridled passion, exclusive sex with a fatal attraction and major ego boosts from several quarters. Make the most of it, especially on the 23rd, 24th, 27th and 28th.

February: You'll feel exposed and vulnerable. But others find you enigmatic and unfathomable. Whilst they're trying to get to the root of it, you can keep a sharp eye on your own sexual interests. Probe deeply to get answers, but be warned: Cancers are not about to reveal all.

March: Your actions are irrational, but you'll be proved right in the long run. If you're fed up, display a different persona. Be a Libra: detached, unemotional and light. You'll pull in birds of a feather and you might even enjoy it. Best days for sex: 17th and 18th.

April: Insane jealousy and possessiveness are taking you over. Get a grip and be objective. A lover's time isn't exclusively yours. Dull Saturn leaves your sign on the 7th. This is fabulous news and heralds a brand new emotional and sexual cycle. Be lucky!

May: Don't play on a lover's weaknesses, it's unnecessary; innate charm, attractiveness and sex-appeal are enough – resorting to underhand tactics won't work. Dynamic planetary movements will make Virgos and Geminis fall under your magical spell. Star dates are the 11th and the 12th.

June: Be willing to let go a little, especially with Libra, Aquarius, and Gemini. Charisma wins through from the 13th onwards. Leos exude eroticism and are worth a one-night stand, so don't hold back. An impromptu meeting around the 22nd/23rd augurs well for your sexual fantasies.

July: Alter routines so you can accommodate a Gemini more easily. The cosmos is decidedly in your favour: if you're hoping for something solidly sexual, strike between the 2nd and the 22nd. A lover will unravel an interesting sex toy in late month, which will improve your sex life no end.

August: Consider your input to others before making romantic or emotional decisions. Not a month to expect steamy sex, but a month to analyse motivations, and to decide what you really want. If you're looking for casual sex, choose the 28th or 29th, under a Piscean Full Moon.

September: A high spot in your sexual calendar. A New Moon on the 12th brings a host of opportunities. Shelve previous plans and act on the spur-of-the-moment. A new friendship brings a sexual fringe benefit in the form of a rampant Capricorn or Cancer with an intimate birthmark.

October: Carnal desires are hard to control, especially from the 4th, when Venus makes stunning connections to your sign. Your love life and sex life perk up considerably. When Mars enters the picture on the 30th, there are few who won't fall prey to your slippery magnetism.

November: You're getting the urge to explore fresh horizons in the shape of an attractive Sagittarian or Aquarian. Vivid imagination and fantasies may get in the way of reality and accelerate to a climax around the 15th, 16th and the 17th. You can be a visionary but be a realist too.

December: A dangerous but thrilling month, when you get lost in a sexual haze. New windows of opportunity beckon strongly but, if you're offered some long-term love, pass it by. Singles will benefit enormously from festive sex, especially from the 15th to the 18th.

Best days in 1997 for sex

January: Jupiter brings illicit affairs. There's nothing you like better. A natural-born lover, you swoop swiftly on your prey, attached or otherwise. Aquarians are a great bet: mutual admiration gives a certain boost to the proceedings.

February: An incisive, rewarding month. You scan the landscape for mates with your keen eyesight and keen sex drive. Lethal accuracy and devastating attacks fill lovers with awe and admiration. Capricorns thrill to your touch and respond magnificently from the 19th to the 28th.

March: Venus in Pisces from the 1st to the 22nd is a lucky omen. You'll flush new lovers out from thick undergrowth. And Venus will greatly increase your sexual success. The force and impact of your love-making has no limits: you're a hard act to follow and impossible to emulate.

April: Top predators have their eye on you. If you want to be caught, act accordingly. If not, lie low and avoid Sagittarians/ Ariens. By mid-month you'll need to fulfil sexual urges: go for gentle Virgos or Librans. But don't be snapped up like a dispensable sex object.

May: Your sex-drive goes ballistic this month, and one partner is unlikely to be enough. Three-in-a-bed marathons may satisfy your lust, provided your bedmates have the stamina of steam engines and the insatiability of hammerhead sharks. The best days for blindfolded group sex are from the 17th to the 23rd, provided everyone's well stocked with rubber.

June: Resist any urge to dive in head first after a particularly stubborn partner. Battering them into submission, or talking them senseless, is not your style. Be subtle and recognize your limitations. If there's no result by the 18th, aim for a different target.

July: The competition becomes vigorous. Satisfying long-stand-ing sex partners becomes difficult. Dream up a new sex angle and you'll have them begging noisily for more. The alternative is to become aggressively territorial, but you could lose more than you gain!

August: You're at your most intense when trying to attract a mate. Although you thrive on the chase, you tire quickly if there's inadequate response. The sun-warmed atmosphere pro-duces an abundance of sexual heat. Extra effort will increase your mating success from the 1st to the 17th.

September: Not a lot going on: be reserved and keep your dignity when it comes to unapproachable lovers. Having fun and living superficially is the way to go. Shelve heavier stuff until later. Perfectly adapted to marine environments, you should seek out sex in coastal resorts.

October: Strengthen love bonds by giving presents and extra sex. Being a notoriously unpredictable Fish, lovers may be suspicious of your motives. They'll savour the memorable, but brief, euphoria that you create. By the 20th you'll be back in pursuit of the new.

November: New planetary movements put the emphasis on long-term relationships, where you are certainly a warm and patient lover. You'll develop an increasingly monogamous preference, but may have to seek out new attachments: old ones have tired of your fickle and inconstant ways.

December: Dig or crawl your way into a new lover's underwear. Humility and submissiveness work splendidly on Geminis/Leos. By Christmas itself you'll feel completely contented with your sexual and social achievements. Allow your body to be guided passively by Scorpios from the 15th to the 28th.

Chapter Seven

....

HOW TO HOLD ON TO YOUR LOVER

INTRODUCTION

If you are a fanatical member of the immoral majority, who regards it as being blasphemously unhygienic to sleep with the same person twice, then you're going to find this chapter really offensive. We would therefore recommend that you give it a miss and move straight to Chapter Eight, where we tell you how to get rid of lovers once they've passed their sell-by date.

However, if your moral standards are less exacting and you're prepared to go so far as to commit yourself to a long-term relationship, then you may find this chapter extremely useful. It will give you detailed advice on how to hold on to a lover; if you follow this advice, we are confident that you will gain maximum mileage out of your present and future relationships.

To give you an idea of how astrology can help you to hold on to your lover, we would like to continue with the story of Monica. In the last chapter, you found out how she used astrology to uncover Mike the Scorpio's hidden sexuality. This information was of great help to Monica, because it helped prepare her for a physical relationship with her new lover. She was able to discover, for example, that she was about to sleep with a sex god who would have no difficulty satisfying her many erotic needs. She was also relieved to find out that Mike had few kinks or peculiarities and that he was unlikely to submit her to obscene practices involving Indian take-aways and stinging insects.

Although a detailed knowledge of Mike's sexuality was very useful to Monica, it couldn't on its own guarantee the long-term survival of the relationship. As you will remember from Chapter Five, Mike and Monica's relationship was still going strong after six weeks. Now one of the reasons it had lasted for so long was that Monica continued to use astrology. She rang Archie up a few times, and asked him to tell her about Mike's attitude to a wide range of subjects, including the home, marriage, children, sex, and more sex. Monica was then able to make adjustments to her behaviour, so as to keep Mike sweet and faithful.

At this stage you're probably dying to know what Archie and Monica talked about, so we now print an unedited, uncensored transcript of one of their telephone conversations.

ARCHIE: Hello?

MONICA: Anyway . . .

ARCHIE: Hello?

MONICA: Archie! Hold on . . . OK . . . bye! Sorry, Archie, can you hold on, someone's trying to get through . . .

[There is a fifteen-second break in the tape.]

MONICA: Sorry about that, but everything's a complete nightmare at the moment. The telephone's gone mad.

ARCHIE: So, you're back.

MONICA: Yeah, we had a great time, and Mike is just amazing. Just like you said. The best lover I've ever had. Brilliant . . . I just feel so happy, and so satisfied.

ARCHIE: Great.

MONICA: But I think you were wrong about Scorpio being the least kinky sign of the zodiac. He's seriously into domination.

ARCHIE: I'm sorry.

MONICA: No, it's not a problem. Actually, I quite enjoy it. But there was this time when we went to this club in Santa Cruz, and I got talking to this guy. Kurt from Stuttgart. Yeah, he seemed to quite like me. He wasn't anything special, but he did have lots of money. I think he was a Capricorn. Somehow, I had this sense of *déjà vu*, as if I'd slept with him before. Maybe I had. Anyway, Mike got really mad. He didn't say anything. He just went very quiet.

ARCHIE: He's a Scorpio. They've got to be treated with respect.

MONICA: Yeah. Anyway, when we got back to the hotel room, he blindfolded me. With a couple of silk ties. It was really scary. It was like I had this wild animal in the same bed as me. I couldn't see him, only feel and hear him. I never knew what he was going to do next. God, it was really far out. The ultimate trip. I think I experienced everything. And when he took the ties off . . . it was like I was being born all over again . . . it was also time for lunch. Amazing. And then, he told me to never flirt again. Or else.

ARCHIE: Or else what?

MONICA: I'm not sure.

ARCHIE: So. You've stopped flirting?

MONICA: Of course.

ARCHIE: But what if he finds . . .?

MONICA: Sorry, I'll have to ring you back.

[There is a two-minute break in the tape.]

ARCHIE: Hello?

MONICA: Hi. Yeah, what I want to know is, how do I hold on to Mike? We're both crazy about each other, and sex is great, and we're really compatible. But I'm afraid that things are going to go wrong. Archie, what do I do to keep him? Tell me.

ARCHIE: Well, Scorpios hate it when their women flirt in front of them, as you've found out. You'll end up dead if you carry on like that.

MONICA: I told you, that's all over. Mike's my man, and I'm not interested in anyone else.

ARCHIE: And then there's honesty. Scorpios are obsessed about it, and they hate it when their partners lie to them. Or deceive them, or do things behind their back. Once they've caught you out once, they'll never forgive you.

MONICA: Aaah . . . I see . . . So it's important not to get caught. I think I can manage that.

ARCHIE: But Scorpios always find out. It doesn't matter how clever you are. They'll always get you.

MONICA: I don't know about that. I've deceived so many men. Hundreds. Thousands. In fact, I think I've deceived every man I've ever met. They're such idiots. Except you, of course. Anyway, what about sex?

ARCHIE: What about it?

MONICA: Well, how do I keep him happy in bed?

ARCHIE: You seem to be doing a good job so far.

MONICA: Yes, but I somehow feel that I'm not doing enough.

ARCHIE: Are you totally surrendering yourself to him?

MONICA: Yes.

ARCHIE: Mind, body and spirit?

MONICA: Yeah. I've let him blindfold me and do all sorts of things. Yeah, definitely.

ARCHIE: What about spirit? When he's making love to you, do you feel possessed by him?

MONICA: Umm . . . I'm not sure what you mean . . . you mean like being possessed by a demon, like the girl in *The Exorcist*?

ARCHIE: That's exactly what I mean.

MONICA: That's . . . umm . . . ridiculous. There's no way that anyone's ever going to possess me. Never.

ARCHIE: Well, Monica, if you are really serious about Mike, it's essential that you allow him to possess you. And it's no good faking possession.

MONICA: Christ, Archie, you're so weird. But I suppose you're right. You usually are. And frequency . . . How often will Mike want sex, once our relationship's settled down?

ARCHIE: Scorpio's a highly sexed sign. So he's going to want it fairly often.

MONICA: How often?

ARCHIE: It's difficult to be precise . . . but I think with Scorpio it's a question of quality rather than quantity. He might be satisfied with sex once or twice a week, provided it's mind-blowingly sensational.

MONICA: I think you're right. Yeah, that's very perceptive of you. Now, I wanted to ask you about moving in with Mike. I'm not sure when, but we've started talking about it.

ARCHIE: Already?

MONICA: Yeah. Joe the Toad reckons I should have no problem selling my flat. Or else I might rent it out. He reckons I could get two hundred a week for it.

ARCHIE: So you're going to live with Mike.

MONICA: Yeah, he's got this huge flat off the Finchley Road. Three bedrooms, and loads of space. His bed's amazing. I don't think there'll be any problems moving in.

ARCHIE: I do.

MONICA: What?

ARCHIE: I think there'll be problems. Scorpios are very private people, and they don't like it when other people get in their way.

MONICA: Yeah, but he says he's happy for me to move in.

ARCHIE: On his terms. You'll have to adjust your bedtimes, mealtimes and sex times to fit in with his lifestyle. And you'll have to give up long phone calls.

MONICA: Oh.

ARCHIE: Then there are your ghastly friends.

MONICA: Archie!

ARCHIE: Come on, a lot of them are pretty ghastly. Anyway, I don't think he'll like them . . .

MONICA: He got on OK with Sandra.

ARCHIE: Yeah, well, I'm sure she's OK in small doses. But the point is, he won't like you bringing your friends round to his flat. Scorpios do, after all, despise everyone . . . except their immediate family and their close friends.

MONICA: Oh, and talking about family, what about children? And marriage?

ARCHIE: So you want to get married to him? Already?

MONICA: I'm nearly thirty. It's time to settle down.

ARCHIE: And become a dutiful housewife?

MONICA: Yes. I don't see why not. I could learn how to sew buttons and darn socks.

ARCHIE: Sure.

MONICA: Anyway, tell me about Scorpio's attitude to marriage and children.

ARCHIE: Mmm . . .

MONICA: I mean, if I marry him, then it's bound to help me hold on to him, isn't it?

ARCHIE: Mmm . . .

MONICA: Oh shit, it's four o'clock. I've got to get my nails done. Bye.

This conversation between Archie and Monica highlights the difference between casual and long-term relationships. If we are in a casual relationship, we don't have to know too much about our partners; their attitude to things like marriage and children will be fairly irrelevant. However, in a long-term relationship, lasting anything from a fortnight to a lifetime, it is important to have a deeper understanding of one's partner.

We saw how Monica thought that she could move into Mike's flat, without changing either her lifestyle or her social habits. As Archie pointed out, this idea was rather naïve. Mike is, after all, a Scorpio, who likes to be in total control of his domestic environment.

Attitudes to marriage and children also need to be considered. If, for example, you tell your Cancerian lover that you want to get married and have children, then you will be strengthening the relationship no end. Say the same thing to an Aquarian and the relationship may never recover. So, if you want to hold on to your lovers, it is always a good idea to look at their Sun signs. That way you'll avoid making costly mistakes.

At the beginning of each section in this chapter, we give you general advice, then detailed information on how to hold on to your lover. We cover the following topics:

Keeping your lover happy in bed

We look at sex and tell you how to keep your lover satisfied. The emphasis is not on single sexual episodes but on the role of sex within a long-term relationship. Amongst other things, we tell you how often you should expect to have sex with your lover.

Keeping your lover happy in the home

If you're in a long-term relationship, you may eventually move in with your lover. At this stage all sorts of frictions can develop – for example, a Virgo will go berserk if you do the washing up in the lavatory bowl, and a Scorpio will go AWOL if you down-load pornographic pictures from the Internet (particularly if you use her computer). To ensure that such frictions don't occur, we tell you how to behave in the home and how not to upset your lover's delicate sensibilities.

Understanding your lover's attitude to marriage

At a certain stage in every relationship, the issue of marriage raises its ugly head. We tell you how your lover likes dealing with this subject and we also give you an idea of whether marriage would increase the life-span of a relationship.

When it comes to timing, we give you an idea of how long you should wait before proposing marriage and how you should go about it. We take the view that, in most cases, women are just as capable of making marriage proposals as men. However, we recommend that our female readers are cautious when dealing with some of the more macho signs.

Understanding your lover's attitude to children

From a biological point of view, the only reason that men and women are attracted to one another is so that they can mate and produce children who will survive long enough to have children of their own. So it is often important to understand your lover's attitude to children, particularly if you're planning on having a relationship which lasts longer than nine months.

Holding on to your lover when all else fails

You've read our book backwards, you've taken every word of our advice and still the ungrateful bastard wants to leave you. What do you do? Well, you should probably let him or her go and find someone else. However, if you're obsessed with your lover, you may not be able to accept this advice; in which case, you'll have to resort to emergency measures. The emergency measures that are recommended for each of the twelve signs are often extreme and should only be used as a last resort. If they backfire, the authors of this book take no responsibility for the consequences.

We would like to point out that in most cases you can hold

on to your lover with money, however bad the relationship is going. The following table gives you an idea of how much it might cost to hold on to each of the signs, in pounds sterling.

Sign	£ (sterling)
Aries	5,000,000
Taurus	250,000 (in cash)
Gemini	10,000 (watch out – they'll take the money and run)
Cancer	50,000
Leo	3,000 (males); 1,000,000 (females)
Virgo	300 (per night)
Libra	25,000 (per month)
Scorpio	10,000,000,000
Sagittarius	5,000
Capricorn	75,000,000
Aquarius	75,000,000
Pisces	50p

One final point we want to make is that a relationship is a two-way affair. If you are going to do everything possible to keep your lover happy, he or she should return the favour. So make sure that your lover reads this chapter and finds out how to hold on to YOU. That way your relationship has the best possible chance of surviving and prospering.

ARIES—GENERAL ADVICE

During the first few months of your relationship with Aries, you won't have to take any special steps to hold on to them (unless you have the misfortune to be dating the abominable Monica). The original passion that first brought you together is likely to linger on and, if you have the odd argument or fight, it won't be the end of the world.

However, as the relationship progresses, you will have to get used to the Rams' mood swings. One week they'll want you to take the initiative, and the next they'll want to walk all over you. At the same time you must always be spontaneous and full of new ideas to keep you both amused. And one other thing. The Rams dislike jealous and possessive partners and they hate being asked questions such as 'What did you do last night? and 'When are you and your secretary coming back from the Seychelles?'

Keeping your lover happy in bed

If you are serious about holding on to your Aries lover, then you must prepare yourself for regular sex sessions. The female Aries will require sex daily, while the male of the species needs

The Aries male needs sex every six hours, or else. . . .

it every six hours. This means that you must always be on stand-by for sex, rather like a Battle of Britain fighter pilot waiting for the Luftwaffe's next raid.

When you do have sex with the Rams, make sure that you are passionate and enthusiastic, even if you have been married to them for thirty years. If you refuse the Rams' sexual advances more than twice in a row, they will start looking elsewhere for satisfaction.

Keeping your lover happy in the home

Once you move in with your Aries lover, you will realize that you are dealing with a selfish person, who likes to have their own way. They will expect you to adapt your routine to fit in with theirs and they will expect you to do as you're told. If you try to order the Rams around, or complain that they are not doing their fair share of the household chores, they will explode and accuse you of being an interfering, ungrateful fascist. None the less, it is unlikely that your relationship with your lover will break down for domestic reasons alone: the Rams often get a perverse kick out of long-running domestic disputes, particularly if their partner-cum-opponent is loud-mouthed and belligerent.

Understanding your lover's attitude to marriage

The Rams have a rather ambiguous attitude to marriage. On the one hand, they hate the idea of being tied down to one partner for life. On the other, they love spontaneity and the idea of a sudden marriage may well turn them on. Your Aries lover may, therefore, propose to you within the first few days of the relationship. However, if you don't accept the proposition immediately, they will quickly change their mind.

If you want to do the proposing, you can do it at any stage in the relationship though, if possible, your proposal should be unexpected and come at a moment of high passion. Try asking

245

the Ram to marry you while you're both lying in bed, having a blazing argument about who should be on top. One final thing to remember: marrying the Rams won't help you hold on to them. Once they're sick of you, their wedding vows will be about as useful as a bent farthing.

Understanding your lover's attitude to children

At the beginning of a relationship with an Aries, it is not a good idea to bring up the subject of children. The Rams will automatically assume that you're planning to take away their freedom.

However, after a year or two, the situation changes and we start seeing some differences between the sexes. The male Aries is very good with children and definitely wants to be a father. If he was in a stale relationship and his partner suddenly announced that she was pregnant, he would be over the moon and he would have a renewed commitment to the relationship.

The female Aries has a rather different attitude. She wants children, but she is horrified by the thought of nine months of restricted mobility and eighteen years of parental responsibility. So it is best that you avoid discussing the subject of children with your female partner. When she's summoned up the courage to bite the natal bullet, she'll let you know.

Holding on to your lover when all else fails

You can do what you like with the Rams. You can blackmail them, you can marry them, you can get them pregnant, you can get them to get you pregnant, you can give them diamonds, you can give them a Rolls Royce, you can get down on your knees and beg. However, once they've had enough of you, that's it. They leave. Short of locking them up in a cage, there is absolutely nothing you can do to stop them and nothing you can do to bring them back. Sorry.

TAURUS—GENERAL ADVICE

The longer that you go out with Taureans, the easier it is to hold on to them. After a few months, they start getting used to you and within a year they regard you as a permanent fixture. However, there is no need to be complacent, because there are still positive steps you can take in order to tighten your grip on your Taurean lover's affections.

For one thing, Taureans are obsessed by beauty; in all likelihood your lover chose you because you looked so good. He or she will expect you to carry on looking good, so you must make sure that you continue to look after your figure and general appearance.

We also recommend that you think back to your first few dates and ask yourself what other things about you seemed to attract the Taurus. If it was the expensive presents that you gave them, then make sure that your generosity continues unabated. If it was your cooking, then carry on going to cordon bleu cooking classes.

Keeping your lover happy in bed

Male Taureans are easy to please. You just submit to their sexual advances, which will come your way two or three times a week. As the relationship progresses, you should find that these advances become as regular as clockwork, so Wednesday and Saturday might, for example, be your Taurean man's regular sex days. After the first six months of the relationship, you can cut down on the amount of time you massage and pamper the Bull. If you're a busy career girl, you'll start having more free slots in your diary to play around with.

Female Taureans are harder to please; they will expect you to give them full sexual attention for the duration of the relationship. They will require sex at least four times a week and they won't be amused if you skimp on the foreplay.

Keeping your lover happy in the home

The home is extremely important to Taureans, so make sure that you pay a lot of attention to the domestic side of the relationship. If you're in a traditional relationship and you're the bread-winner, make sure that you spend a lot of money on making the home look beautiful. Buy new kitchens every few years and, if possible, give your Taurean partner regular blank cheques so that they can splash out on redecoration and landscape gardening.

If, on the other hand, it is you that is staying at home and the Taurean is the one earning the money, then you'll have a fairly easy life, though you will, of course, be expected to provide superb meals on a regular basis.

Understanding your lover's attitude to marriage

Taureans believe that marriage is a good thing and, if you are in a relationship with them for longer than a week, they will expect you to join them at the altar. However, you must appreciate that Taureans are traditionalists, who expect the man to do the proposing. So if you're a man, and you've been going out with a Taurean girl for a few months, it is probably time that you popped the question. Assuming, of course, that you can afford an extremely expensive engagement ring.

Taurean men will propose to their partners within the first year of a relationship, provided that they feel financially secure. If your Taurean man is a millionaire and you're still waiting for a proposal after eighteen months, then ditch him; he's either got a wife or a mistress, or he's lying about his Sun sign.

Once you do get married to the Bulls, either male or female, your chances of holding on to them will definitely improve, so if you're serious about your Taurean lover, get married as soon as possible.

Understanding your lover's attitude to children

When it comes to children, Taureans are extremely responsible. They believe that children need to be looked after in a stable family environment, where there is enough money around to feed, cloth and educate them.

At the same time, many Taureans are moralistic and don't like the idea of children being born out of wedlock. You should therefore avoid getting too serious about children at the beginning of a relationship, because otherwise your partner will regard you as being an irresponsible, immoral fool. It is best to keep your comments vague, and say things like, 'I hope we win the jackpot on the lottery, because then we could get married and have lots of children.'

However, once you are married, and relatively prosperous, children are an excellent idea. They ensure that you are able to hold on to your Taurean lover for as long as you want.

Holding on to your lover when all else fails

If your lover is on the point of walking out on you, then cook a gourmet meal. If you can't cook, which is probably one of the reasons why you're being dumped, then hire a French chef for the day. After that, lie on your dining-room table and have the food laid out over your naked body. Don't forget to clasp a bottle of finest claret between your thighs. When your lover sees, smells and tastes you, he or she will go crazy and you'll be given one more chance to prove yourself. Don't blow it!

GEMINI—GENERAL ADVICE

Holding on to a Gemini is hard work, so before you throw all your resources into maintaining your relationship with the Twins, you should ask yourself whether it's worth it. After all,

Geminis are unreliable and inconsiderate people who tend to get bored with their partners after a couple of months.

If you want a lasting and caring relationship, wouldn't it be better to choose a more stable sign, such as Taurus or Cancer? However, you may be addicted to your lover's phenomenal intellect and sparkling charm, in which case you'd better read the following few pages very carefully. If you follow what we say to the letter, then you will hold on to your lover, provided that you have patience, resilience, and above all, flexibility.

Keeping your lover happy in bed

Geminis are appalling insomniacs and if you're sharing a bed with them for longer than a few days, you'll notice that they do a lot of tossing and turning. Gemini also has a rather annoying habit of getting up at 4 a.m. to check up obscure facts in the encyclopaedia. Given these circumstances, we recommend that you have separate beds, or even separate rooms, unless you are a heavy-sleeping sign such as Taurus or Scorpio.

As far as sex is concerned, you must remember to constantly change your sexual style, so that your lover doesn't get bored with you. You must also be prepared to participate in Gemini's outrageously perverted sex games. Be enthusiastic when your lover suggests that you play a new game, which involves two dice, the couple next door and a frozen turkey.

When it comes to frequency, you must appreciate that Geminis go through phases. When they're going through a 'hot' phase, they will want sex every couple of hours. During a 'cold' phase, it may be once a month. However, you have to be careful during cold phases, because they may indicate that your lover is having it off with someone else.

Keeping your lover happy in the home

Geminis like dividing things up. King Solomon, who was almost certainly a Gemini, settled a dispute between two women about ownership of a baby by suggesting that the child be cut in half. The genius who thought up the idea of the Berlin Wall, which divided East and West Berlin, was another Gemini.

So, when you move in with your Gemini lover, you should immediately set about dividing up the house or flat. Decide which rooms you control and which rooms your lover controls. That way you'll both know where you are with each other.

Once you have done that, you've got to keep the Gemini amused. You can do this by inviting interesting people round for dinner, such as mass murderers and disgraced politicians.

One final thing to remember is that Geminis like moving house as often as possible. You should therefore make sure that your suitcases are always half-packed.

Understanding your lover's attitude to marriage

If your relationship with your Gemini lover is in the doldrums, then it's worth getting married. Although marriage won't in itself save the relationship, it will at least allow you to hold on to your lover for a few extra months. The reason for this is that Geminis are curious people who enjoy new experiences. Gemini women are particularly fond of getting married, because it gives them an opportunity to change their name.

However, before you get married to a Gemini you must do some careful research because, as we said earlier in the book, the Twins have a penchant for bigamy.

Understanding your lover's attitude to children

Geminis' approach to children is much the same as their approach to marriage. They regard having children as an exciting adventure that might spice up their lives. You should, therefore, have no worries about bringing up the subject of children.

Another point about Geminis is that they are arrogant and

have a fantasy of creating human beings who match their own intelligences. Having children is, of course, the perfect way of realizing this fantasy.

So overall it will be easier to hold on to your Gemini lover, male or female, once your relationship produces a child. If twins are produced, then you'll be able to hold on to your lover for life.

Holding on to your lover when all else fails

There are a number of ways of holding on to Geminis in an emergency situation. One very simple method is to wait until the Twins are just walking out of the door and then say, 'Before you go, could you possibly tell me how gravity works?' Geminis love showing off their knowledge; they will spend the next few hours trying to explain to you the laws of physics. If that method doesn't work, then you'll have to use the secret weapon, which is certain to bring back your lover. You simply say, 'It's such a shame you're leaving. You'll be missing the eight-in-a-bed sex and flagellation session that I've organized for tonight. We're going to be using the model DZ666 computerized whipping machine, which has just been shipped over from Japan.'

CANCER—GENERAL ADVICE

It's very easy to hold on to Cancerians, provided that you're neither an idiot nor a Gemini. You just have to accept that you and your Cancerian lover are in a parental relationship in which roles are constantly switching back and forth. There will be times when Cancerians want you to mother and protect them and other times when they want to mother and protect you.

Throughout the relationship you should show Cancerians that you are a warm and emotional person. If they are ever in trouble you should immediately go out of your way to help them.

If you are having a relationship with a female Crab, then you will find that she is quite bossy and in most cases she expects to get her way. Male Crabs are not so strong; they often appreciate a domineering partner who is prepared to take over and control their lives.

Keeping your lover happy in bed

According to Sigmund Freud, we are sexually attracted to people who resemble our opposite-sex parents. So, men will find women who resemble their mothers to be irresistible and woman will go for men who are like their fathers. Now, you may think that this theory is complete rubbish, and perhaps for most signs it is. However, Cancerians' sexuality invariably conforms to the Freudian model. You should therefore make sure that, when you're in bed with the Crabs, you smother them in a protective, parental cocoon.

As far as sex is concerned, Cancerians are fairly moody and you should never force yourself on to them, otherwise they might think that you're using them as a sex object. Female Cancerians are particularly temperamental and can go for at least a week without having sex. However, around the four-teenth day after their period, their passions soar and they start wanting it three or four times a day.

Cancerian men don't need sex that often: twice a week is usually enough to keep them quiet.

Keeping your lover happy in the home

The Crabs are domestic animals; if you can keep them happy in the home, then you will have no difficulty holding on to them. To keep them happy, you don't have to spend a fortune on interior design, or on expensive domestic appliances. Nor do you have to be a slave to the kitchen sink. You just have to make sure that you are always there for them, in a supportive role.

If you're hitched up to a male Cancerian, he will want you to stay at home, because that way he'll always know where you are. The female Cancerian is slightly more relaxed, but she does expect her partner to spend all his spare time with her.

When you're at home with a Cancerian you should help with the domestic chores, do the occasional bit of cooking and be soft and emotional. Easy, isn't it?

Understanding your lover's attitude to marriage

Cancerians regard marriage as the crowning moment of a relationship, when they finally gain full control over their partner. So don't get married to Cancerians, unless you're prepared to completely surrender to them. However, if you are reckless enough to take the plunge, then you can safely propose to the Crab when you're about six months into the relationship. If you're dating a male Crab, feel free to make the proposal yourself. In fact, he usually prefers it that way.

Once you're married to your Cancerian lover, the relationship will definitely become stronger and you will both feel a growing confidence that you can hold on to each other until death you do part.

Understanding your lover's attitude to children

Your Cancerian lover dreams of having a family, so it is important that within the first few weeks of the relationship you let him or her know that your main ambition in life is to have six or seven children. But you should bear in mind that the Crabs are cautious animals who believe that it is essential to plan for the future, so they won't want to bring baby Crabs into the world unless they have a secure and stable home in which to bring them up.

254

When it comes to looking after children, Cancerians make excellent parents. The male Cancerian is just as effective as the female and he won't hesitate to do his fair share of the child-rearing – even if this means taking time off work.

Holding on to your lover when all else fails

If your Cancerian lover has left you, you must have done something really stupid. Perhaps you were caught having a steamy affair with his brother or her sister. Or maybe you burnt the house down. Anyway, whatever you've done wrong, it is quite easy to get your lover back. You just use emotional blackmail. This means telling the Crabs that life without them is unbearable and that if they don't come back to you you'll either join the Foreign Legion, or become a Trappist nun.

LEO—GENERAL ADVICE

If you want to be sure of holding on to Leos, then make sure that every morning, before breakfast, you remind yourself of how lucky you are to be going out with one. So when you get out of bed and first catch sight of your lover's king-size photograph (which we assume is hanging from your bedroom wall), you should bow down, and silently thank the gods for giving you such a perfect partner. By doing this simple exercise, you will be ensuring that you maintain a healthy respect for your lover and that you never make the mistake of taking him or her for granted.

When you're in the company of Leos, you should pay careful attention to them; when they're talking, listen to what they say; when they're not talking, massage their egos with lavish compliments. Another thing to bear in mind about Leos is that they like getting presents, so make sure that every few weeks you give them a special gift, as a token of your undying appreciation.

Keeping your lover happy in bed

Every time Leos are flattered and praised, they get a mini-orgasm. When they are given a major honour, such as an Oscar or a knighthood, they get a super-orgasm. This means that the more successful and more highly praised they are, the less they need sex. To take an example from history: if you were Josephine and Napoleon, your Leo lover, had just won another famous victory, you probably wouldn't have to have sex with him. However, if it was the day after the Battle of Waterloo, it would be your job to restore his shattered ego, by letting him conquer you in bed.

So, what we're suggesting is that you look very carefully at your Leo lover's life. If it is going well, then you won't have to bust a gut to keep him or her happy in bed. If, on the other hand, things are going badly, the sexual aspect of the relationship will become vital.

As far as frequency is concerned, it is difficult to be precise, but on average the female will want sex five or six times a week, while the male will want it every other day.

Keeping your lover happy in the home

Keeping Leos happy in the home is expensive, on account of their extravagant tastes. Leo women are particularly demanding and they expect their partners to foot the bill for the services of the most fashionable Californian interior designers. Once their homes are looking fabulous, Leos like to show them off to their celebrity friends. So when you're organizing a party, make sure that everyone on the guest list is a household name.

On a more mundane note, Leos love cats, particularly those white, fluffy things you see in James Bond films. So make sure that you treat the family cat with loving respect and remember that you'll be held personally responsible if it gets run over by a truck.

Understanding your lover's attitude to marriage

When it comes to casual relationships, Leos are not that fussy. If you're reasonably attractive, reasonably well off and reasonably good at flattering the Lion's ego, then you'll probably do, at least for the time being.

However, when it comes to marriage, Leos are more discriminating. At the very least, they will want someone who is charming and beautiful enough to be displayed at society events without any fear of embarrassment.

Leos who don't regard themselves as breadwinners will also expect their spouse to be rich enough to support their expensive tastes over the course of a lifetime. We would therefore suggest that you don't propose marriage to a Leo unless you think you're something special.

On a more positive note, Leos take their marriage vows very seriously, at least to begin with, so if you can persuade the Lions to marry you, it will almost certainly increase the lifespan of the relationship.

Understanding your lover's attitude to children

If you read most books on astrology, you will be told that Leos love children and that they love playing with them and looking after them. Well, this isn't true. Leos are completely into themselves and they resent it when children steal the show for longer than five minutes. This is particularly the case with the Leo man, who is often devastated, and even permanently traumatized, when his partner starts switching all her attention to a new-born baby.

So, if you are going out with a Leo man, you should spend a few years boosting his confidence before you start introducing babies into his life. Female Leos are probably better able to deal with children than the males, provided that they've got an army of servants and wet-nurses to help them out.

Female Leos are able to deal with children, provided that they've got an army of servants.

Holding on to your lover when all else fails

If you've flattered the Leos into a coma and still they want to walk out on you, then you'll have to take emergency measures. If you're a man, then tell the Lioness that your father, the Baron of Barking and Dagenham, has just died, and you've now inherited the title. If she wants, she can become the Baroness of Barking and Dagenham.

Alternatively, you could kidnap the Leo's pet cat and warn him or her that unless he or she comes back to you, you'll send it to a furrier for processing.

VIRGO—GENERAL ADVICE

If you want to hold on to Virgos, you should take advantage of the fact that they are born worriers desperate for reassurance. Every time they start worrying, stop what you're doing, listen to their fears, and then tell them that the Iraqis aren't going to launch a combined nuclear and chemical attack, that they will get the blackcurrant stain out of their white jacket and that there's no danger of catching genital lime-scale from soft water.

Over a period of months, the Virgins will begin to rely on your counselling skills and before you know it, they'll be completely hooked on you. However, if you want to be sure of maintaining a Virgo's affection over a long period of time, you must also make sure that you wash regularly, and that you change your underwear at least twice a day.

Keeping your lover happy in bed

Starting with the bed itself, it is important that you keep the sheets clean. So, when you go to bed with a Virgo, take your muddy boots off first and make sure that you have washed your hair with a good dandruff shampoo. You should also avoid climbing into Virgins' beds when you're naked: they regard raw flesh as being rather unhygienic and they would prefer it if you wore pyjamas, a nightgown, or even an army surplus body-bag.

As far as sex is concerned, Virgos of both sexes like it to be well organized. You should give them a couple of weeks' notice, so that they can check in their diaries that they're not already booked up. It would also help Virgo if you gave them some idea of how long you wanted to have sex with them for and what positions you wanted them to assume.

When it comes to frequency, male Virgos like it once a month, while the females are happy with it once a year, on their birthdays.

Keeping your lover happy in the home

Virgos like their homes to be immaculately clean. So, if you want to keep your Virgo lover happy in the home, spend at least four hours a day doing housework. If you are a messy person, who can't handle doing housework, then don't, whatever you do, move in with your lover because it will kill the relationship.

Domestic chores aside, you can make Virgos happy by healing them. You could go into the kitchen and brew up a herbal concoction to relieve their stress. Once they've drunk that, have them lie on the floor and give them an aromatherapy session. While you're rubbing the essential oils into their backs (don't forget to wear surgical gloves), you can reassure them that you haven't poisoned them with deadly nightshade, at least not deliberately.

Understanding your lover's attitude to marriage

Virgos are not particularly romantic, therefore you shouldn't expect them to get too excited about the prospect of marriage. At the same time, Virgos are practical people who know only too well that weddings are expensive events, which are extremely difficult to organize. So, when you propose marriage to your lover, you should expect a matter-of-fact reply, such as, 'Yeah, I'll marry you, provided we do it by post and you foot the bill.'

As far as timing is concerned, you shouldn't get married to Virgos until you've lived with them for a few months. This is because they often have strange habits and obsessions, which you should experience at first hand before committing yourself to a lasting relationship.

Understanding your lover's attitude to children

Children are very important to Virgos, and they often feel incomplete if they don't have children of their own. However, this doesn't mean that you should get yourself, or your partner, pregnant on the first date, because Virgos like to plan their family according to a rigid schedule. They might decide, in their mid-teens, that they want their first child at the age of twenty-five, the second child at the age of thirty-one and the third child at forty-one and a half. You should therefore familiarize yourself with your lover's natal masterplan before putting forward any specific suggestions.

Once Virgos have children, they turn out to be good parents, particularly when it comes to matters of health and education. If you want to hold on to your Virgo lover, then introducing children into the relationship will definitely help, because your lover will be so busy worrying about the kids that he or she will no longer notice your own many imperfections.

Holding on to your lover when all else fails

If you want Virgos to think twice about leaving you, then the best thing to do is to throw a worry into their minds. So you might warn the Virgins that if they walk out on you, you'll tell the tax man about the fifty pounds of income they forgot to declare five years ago. Alternatively, tell your Virgo lovers that unless they receive regular foot massages from you personally, they'll start developing pattern balding.

However, if these methods don't work and you're absolutely desperate to get your Virgo back, then you'll have no choice but to steal their heart pills.

LIBRA—GENERAL ADVICE

Holding on to Libran lovers for longer than a few weeks can be difficult – Librans get bored easily and, once their relationships slip into a routine, they get increasingly restless.

Make sure to always excite and surprise Libran lovers so that they are never able to predict your next move. Another thing to bear in mind about Librans is that they love going out to parties, restaurants and theatres and expect their partners to keep up with the frantic pace of their social lives. This means that, if you've gone out to a party with your Libran lover, you don't go home when things start stagnating at three o'clock in the morning. Instead you should whisk your lover off to another, more exciting party.

Keeping your lover happy in bed

One area of your relationship which you must never allow to slip into a routine is your sex life. You should never take it for granted that Librans will have sex with you, even if you've been going out with them for a decade. Instead, you should constantly flirt with them, trying all the time to entice and allure them into your bed with new tricks and new turn-ons.

As far as the actual sex is concerned, you must always be enthusiastic and spontaneous and you should avoid adopting the same sexual position two nights in a row. It is also import-ant that the balance of sexual power is reasonably even and that neither you nor your Libran lover becomes too passive or too aggressive.

When it comes to frequency, Librans, on average, like to make love four times a week. However, we must warn you not to get into a fixed sexual routine, where you insist on having sex on the same days every week. Librans find this very boring and, if you continue with your routine for longer than a month, you'll find that your lover becomes unresponsive on your sex days and unfaithful on your chaste days.

Keeping your lover happy in the home

Librans hate untidiness nearly as much as they hate doing housework. So, if you're living with a Libran, don't complain about their mess: instead, you should get down on your knees and clear it up yourself. If you find it demeaning to constantly clear up after your partner, then you'll have to hire some domestic help.

Once Librans have moved in with you, they expect their home to become a major social centre. They will invite their many friends round for regular soirées and parties and they will expect you to be a willing and open-minded host. You'll find that many of your lover's friends are pretty weird and they will include astrologers, clairvoyants, rock stars and glamour models.

Understanding your lover's attitude to marriage

Feel free to propose marriage to your Libran lover, even if it's only the first date. He or she will not only be flattered, but be proud to have notched up another romantic conquest.

However, if you are serious about marrying Librans, we would recommend that you wait a few months. That gives them time to discover that you're a fascinating person, who will under no circumstances bore them to death. None the less, the key factor which determines whether or not Librans will accept your proposal is the quality of the wedding. If they think that it's going to be a huge social event, which will be attended by everyone who's anyone, then they'll definitely say yes.

Once you are married, they will be loyal to you at a mental level – in other words, they'll stick up for you in an argument. As far as the sexual level is concerned, marriage is no guarantee of your partner's fidelity.

Understanding your lover's attitude to children

Librans like children – provided that they are sweet, cuddly and well-behaved, and someone else is looking after them. So, if you are going to have children, don't expect much help from your Libran partner.

Libran men are particularly useless with children: as soon as the baby starts screaming, they go down to the pub. Libran women are more competent but, like their Leo counterparts, they do need help from a childminder, a nanny or a male Cancerian.

If you and your Libran lover do decide to have children, it is essential that he or she has nothing to do with naming them. This is because Librans have a nasty habit of giving their children silly names, such as 'Mountain', 'Snowdrop Surprise' and 'Lightswitch'.

Holding on to your lover when all else fails

By and large, Librans only get involved in a relationship if they can see a tangible benefit for themselves. Usually it's money, though it can sometimes be sex or status. So, if your Libran lover is about to leave you, it is essential that you dangle a very big carrot in front of their nose. One trick you can pull is to say that you've only got three months to live, and that when you die they'll inherit your entire fortune.

SCORPIO—GENERAL ADVICE

This chapter has so far assumed that there are positive steps you can take to help you hold on to your lover – you just look at his or her Sun sign, and behave accordingly. When you're dealing with a Scorpio lover, there are certainly right and wrong ways to behave that may influence the long-term survivability of the relationship.

However, you must appreciate that Scorpios are powerful people who like being in full control of their love life. They hate it when their partner tries to manipulate them and under no circumstances will they succumb to blackmail or bribery. So, if you want to hold on to a Scorpio, you shouldn't try to be too clever but instead be patient and understanding. If you possibly can, you should also fine-tune your sensitivity. That way you'll be able to harmonize your conversation and your behaviour with the Scorpio's intensely powerful feelings.

Keeping your lover happy in bed

Sex is the only sure way that Scorpios can release their pent-up emotions. If Scorpios are starved of sex for a few weeks, they become tense and irritable. If the starvation continues for longer periods, their sexual energy sublimates into spiritual delusion. People who report seeing ghosts, UFOs and Elvises are often sex-starved Scorpios in disguise. You can now see why it is important that you keep your Scorpio lover happy in bed. Your body must always be available to them and you must never play hard to get, otherwise your lover will turn into a religious nutcase.

When it comes to frequency, Scorpios prefer to have sex four or five times a week. However, if they have busy lives, then once or twice a week may be enough, provided that you are a superb lover who knows how to give your partner total satisfaction.

Keeping your lover happy in the home

Ask yourself three questions. First, are you sick of being independent? Second, are you tired of making your own decisions? Third, do you hate choosing your own bedtime? If you answer 'yes' to all these questions, then you're ready to move in with your Scorpio lover.

Once you're living with Scorpios, they will expect you to do what you're told and to adjust your routine to fit in with theirs. If you want to take any initiatives of your own, such as rearranging furniture, or inviting friends around for coffee, always make sure that you get Scorpio's permission. Although Scorpios regard their whole home as being their territory, they usually have one room which is their inner lair. You must never enter this room, or even ask questions about its use, on pain of instant death.

Understanding your lover's attitude to marriage

Imagine that you're with a group of friends, sunning yourself on the banks of the River Congo. All of a sudden, a huge crocodile pokes its head above water, catches your eye and decides that it wants to eat you. From then on, the crocodile will relentlessly pursue you, until it finally runs you to ground. It won't be interested in eating any of your friends, even if they're easier to catch, because you're the chosen one.

When it comes to marriage, Scorpios are just like this crocodile. They'll make a decision to marry you and that will be that. They won't be interested in marrying anyone else and, if you're stupid enough to turn down their first marriage proposal, the next one will be at the end of a shotgun. However, we should warn you that there is no point in using marriage to prolong a relationship with a Scorpio; once your Scorpio lover becomes sick of your taste, they'll immediately spit you out.

Understanding your lover's attitude to children

If your Scorpio lover is not a parent, then you shouldn't bring up the subject of children until you've been living with each other for at least a year. This is because Scorpios are not very trusting and they may suspect that you're trying to trap them into making a lifetime commitment to the relationship.

However, once Scorpios become mothers or fathers, they become devoted parents who will die for their children and even kill for them. If you and your Scorpio lover do have children, then it is likely to strengthen the relationship, provided that you yourself are a good parent.

Holding on to your lover when all else fails

Once Scorpios have decided to blow you out, there is very little you can do to change their mind. If you have children, then you might try to persuade them that you should stay together for the children's sake. However, Scorpios are good psychologists and they would probably argue that children are less damaged by an amicable divorce than they are by a troubled marriage.

One other way of holding on to a Scorpio, if you're really desperate, is to ask a witch or a magician to cast a love spell. This is a dangerous option that will cost you a lot of money in the short term, and eternal damnation in the long term.

If you're really desperate to hold on to a Scorpio, ask a witch to cast a love spell.

SAGITTARIUS—GENERAL ADVICE

Sagittarians are freedom-loving people who hate being tied down. If anyone tries to restrict this freedom, they run a mile. So, if you want to hold on to your Sagittarian lovers, you must on no account let them know that you're trying to hold on to them. You must allow them to come and go as they please and, if they go walkabout for months on end, you mustn't embarrass the Sagittarian by sending out search parties.

On a day-to-day basis, Sagittarians have many different interests, which they insist on indulging. So, on Monday they might want to go to the ballet, on Tuesday to a yoga class, on Wednesday to football practice, on Thursday to an art exhibition and on Friday to a horse race. If you want them to devote Saturday and Sunday to you, it is essential that you take a positive attitude to these interests and that you don't moan about not getting enough attention.

Keeping your lover happy in bed

Your Sagittarian lover wants to have fun in bed, for the duration of the relationship. You must, therefore, be playful and enthusiastic. If the Sagittarian wants to do something to you which you find shocking (perhaps because you have a low kinkiness rating), under no circumstances should you express moral outrage. Instead, be constructive and say something like 'I don't think it would be much fun if we did that. In fact, I think it would be rather boring. No, let's try the Cape Canaveral position instead.' Once you manage to achieve sexual lift-off, it is important that you shout, scream and crash around as loudly as possible, otherwise your Sagittarian lover might worry that you're not enjoying yourself enough.

As far as frequency is concerned, both male and female Sagittarians like going into orbit at least five times a week.

Keeping your lover happy in the home

If you want to keep your Sagittarian lover happy in the home, you should make the domestic environment as exciting and exotic as possible. You can do this by allowing wild animals to roam around your house and garden. The tiger sunning itself on the front lawn will remind the Sagittarian of last winter's safari in Nepal, while the funnelweb spider on the lavatory seat will bring back fond memories of the Australian outback (see Chapter Five, 'Locations where they most enjoy having sex', for further details).

It is also worth noting that male Sagittarians are sports fanatics and they often spend hours on end watching football and wrestling on the sports channel. While they're glued to the TV, they will expect you to form a human chain from their armchair to the kitchen, so that they are supplied with a constant flow of beer, pizza and cigarettes.

Understanding your lover's attitude to marriage

There's no point in trying to have a serious conversation about marriage with your Sagittarian lover. This is because Sagittarians don't understand marriage and they don't understand the responsibilities involved. None the less, you shouldn't have too many problems persuading Sagittarians to marry you. You start off by telling them that marriage is an opportunity to have a big party, called a 'wedding', in which everyone stuffs their faces with food and gets obscenely drunk. You then describe the extended world tour which follows the wedding, which is sometimes known as a 'honeymoon'. If they still don't see the point of getting married, then tell them that marriage is a lifetime of non-stop fun, before pouring them another drink.

Understanding your lover's attitude to children

When it comes to attitudes to children, there are two types of Sagittarian. One type has absolutely no affinity with children and regards them as being a loathsome burden. These Sagittarians expect their partner to do all the child-rearing and, if their kids get too troublesome, or too expensive, they tend to flee the country. The other type are rather different. They are fascinated by children and love watching them grow up. They also see it as their personal responsibility to guide and teach their offspring and to show them what is right and what is wrong.

So, if you want to hold on to your lover, you'd better ask yourself what kind of Sagittarian he or she is. If they're of the first type, then avoid having children. If the second type, then the introduction of children will definitely help hold the relationship together.

Holding on to your lover when all else fails

If your Sagittarian lover is about to leave you, don't panic and don't get nasty. Instead, you should suggest that you both hold a massive party, to celebrate the end of the relationship. You should then tell the Sagittarian that you find him or her rather boring and that you need a partner who's more exciting and more adventurous. Your Sagittarian lover will be devastated by your attitude and within a week you'll both be hacking your way through the New Guinea jungle, in search of the Bird of Paradise.

CAPRICORN—GENERAL ADVICE

If you want to hold on to Capricorns, you have to show that you're a good, long-term investment. This means that you must be well behaved and you must avoid doing anything unusual or eccentric. You also need to show them that you are good with money. Tell them that you've been saving up for your retirement since you were four, and that by the age of six you were hiring out your Dinky cars for threepence an hour.

If your relationship gets really close and your Capricorn lover trusts you enough to open a joint bank account, you should still get his or her permission before you write out a cheque. Otherwise, your lover will give you a regular grilling, in which you're forced to justify and explain every debit entry on the monthly bank statement.

Capricorns are also very concerned about their public image; they expect their partners to have an unblemished past. It is, therefore, not a good idea to go out with a Capricorn if you've ever had a publicized affair with a cabinet minister, or if you've ever been convicted of drug smuggling.

Keeping your lover happy in bed

As your relationship with your Capricorn lover progresses, the bed takes on an increasingly important role. Your lover will lie on the bed, after a hard day's work, and expect you to provide a thorough massage. As you stimulate the Goats' erogenous zones, they will tell you about their career problems and expect you to soothe them with words of sympathy and understanding. The purely sexual aspect of the relationship will still be important, but after a few months it will lose some if its manic passion. This is a good sign: it shows that the relationship is becoming more rounded and that the Capricorn is beginning to treat you as a trusted companion, rather than just a sexual animal.

As far as frequency is concerned, both male and females are able to go without sex for months at a stretch. However, if they're in a healthy relationship, they like to get it at least four times a week.

Keeping your lover happy in the home

Once you move in with your lover, you should avoid making decisions about either furniture or decoration. This is because Capricorns have a refined taste, which you won't be able to match. They'll know exactly what kind of oak panelling to put in the dining room and they'll relentlessly track down the best, and the cheapest, antique furniture in town. However, if you're dead set on buying something for the house, make sure that it is practical, and that it doesn't draw unwelcome attention to itself. In other words, buy the mahogany chest of drawers rather than the Mickey Mouse hatstand.

Another point about Capricorns is that they do a lot of work at home and they usually expect their partner to double up as a personal assistant. You should, therefore, make sure that your typing and shorthand are up to scratch before you move in with your Capricorn lover.

Understanding your lover's attitude to marriage

Capricorns regard marriage as a lifetime commitment, so they will marry you only if they are sure that you're the right person. You must, therefore, demonstrate to the Goats that by marrying you they will be improving their career, their finances and their status. Your task will be made easier if you come from a wealthy family, or if you are related to your Capricorn lover's boss.

In some cases, Capricorns prefer to have an arranged marriage. In which case make no effort to seduce them. Instead, send your photograph, curriculum vitae and an unexpired virginity certificate to the Capricorn's family. Allow twenty-eight days for a reply.

Once you do manage to marry a Capricorn, he or she will remain loyal to you, provided that your social and financial performance continues to impress them.

Understanding your lover's attitude to children

Like Taureans and Virgoans, Capricorns are aware of the enormous responsibility that comes with having children. They know that children are expensive and that they require 24-hour attention. Female Capricorns are also aware that having children may lead to the disruption, and perhaps even destruction, of their careers. So you shouldn't discuss children with Capricorns, unless their material situation is healthy enough to take the strain.

When they do finally become parents, the Goats take to their responsibilities like ducks to water and very often discover that they can look after their children without their partner's support.

Holding on to your lover when all else fails

If you want to hold on to your Capricorn lovers in an emergency, then bribery or blackmail are often effective techniques, so offer them either a large sum of money, or else threaten to sell their business secrets.

If you're married to a Capricorn and you've got the body of a beached walrus, you might threaten to pose for a centrefold shot in a pornographic magazine: your partner would never be able to live down the humiliation and the embarrassment.

AQUARIUS—GENERAL ADVICE

If you want to hold on to Aquarians, it is essential that you respect them. This means that you must make a real effort to understand their unique view of the world and under no circumstances should you accuse them of being cranks or weirdos. Indeed, you should do your best to reassure Aquarians that they are not cranks and that their supreme genius will eventually be recognized. You should also remember that Aquarians are not very comfortable in close relationships. They find the emotion and the passion overwhelming and they often leave relationships when things get too intense.

So make sure that when it comes to emotions, you always keep a respectable distance from your Aquarian lover.

One other point about Aquarians is that they are suspicious of people who are normal. You should, therefore, make sure that your behaviour and your clothes are unusual and that your attitudes and beliefs are controversial.

Keeping your lover happy in bed

At the beginning of a relationship it can be very difficult to keep Aquarians happy in bed. They are very demanding and frequently want to do unorthodox things to their partners' bodies. However, as the relationship progresses, sex becomes more routine and more predictable. Your lover will start choosing the same position, night after night, in the same way that he or she always orders the same pizza, from the same place, with the same topping. If this routine continues for longer than a few months, you should take positive steps to change it, because otherwise the Aquarian will start accusing you (quite unfairly) of being boring in bed.

One step you and your partner could take is to join a tantric sex cult. This will not only lead to a massive improvement in your sex life, but it will also motivate your Aquarian lover to install special panels under your bed, which enable the central heating system to be powered by your joint orgasm energy.

Keeping your lover happy in the home

Once you move in with Aquarians, it is important that you are tolerant because they are sloppy and absentminded about the house and are usually terrible cooks. However, the domestic situation can be improved, if you are prepared to provide your

Aquarian lover with numerous labour-saving devices, such as self-cleaning carpets and saucepans which automatically turn the cooker off when they've boiled dry.

Aquarians are often self-employed, or else engaged in a secret project, so it is very important that one room is set aside for their exclusive use. You should avoid disturbing Aquarians while they're working, unless the radiation detector in the living room goes into the danger zone. This means that the atomic bomb your lover is building (with money and materials supplied by a Middle Eastern Government) is about to explode, and you have five minutes to evacuate the house.

Understanding your lover's attitude to marriage

Many Aquarians believe that marriage is a barbaric institution, which has about as much place in civilized society as torture, slavery and public hanging, so be very careful how you broach the subject, particularly during the first year of the relationship.

If your lover is a marriage-hater, you shouldn't be unduly worried: such Aquarians are often prepared to spend a lifetime with their partners in glorious, unmarried bliss. Those Aquarians that are prepared to marry will want an unusual wedding. Don't be surprised if your lover whisks you off to Iceland and marries you on top of a geyser, where a pagan priest officiates at the ceremony.

Understanding your lover's attitude to children

Male Aquarians often have no understanding of children and want nothing to do with their upbringing. If your lover is this kind of person, you shouldn't talk to him about children. Instead you should get pregnant when you're ready, using a man whose genes you fancy. You then tell the Aquarian that you're taking up mothering as a hobby and that what you do with your life and your body is nothing to do with him.

275

Many Aquarians believe that marriage is a barbaric institution, which has about as much place in civilized society as torture, slavery and public hanging.

However, there are other Aquarians, both male and female, who take a keen interest in child development. They want to have lots of children, as quickly as possible, so that they can test out their latest theories about diet and education.

These Aquarians need to be watched, because otherwise your children will grow up to be fruitarian anarchists, with genius-level IQs and moron-level common sense.

Holding on to your lover when all else fails

If an Aquarian has left you, it probably means that they think that you're boring and conventional. You must therefore prove them wrong. You can do this by changing your name to 'Alpha Centauri' and then setting up a world religion, with you as its leader. Once you've established yourself and you've got a few million followers, offer to make your ex-lover Archguru of Southern California.

PISCES—GENERAL ADVICE

If you want to hold on to Pisceans, you must be firm with them and you must never show any sign of weakness. This means that, on day one of the relationship, you should make it quite clear to the Fish what kind of behaviour you expect from them. If they do what they're told, then you can reward them with a kiss and a cuddle. However, if they misbehave, you must punish them, either by withholding affection, or by giving them an ice-cold shower. Once your lover is behaving perfectly, it is important to keep up the pressure. So every now and then tell them that they're useless, and threaten to leave them if they don't get their act together.

In order to guarantee the Pisceans' loyalty and respect, you must exercise control over all aspects of their lives. You should tell them what clothes to wear, what food to eat and what books to read. You should also stop them watching TV programmes which contain too much sex or violence. In this way, they'll come to see you as being the super-dominant parent that they have been secretly yearning for since early childhood.

Keeping your lover happy in bed

Pisceans are obsessed with the idea of pleasing their partners so, if you want to keep *them* happy in bed, you must train them to make *you* happy in bed. You must, therefore, tell them about your perfect sexual experience and about your secret fantasies.

If, at any stage in the relationship, you find that you are not enjoying sex, it is important that you tell them straight away and force them to improve their performance. Pisceans are sensitive people who are quick to pick up their partner's true feelings and, if you fake your orgasms, they will quickly suss you out and start looking for partners who are easier to satisfy.

As far as frequency is concerned, your Piscean lover, male or female, will want sex as often as you do. If you are Pisces and your lover is also a Pisces, then you'll probably want sex once a week if you're a man, and three times a week if you're a woman.

Keeping your lover happy in the home

Pisceans are disorganized people who are desperate to find a partner who can provide them with discipline and structure. If you remember this, then you should have no difficulty keeping your Pisces lover happy in the home. You must insist that they stick to a strict routine and you must also make all their decisions for them. Indeed, you should be able to look at your watch, at any time of the day or night, and immediately know what your lover is doing. So you might notice that it's 2.57 p.m. on Wednesday afternoon – in which case you'll know that he or she is in Safeways and is about to put a 200 gramme jar of coffee into the shopping trolley.

On a different note, Pisceans like water. If you want them to feel secure in their domestic environment, you should have a swimming pool or a pond in the garden and have a marble fountain in the living-room. You might also consider buying some tropical fish: your Piscean lover will be fascinated by them and will enjoy cleaning out their tank.

Understanding your lover's attitude to marriage

Your Pisces partner is an extremely romantic person, who loves getting married, the more times the better. So, propose marriage to the Fish whenever you like, even if you've known each other for only five minutes.

However, we would give you one piece of advice. Don't *ask* Pisceans to marry you, because otherwise you may get a vague reply, such as, 'I've already promised to marry someone else.' Instead, you should *instruct* them to marry you, using words such as 'By the way, I've decided that it's time for us to get married. I've booked an appointment at Chelsea Register Office, for ten o'clock tomorrow morning. I'll pick you up at eight.' At this point, we must stress that a simple marriage ceremony will not guarantee your Piscean lover's loyalty. No, what really counts is your willingness to dominate your lover for the duration of the marriage.

Understanding your lover's attitude to children

Pisceans like children and look forward to having offspring of their own. The female Piscean is particularly keen on children; when she becomes a mother, she is prepared to martyr herself for them. The males are not quite so conscientious and, if you want to turn them into dutiful fathers, you may have to resort to a bit of gentle violence.

Once your lover becomes a mother or a father, it is important that you give them plenty of support. This is because Pisceans are weak parents, who haven't a clue how to control their children. They do whatever their children want and they have no hesitation in shutting up a rowdy nine-year-old by giving him or her the keys to the family car.

Holding on to your lover when all else fails

If your Pisces lover has walked out on you, it probably means that you're a Pisces yourself, or else you allowed your lover too much freedom. Fortunately, it's easy to get your lover back. Just get on the phone, and order them back. If that doesn't work, then threaten to poison their beloved tropical fish with drain cleaner.

Chapter Eight

··

HOW TO GET RID OF YOUR LOVER

INTRODUCTION

This book was specially written to help you improve your
romantic prospects. We wanted to show you how astrology can
be used to track down and seduce the perfect lover. Being
romantic people, it was also our hope that astrology could help
you hold on to this perfect lover for years, even decades.

However, we must be realistic and accept that all good
things must come to an end, including love. The gorgeous
hunk of meat that you fell in love with last week may now have
the sex appeal of a rotten, stinking, maggot-infested carcass
and you may be desperate to butcher the relationship. In most
cases this shouldn't be a problem. You just tell your lover that
the relationship's over and that's that.

Unfortunately, there are some people who are irrational and
obsessive. They believe that love is forever and they can't
accept it when their partners give them the elbow. It can be
very difficult to get rid of such lovers: they stick to you like
napalm, burning away at your individuality and your will to
resist. Indeed, the situation can sometimes get so bad that you
need to resort to desperate measures, such as hiring a hitman,
or reading this chapter.

This chapter tells you how to get rid of your lover, using the
power of astrology. We hope that you don't have to read it too
often, but in an emergency it may save you the price of a bullet.

Getting rid of your lover can be difficult, but only hire a hitman as a last resort.

One person who used the power of astrology to get rid of a lover was Sandra. If you remember from Chapter Five, she's a friend of Monica. At the time Sandra rang Archie up, she was in a relationship with a Taurus, whom she was heartily sick of. As you can see from the following telephone dialogue, Sandra was finding it difficult to get the Taurus out of her life.

However, the situation wasn't that bad; by the end of the phone call, Archie had sorted the problem out.

ARCHIE: Hello?

SANDRA: I wondered if you could help me? I'm a friend of Monica. My name's Sandra.

ARCHIE: Oh yes . . . you're a Sagittarian, aren't you?

SANDRA: Yeah . . . that's amazing . . . you could tell that from my voice?

ARCHIE: I wish I could. No, Monica talked about you. You were born on the 2nd December, weren't you?

SANDRA: The third. Oh yes, that was the other thing I wanted to ask you. I saw on the telly that I am no longer a Sagittarian, that they've discovered a thirteenth sign. What's it called?

ARCHIE: Ophiuchus.

SANDRA: That's right. Monica said it was all a load of rubbish, but I'm not sure.

ARCHIE: You're the tenth person this week to ask me about the bloody thirteenth sign. The point is, astrologers don't use the constellations. We use the seasons. So the first sign of the Zodiac, Aries, starts at the beginning of spring, on the 21 March. The second sign, Taurus, starts a month later and Gemini a month after that. Cancer, the fourth sign, starts on the longest day, which is the 21 June. Libra, the seventh sign, starts at the beginning of autumn, on the 23 September. Scorpio starts a month after that, on the 23 October, Sagittarius on the 22 November, and Capricorn on 22 December, which is the shortest day. Ophiuchus doesn't come into it.

SANDRA: So I'm definitely a Sagittarian?

ARCHIE: Definitely.

SANDRA: But what if I wasn't? What if I was an Oph . . .

ARCHIE: Mmm . . . I suppose you'd have the traits of Rasalhague, the brightest star in the constellation of Ophiuchus.

SANDRA: Yeah?

ARCHIE: You'd be immoral, decadent and perverse and you'd be almost certain to have an alcohol or a drug problem. You'd frequently get involved in fights and you'd be vulnerable to the bites of rabid dogs and poisonous snakes.

SANDRA: No, that doesn't fit me at all. I must be a Sagittarian.

ARCHIE: I think so.

SANDRA: Right. Now, the other thing I want to know . . . you don't mind me asking? I'll pay you.

ARCHIE: It doesn't matter.

SANDRA: Well, it's my boyfriend . . . my ex-boyfriend . . . Vernon. I can't get him out of my life. He's obsessed by me.

ARCHIE: Tell him you're not interested in him.

SANDRA: I've tried that. He doesn't hear me.

ARCHIE: Well, just don't have anything to do with him.

SANDRA: But he's always there. And I find it difficult to say no to him. He's a very persuasive and persistent person. And he's also quite good in bed.

ARCHIE: Is he a Scorpio?

SANDRA: No. A Taurus.

ARCHIE: Why do you think that he's so obsessed by you? Taurus and Sagittarius aren't a particularly compulsive combination.

SANDRA: Well, I'm very attractive. At least Vernon says I am. And I always make sure I wear nice clothes. I always wear what he likes.

ARCHIE: Is that wise?

SANDRA: I don't really have a choice. Practically every

stitch of clothing I wear was bought by him. We have been going out for three years.

ARCHIE: Look, I think you need to do something about your appearance.

SANDRA: Like?

ARCHIE: Put on weight. As much weight as possible. Eat plenty of double cream, cheese, and bananas. Make sure that you eat a fried breakfast every day. And drink a gallon of stout a day. A few weeks on that diet, and Vernon will be retching at the sight of you.

SANDRA: No way! I'm ... I'm a model. Part-time. My figure's very important to me.

ARCHIE: Well, you could at least dress like a tramp. Buy some old clothes from a charity shop and make sure that your underwear is as filthy and rancid as possible.

SANDRA: But Vernon would hate that!

ARCHIE: Of course.

SANDRA: But ...

ARCHIE: I thought you wanted to disgust and revolt Vernon, so that he could no longer stand the sight of you?

SANDRA: I suppose.

ARCHIE: Now, tell me about your cooking.

SANDRA: Oh, I love cooking. I'm a brilliant cook. I did a year's cookery course in France when I left school. One day I'm going to open a restaurant. Vernon's promised to put up the money.

ARCHIE: You said you wanted to get rid of him.

SANDRA: I do. But Vernon's very rich. And he does appreciate my cooking. He says my *crème brûlées* are the best in the world.

ARCHIE: Well, you're going to have to cut them out.

SANDRA: What?

ARCHIE: Taureans love food. If you carry on stuffing Vernon with your choicest delicacies, you'll never get rid of him.

SANDRA: Oh.

ARCHIE: Start feeding him boiled Spam and vinaigretted baked beans, washed down with tinned peaches and lumpy custard.

SANDRA: He'll kill me.

ARCHIE: That's a risk you'll have to take.

SANDRA: Well, I don't mean he'd literally kill me. No, he wouldn't do that. He's quite a gentle man really. And he's only five foot four.

ARCHIE: How tall are you?

SANDRA: Five foot eleven.

ARCHIE: So you're stronger than Vernon?

SANDRA: Sort of. But he's the dominant one. I always do what he says.

ARCHIE: In bed?

SANDRA: Especially in bed.

ARCHIE: Yeah, male Taureans do like to be in control. They like their women to be weak and submissive.

SANDRA: Yeah.

ARCHIE: Sandra, I think you're going to have to use your height advantage.

SANDRA: What do you mean?

ARCHIE: Be aggressive. Start dominating Vernon.

SANDRA: I don't know if I can do that.

ARCHIE: But . . . Monica said that you stubbed a cigarette out on someone's wrist?

SANDRA: Oh, that. I was drunk . . . and being molested by a disgusting stranger. Vernon's different . . . he has a hold on me. He expects me to behave in a certain way.

ARCHIE: I don't think you really want to get rid of Vernon.

SANDRA: I do!

ARCHIE: Really?

SANDRA: I hate him. I mean, I can't stand him.

ARCHIE: OK, get rid of him.

SANDRA: I'll try. But it's so difficult. Look, thanks for all your help.

ARCHIE: No problem.
SANDRA: I'll send you some money.
ARCHIE: It doesn't matter.
SANDRA: Are you sure?
ARCHIE: Yeah.
SANDRA: Thanks. I'll speak to you soon.
ARCHIE: OK. Good bye . . . and good luck.
SANDRA: Thanks. Bye.

Two days after this phone conversation, Vernon went round to Sandra's flat, for a romantic, candlelit dinner. Sandra gave him fish fingers and chips, followed by a pot of pre-packaged strawberry mousse. While Vernon was eating, Sandra drank six cans of Crucial Brew and insisted on playing Motorhead at full volume. Eventually, Vernon lost his temper and attacked Sandra. In the ensuing fight, Sandra managed to tear his clothes off and to tie him to the banisters with her stockings.

She then went off to an all-night party, to look for a new lover. When Sandra finally cut Vernon free, at two o'clock the next afternoon, he told her that she was a disgusting pervert and that he was ending the relationship forthwith. Vernon then walked out of her house and out of her life.

From an astrological point of view, it's quite obvious why Vernon left Sandra. He was a Taurus and he liked good food. The experience of eating fish fingers and chips would therefore have been very distressing. He also expected women to behave as women and not to guzzle high-strength lager. However, what really upset Vernon was being stripped and tied to the banisters. As you will remember from Chapter Five, Taurean men have a one-star kinkiness rating: they can't handle anything that is remotely kinky. By tying Vernon up for sixteen agonizing hours, Sandra had dealt the relationship an effective *coup de grâce*.

The basic philosophy of this chapter is that you can use astrology to break up any relationship. Simply find out the Sun sign of your lover and act accordingly. We will be going through each of the twelve signs, giving you detailed instructions on how to blow each one out of your life. You will find that our instructions come under four main headings:

Dumpability rating

We accept that some signs are more difficult to get rid of than others. We therefore give each sign a set of ratings. A five-star dumpability rating represents a sign which is easy to get rid of, while a one-star rating represents a serious challenge. We give the ratings after a week, after six months and after three years. This takes account of the fact that dumpability can vary as the relationship progresses. So, a lover can be easy to get rid of if you have been going out with them for only a week, difficult to get rid of after six months and very difficult to get rid of after three years.

How to upset your lover

We give you tips on how to aggravate your loved one. For example, if you're trying to aggravate Taureans, you might serve them disgusting food, or consistently turn up late for dates.

How to turn off your lover

If you want to get rid of your lovers, it is important that they lose sexual interest in you. In this section we tell you how to disgust and revolt the twelve signs.

How to give your lover the final push

Having upset your partners and turned them off, you'll probably want to give them the final push. This often represents a single act in which you go completely over the top. If the act is sufficiently outrageous, your lover will end the relationship there and then.

We saw how Sandra was able to give Vernon the final push by means of a supreme act of bondage. However, there are wide variations amongst the signs. If, for example, you tied Pisceans to the banisters for sixteen hours, you'd never get rid of them.

Before you read the rest of this chapter, we request that you exercise caution and don't cause your partner needless suffering. We must also make our usual point: the authors of this book take no responsibility for the consequences of *your* actions. Indeed, if you are having genuine difficulties getting rid of a partner, we would advise you to consult a lawyer, a marriage guidance counsellor or a psychotherapist. However, if you want to give astrology a whirl, then read on . . .

ARIES

Dumpability rating

After one week: **
The Rams enjoy the excitement of a new relationship and you are therefore going to find it difficult to get rid of them during the first week.

After six months: ****
After six months your Aries lover will be finding the relationship rather tiresome, so it is unlikely that you'll face much resistance if you break the thing up.

After three years: **
If the Ram is loyal to you for over a year, it means that you're morally and sexually compatible with each other. To destroy the relationship, you'll have to change both your political opinions and your sexual behaviour.

How to upset your lover

Your Aries lover has strong political opinions and a rigid ethical code. It is important that you find out what these opinions are and then adopt a contrary position. For example, if your lover hates the death penalty, you should not only harp on about the benefits of hanging, but you should also get into the habit of watching lethal injections on the execution channel.

Another way of grinding down your lover's respect for you is to be lazy and unenthusiastic. Stay in bed as long as possible and if the Ram suggests doing something, say 'What's the point?', or 'I can't be bothered.' When you do finally get out of bed, flood the bathroom, leave strands of your hair all over the bath and use up all the hot water. This act of supreme selfishness will drive the Rams mad, because they love having quick, no-nonsense showers, in immaculately tidy bathrooms.

How to turn off your lover

Turning off a female Aries is easy. You refuse to take any initiatives and, when you're in bed with her, you lie still and you wait to be told what to do. Another thing to remember is that Aries women hate weak men, so you might cry on her shoulder and tell her all about your miserable childhood.

Both male and female Rams are extremely impatient people and when they want sex, they want it NOW. You could play on this impatience by refusing to have sex or, if you really want to wind them up, you could go back to the bathroom (which you flooded earlier in the day) and tell your lover that you'll be ready for sex in five minutes. When you come out of the bathroom six hours later, make sure that you're wearing body armour, because the Ram's sexual frustration will have reached psychotic proportions.

How to give your lover the final push

Giving your Aries lover the final push can be difficult. The reason for this is that the Rams like fights and arguments and if you have a screaming row with them about sex or ethics, this row might rekindle the flames of their passion. However, if you go out of your way to humiliate and outrage your lover, then you should get a result.

We therefore recommend that, if your lover is a man, you charge him a hundred pounds every time you have sex. If your Aries partner is a woman, then treat her like a whore. In other words, have sex with her, then toss her a bundle of cash for services rendered. She'll never forgive you.

TAURUS

Dumpability rating

After one week: ****
The longer you're in a relationship with a Taurean, the harder it is to get rid of them. So if you have any doubts about the Bulls, dump them in the first week, before they've had time to fall in love with you.

After six months: **
After the first few months of a relationship, the Taurean will start seeing you as a permanent fixture. This means that if you want to get out of the relationship, you'll have to take decisive action.

After three years: *
As Sandra demonstrated, it is possible to free oneself from a Taurus after three years. However, to be sure of success, you may have to use sledgehammer tactics.

How to upset your lover

Generally speaking, Taureans are reliable and honest people, who keep their word and arrive punctually for dates and appointments. By the same token, they expect their partners to behave in the same way so, if you're meeting a Taurean, make sure that you're an hour or two late. However, if you've got a date in the Taurean's own home and you know that he or she has gone to great trouble and expense to cook you a gourmet meal, then make sure that you give it a total miss, without giving any warning or notice.

If you're living with a Taurus and you do most of the cooking, then the meals you give them should be disgusting. Never use fresh ingredients, except raw chillies, and, where possible, use canned food. When serving meat, cheese or bread, it is your responsibility to ensure that it is visibly mouldy.

How to turn off your lover

Taureans are obsessed by beauty and by physical form so, if you want to turn off your Taurus lover, you should make yourself as unattractive as possible. This may mean putting on weight, either by going on a balloon diet, or else by getting a blubber transplant. You should also get blind drunk before you put on make-up; if you're a man, you should only shave once a fortnight.

When it comes to underwear, you should have one pair of knickers or underpants which you never wash. Always wear them when you're with your Taurean lover and make sure that he or she has plenty of opportunity to savour their delicate bouquet.

How to give your lover the final push

The Bulls are thick-skinned animals who are slow to take hints. However much you upset them and however much you turn off, they may not understand that you're trying to get rid of them. And even if the Taureans do get the message, they are creatures of habit, who will do everything they can to carry on with a relationship, regardless of its absurdity. This means that you often have to give Taureans a huge push. As you saw with Vernon, the males hate kinkiness; if you are prepared to inflict on them a night-long orgy of relentless domination, you'll soon be rid of them.

The female's Achilles' heel is money, rather than kinkiness. So take the Taurean woman out for an expensive meal and at the end of it tell her that you're bankrupt and that she'll have to pay the bill. By the time you leave the restaurant, your relationship with her will be dead and buried.

GEMINI

Dumpability rating

After one week: ★★
Geminis won't want to let go of you until they've had a chance to thoroughly investigate your personality and your body. It can take them a few weeks to finish their inquiries.

After six months: ★★
The ideal time to dump Geminis is after a month. They'll be bored with you, without being emotionally attached to you. After six months Geminis' love for you will be hitting a peak and as a result you may find it very difficult to get rid of them.

After three years: ★★★★★
Every three years Geminis like to make radical changes to their lives. They like to change their jobs, their beliefs and their friends. So if you want to dump them at this crucial juncture, then go ahead.

How to upset your lover

Most Geminis leave their partner because they're bored, so it is essential that you bore your Gemini lover to death. You can do this by talking about the same subject day in, day out. If possible, this subject should be really trivial, such as your favourite soap opera or the price of new curtains. You should also spend hours on the telephone, talking endless drivel to your boring little friends. This activity will drive your lover mad because Geminis are addicted to telephones and, if they're not on the phone, it means that they're waiting for an important call.

How to turn off your lover

If you want to turn off your Gemini lover, then you need to adopt a dual strategy. The first thing to do is to show absolutely no creativity or imagination in the bedroom. You must refuse to co-operate with the Gemini's sex games and you must always adopt the same sexual position. And, when you're actually having sex with the Twins, you should yawn as much

If you spend hours on the telephone, talking drivel to your boring little friends, you will drive your Gemini lover mad.

as possible. This is because yawning is infectious and it won't be long before they start yawning too.

The second plank to your strategy should be to send your lover's details to a dating agency. Make sure that you request, on your lover's behalf, a super-intelligent, super-kinky partner. When the Gemini starts receiving weird letters from a quantum physicist who wants to go time-travelling through sexual black holes, he or she will zap out of your life at the speed of light.

How to give your lover the final push

After the first year of a relationship, Geminis become very easy to get rid of, so it is unlikely that you'll ever be driven to desperate measures. However, if the Twins are proving troublesome, you should wait until they've gone out for the day and then make a huge bonfire out of their books. After that, move on to their computer and erase its hard disk; this simple act will wipe out a year or two of the Gemini's life.

When the Twins return home and realize the enormity of your crime, they will go completely ballistic. You will experience a barrage of brutal invective, which will go on for at least six hours. When the Twins have finally calmed down and are beginning to rationalize the situation, look them in the eyes and tell them that they're boring.

CANCER

Dumpability rating

After one week: **
During the first month of a relationship, Cancerians are still feeling their way around. If they find anything they don't like, they'll run a mile, so getting rid of the Crabs after a week is a fairly straightforward matter.

After six months: ★★★

After six months, your lover is beginning to get used to you. You should, therefore, get out of the relationship as soon as possible, otherwise you'll start getting into romantic quicksand.

After three years: ★

That was careless, wasn't it? You're now part of the family and you've no doubt got several *bambini*, with more on the way. While it is possible to get out of this relationship, it may cost you your neck.

How to upset your lover

Cancerians love their families, in particular their mothers. So whenever you're being entertained by the Crab's family, be extremely abusive and make sure that you tell their mother, to her face, that she's fat and that her cooking tastes like vomit.

Your Cancerian lover also cares about *you* and will need constant reminders that you're safe and well. This means that you should, first, take up a dangerous sport, such as shark-wrestling and, second, keep your lover in the dark about your movements. For example, tell your lover that you're going to the shops to buy some milk and then disappear for a month.

One other thing to remember about Cancerians: they are sentimental creatures, so always forget birthdays and wedding anniversaries and make sure that, over Christmas, you work as much overtime as possible.

How to turn off your lover

From a sexual point of view, it is very difficult to turn off a Cancerian. They are attracted to your personality rather than your body, so there's no point in adopting the physique of an East European weight-lifter. However, if you alter your behaviour, it may be possible to turn your lover off, provided that you are patient. To begin with, you should use more swear words, particularly when you're in bed with the Cancerian. At the same time, you should become obsessed with sex and demand it as often as possible. If you're really cunning, you'll take advantage of the Crabs' early morning grumpiness and force your sexual attentions on them at 6.30 a.m., day in, day out. After a week or two of this routine, they'll insist on separate bedrooms.

How to give your lover the final push

Your Cancerian partner is an extremely jealous person. So, early one morning you and your secret lover should both climb into the Cancerian's bed, while he or she is still asleep, and start having sex.

When the Crab wakes up, and catches you both *in flagrante delicto*, you should stop what you're doing and hand over the remains of his or her favourite teddy bear (the one their mother gave them for their third birthday). Explain to the Cancerian that you always hated the animal and that the night before, you disembowelled it with a carving knife. Your Cancerian partner will then disembowel *you*, so bringing the relationship to a timely, if bloody, end.

LEO

Dumpability rating

After one week: *
During the first week of a relationship, Leos will tell you how lucky you are to be going out with them. If you try to dump them at this stage, they'll think that you're either joking or mad.

After six months: ***
After six months, the Lions will have finished telling you

about their many achievements. If you're unimpressed, then feel free to leave the relationship.

After three years: ***
If you want to split up with Leo lovers after three years, you must make it quite clear that you're leaving the relationship because you're not good enough for them.

How to upset your lover

At heart the Lions have very little self-confidence (particularly the men). You should therefore do everything in your power to further undermine their fragile egos. At every available opportunity you should tell the Lions that they're stupid and you should always discuss their failures. If your Leo lover is an actor who's just got terrible reviews for his latest play, make sure you cut the reviews out and frame them. If, on the other hand, your lover's a footballer, keep reminding him that, if he hadn't missed six penalties in a row, his team wouldn't have been booted out of the league.

However, the way to really upset Leos is to attack their looks and their appearance. You should tell them that they are ugly and that it doesn't matter what they wear, or which plastic surgeon they visit, because they'll always look like a bloated slug crawling through an oil slick.

How to turn off your lover

When you go to bed with Leos, you should do everything you can to shatter their self-esteem. You can do this by criticizing their sexual performance and by giving them books with titles such as *Traditional Herbal Remedies for Impotence* and *Frigidity Explained*. When the Lions start denying that they've got a sexual problem, you should start producing medical statistics and averages, which prove that they do.

Another way of turning Leos off is to talk about your ex-lovers and how wonderful they were in bed. And if you're really vicious, you'll say to the Leo, 'Whenever I make love to you, I close my eyes and try to imagine that you're someone else. Unfortunately, it's impossible to confuse your performance with anyone else's: only you would make such an appalling mess of things.'

How to give your lover the final push

In order to give Leo lovers the final push, you have to humiliate them in public. If they are celebrities, this is easy. You arrange an interview with a tabloid newspaper, in which you give an agonizing account of what it's like to be going out with a sexual failure. If your lover is a man, don't forget to mention his microscopic size and his miserable staying power.

You can still use the mass media to humiliate your Leo lovers even if they're not celebrities. You simply drag them along to a live network TV show, which allows audience participation. When the host asks you for your opinion on Northern Ireland, give a detailed description of your lover's sexual inadequacies. Make sure you show the nation some explicit photos of your lover, for extra impact.

VIRGO

Dumpability rating

After one week: ★★
At the beginning of a relationship, Virgos do everything they can to please their partners. So it may be difficult to find a good reason for dumping them.

After six months: ★★★★
After six months, Virgos start becoming very critical of their partners. If they see anything they don't like, or which disgusts them, they often end the relationship.

After three years: ***

If the Virgos are still going out with you after three years, then you can't be that disgusting, therefore you will have to adopt some new habits and reduce your general standard of hygiene.

How to upset your lover

There are a number of ways of upsetting your Virgo lover, all of which involve health, hygiene, tidiness and organization. You should at the very least be untidy around the house and leave dirty clothes and dirty washing-up everywhere.

If your Virgo lover is a non-smoker, then you must take up smoking immediately. Smoke sixty cigarettes a day; when you fill an ashtray, make sure that you empty it either on the floor, or over the Virgo's head. At the same time, you should

When you fill an ashtray, empty it over the Virgo's head.

constantly warn your lover about the dangers of passive smoking.

If your Virgo lover is a smoker, you'll have to find another way of stimulating their health worries. You could write to the local council and ask for planning permission to build a toxic waste dump in your lover's back garden. Or else you could take them on a fishing holiday to Chernobyl.

How to turn off your lover

You shouldn't have any difficulty turning off your Virgo lover. To begin with, you stop washing. In other words, you stop washing the dishes, your clothes and your body and you also stop cleaning your teeth. You should then start polluting your breath. When you're not smoking a cigarette, you should be chewing a clove of garlic, or drinking methylated spirits. However, we must warn you, first, that methylated spirits are poisonous and, second, that you must never smoke and drink methylated spirits at the same time, otherwise you'll catch fire.

If you want to really turn off a Virgo, it is a good idea to cultivate a colony of insects, preferably fleas, lice or bed bugs, on your own body. Once this infestation spreads across the bed, your lover will finally accept that you're a permanent health hazard.

How to give your lover the final push

The best way of giving Virgo lovers the final push is to give them a nicotine kiss. A nicotine kiss involves sticking a lighted cigarette into each of your nostrils and then kissing your lover.

Once the two pairs of lips are locked together, you inhale an air and smoke mixture through your nose and then exhale it into your lover's mouth. You must repeat the inhale–exhale cycle every ten seconds: if you get the rhythm right, you and your lover should find that you throw up at exactly the same time, into each other's mouths.

We know it's disgusting, but you did say that you wanted to get rid of your lover.

LIBRA

Dumpability rating

After one week: *
During the first weeks of a relationship, the Librans will size you up, to see if you can be of any social or financial use to them. At this stage, their manipulative skills will be on peak form, so you may find it very difficult to dump them.

After six months: ****
After six months there is an excellent chance that the Librans are being unfaithful to you. You would therefore be advised to assume the worst and to walk out of the relationship.

After three years: *****
After a few years your Libran lover will become extremely lazy. If you try to leave the relationship, he or she won't have the energy or the motivation to stop you.

How to upset your lover

Librans hate hard work, particularly in a domestic environment, so it is important that you keep your Libran lover busy around the house. If they refuse to do anything, you may have to give them some extra encouragement, either with a bull-whip or an electric cattle prod.

Like Cancerians, Librans don't like getting out of bed in the morning: you must make sure that by 7.00 a.m. they're on their knees, scrubbing the kitchen floor. Once you've broken your lover into a harsh domestic routine, you should start destroying their social life. Whenever the phone rings, tell the caller that your lover's not in. You should also throw away the Libran's post (except bills and junk mail). If an invitation does accidentally get into the Libran's hands and you end up going to a party, you should remember to behave as badly as possible and to physically attack your lover's friends. That way neither of you will ever get invited again.

How to turn off your lover

Your Libran lover believes that table manners are very important. So when you and your lover are out at a restaurant, or at a dinner party, behave like a pig. Make sure that you eat with your mouth wide open and that every now and then you spit out lumps of half-digested food. It is also important that you pick your nose at the table, in a way which is both ostentatious and productive.

When your romantic meal is over and it is time for sex, you need to take a down-to-earth approach. You should tell the Librans that sex is something that all animals do and that humans are no different. After that, you should give the Librans an in-depth biology lesson, just to remind them what sex is really about. Talk about conception, contraception and body fluids in vivid medical detail and, when you see your lover becoming visibly pale, give a detailed description of your last visit to the VD clinic.

How to give your lover the final push

If you follow the instructions we have just given, on turning Librans off, you will effectively be giving them the final push. However, if you want to add insult to injury, you should turn on your bedroom's floodlights and take your clothes off. Allow the Libran to see and experience the full horror of your naked body, stripped of make-up, silk underwear, girdles and toupets.

If you're massively overweight, it might also be a good idea to jump up and down, so that your Libran lover can see your rolls of fat flopping around. You should then tell your lover about your external piles and perhaps ask him or her to rub haemorrhoid cream into them. On second thoughts, you'll have to rub it in yourself, because the Libran will have fled hours earlier.

SCORPIO

Dumpability rating

After one week: *
It is very difficult to dump Scorpios, at any stage of a relationship. In the first week it is particularly difficult, because you will be overwhelmed by their devastating sexual magnetism.

After six months: *
After six months you may feel confident enough to make a dash for freedom. If you're lucky, you may reach the perimeter fence before you're recaptured.

After three years: ***
After a couple of years of going out with Scorpios, you'll begin to realize that they do have a few weak points. If you exploit these weak points to the full, you may eventually rid yourself of your lover.

How to upset your lover

Scorpios are often terrifying people; the thought of deliberately upsetting them may chill you to the bone, which is probably why you've been going out with your Scorpio lover for the last twenty years. However, if you're serious about dumping the Scorpion, you'll have to bite the bullet; in other words, you'll have to start lying and cheating.

If the Scorpios give you a twenty-pound note with which to buy some groceries, and the groceries cost fifteen pounds, tell them that the bill was twenty-five pounds and that they owe you a fiver. It is also essential to have no respect for Scorpios' privacy. You should therefore go into their study and rifle through their private papers. When the Scorpios uncover your crime, make sure that you protest your innocence, even when they show you the video recording taken by the surveillance camera.

How to turn off your lover

Broadly speaking there are three methods of turning off your Scorpio lover, which we will call plans one, two and three. Plan one involves telling the Scorpio that you've given up sex. If you are serious, and you manage to resist your lover's advances for a month or two, you should find that the relationship starts winding down.

If and when plan one fails, you move to plan two. Plan two is easier, in the sense that you agree to have regular sex with your lover. However, when you are having sex, you show complete disinterest. So, while the Scorpio is on top of you, or underneath you, you might be watching TV, peeling potatoes, or even reading this book.

Plan three is rather unusual, but it can, none the less, be very effective. You announce to your lover that you have become a born-again exhibitionist and that you'll only have sex in a public place, where you're being watched by at least fifty people.

How to give your lover the final push

Before giving Scorpios the final push, you must make sure that you're not reliant on them for anything and that there is no way they can hurt you. Alternatively, you may take the view that your relationship with the Scorpio is so intolerable that you're prepared to risk their revenge. Anyway, when you're ready, engineer a flaming argument with the Scorpios, in which you tell them why you hate them so much and why you think they're such appalling people. Be tactless, merciless and utterly brutal. When you've said your piece, walk out of their lives, without ever turning back (if you do turn back, the Scorpios will instantly turn you into a pillar of salt).

SAGITTARIUS

Dumpability rating

After one week: *****
Sagittarians have a high turnover of partners. So if you give them the elbow, particularly at the beginning of a relationship, they'll shrug their shoulders and find someone else.

After six months: ****
After six months, you may feel physically exhausted, in which case you tell the Sagittarians that you can't keep up with their breakneck sexual pace; you should then book yourself into a retirement home and tend to the roses.

After three years: ****
As far as Sagittarians are concerned, marriages and relationships are founded on mutual consent. You can therefore dump your Sagittarian partner the moment you fall out of love: if you're married, the divorce will be quick and painless.

How to upset your lover

Your Sagittarian lover is a spontaneous and enthusiastic person who wants to live life to the full. This means that you must do everything you can to extinguish your lover's natural spark. Make sure that you become very serious and you never laugh at his or her jokes.

When Sagittarians suggest that you both do something exciting, like going to a party, or sailing round the world, it is
important that you pour cold water on the idea. Tell them that
they're being immature and that it's time they faced up to reality.

If you want to really upset Sagittarians, you should wait
until they're down in the dumps and then go out of your way
to undermine their confidence. Remind them that they're not
getting any younger, and bemoan the fact that their career is at
a complete standstill. If possible, you should also erect a
gravestone, with your lover's name on it, in the garden. That
way he or she will be reminded that the Grim Reaper can
strike at any moment, without warning or apology.

How to turn off your lover

If you want to turn Sagittarians off, you must be cool and
restrained. You should therefore avoid crude behaviour and
you must never swear. When you're in a restaurant or a pub
with Sagittarians, don't allow them to get you drunk: after the
first glass of white wine, stick to orange juice.

As far as clothes are concerned, you should wear things
which cover up and obscure your sexuality, such as boiler suits
and anoraks. You should also make sure, when you go to bed
with your lover, that you wear a shark suit. These are chain-
mail outfits, which divers wear to protect themselves from the
bites of medium-sized sharks. Not only will the shark suit be a
real turn-off, but it will, in most cases, stop the Sagittarians
getting their teeth into you.

However, if your lover is a 30-foot carnivorous monster, the
best way of turning off their sex drive is to impale them with a
cyanide-tipped harpoon.

How to give your lover the final push

Sagittarians value their freedom of movement. So if you want
to give them the final push, you should burn their passport

and crash their car. You should also lock them in a cage, and tell them that you won't let them out until they've written 'I never want to see or speak to you ever again' ten thousand times (this should take a week, according to our calculations). However, we must emphasize that Sagittarians are easy people to get rid of, so it shouldn't be necessary to give them a final push – unless you're a sadist or a Scorpio.

CAPRICORN

Dumpability rating

After one week: *****
During the first week of the relationship your lover will sound you out, to see whether or not you'd make a good husband or wife. At this stage it's easy to get rid of the Goats: you just give them a detailed description of your sleazy past.

After six months: ****
The Goats regard the first six or seven months of a relationship as being a trial period. If, during this period, you prove yourself to be utterly incompetent, then you should have no difficulty scaring your lover off.

After three years: *
After three years, you are a full-time employee of Capricorn plc. If you want to hand in your notice, you'd better have a very good reason.

How to upset your lover

Capricorns find it difficult to express their true feelings, so if you're trying to upset them, be patient and allow their anger and irritation to slowly boil to the surface. As far as technique is concerned, your first line of attack should be to talk, talk and talk. Just carry on talking, regardless of the situation, and don't allow your lover to get a word in edgeways. This strategy will be particularly effective if you're as thick as two short planks, because Capricorns hate it when people talk rubbish.

You can also upset Capricorns by adopting expensive tastes. Always insist that they take you out to the most expensive restaurants and when it's your birthday, ask for a diamond-studded, solid platinum Swiss wrist-watch. And when it's the Capricorns' birthday, make sure that you spend a fortune on their presents, using *their* credit cards.

How to turn off your lover

If you're richer than your Capricorn lover, then it is a fair bet that he or she is sleeping with you for your money. If you want to turn them off, simply tell them that you're broke and that everything you own belongs to the bank.

Another method of turning the Capricorns off is to worry them. This method is most effective when they're about to have sex with you. You wait until the Capricorns are firmly aroused and you then inform them that interest rates have just gone up by a quarter of one per cent. Their enthusiasm will immediately deflate and they'll spend the rest of the night recalculating their profit-and-loss account.

How to give your lover the final push

As you now appreciate, Capricorns are obsessed about money. They will therefore take extreme measures to safeguard their finances and will ruthlessly eliminate anyone who poses a financial threat; so, the best way of giving Capricorns the final push is to devastate their finances. You might, for example, find a way of donating their entire fortune to charity. Or else you could take out a second mortgage on their house and spend the money on Caribbean holidays, fast cars, champagne and gambling.

However, if you really want to blow the Goat's mind, you

should have two simultaneous secret affairs: one with the taxman and the other with the Capricorn's bitterest business rival. You'll be pleased to know that once your lover uncovers your deception, he or she will terminate the relationship with extreme prejudice.

AQUARIUS

Dumpability rating

After one week: ***
During the first week of a relationship, the Aquarians will expect their lovers to dump them. So hire a dumper truck and drive your favourite Aquarian to the nearest rubbish dump.

After six months: ***
After six months you will regard your Aquarian lover as a close friend who you can trust with your deepest secrets. You can therefore tell the Aquarian that you secretly hate him (or her) and that you want to end the relationship as soon as possible.

After three years: **
After three years it can be very difficult to get rid of Aquarians. This is because Aquarians are rather reclusive and when you have finally summoned up the courage to tell them that the relationship is over, you will have trouble finding them.

How to upset your lover

If you want to upset Aquarians, it's important that you have no respect for their time or their space so, whenever you're bored, you should wander into the Aquarian's study or office, without knocking. Ask them what they're doing and then chat to them about the weather.

When the Aquarians go out anywhere, always ask if you can come too. If you carry on with this strategy of gentle interference, the Water-carriers will soon regard you as being a mill-stone round their neck and in the end they'll get rid of you.

However, if you want to speed things up, it's a good idea to patronize the Aquarians. Tell them that you think their latest project or hobby is fascinating and that you're so glad they've found something useful to do with their spare time.

You should also make it clear to your lover that you have no vision and no imagination; so every now and then, you should sigh, and say 'when are you going to stop chasing idle fantasies and start looking for a proper job?'

How to turn off your lover

The quickest way to turn an Aquarian off is to act like a Cancerian. In other words, you should be sentimental, clinging and emotional. Every five minutes tell the Aquarians how much you love them and at regular intervals you should smother them in wet, slobbery kisses. When you're out in public with the Water-carriers, make sure that your behaviour is super-emotional. Put your arm around their waist, stroke their hair and burst into tears at the least provocation.

Another useful tip is to wear plenty of pink clothes. This is because Aquarians HATE the colour pink: not only does this colour make them feel nauseous, but it also short-circuits their sex drive.

How to give your lover the final push

Aquarians are similar to Geminis, in the sense that their books, computers and scientific equipment are essential to them. You should therefore auction off the contents of your lover's laboratory and library, using the proceeds to buy a three-piece suite. Alternatively, if the Aquarians are single, you could con them into marrying you. Perhaps you could hypno-tize them, or else slip a short-acting aphrodisiac into their coffee. Once the Aquarians come round and realize what's been done to them, they'll file for divorce faster than you can say 'non-consummation'.

PISCES

Dumpability rating

After one week: *****
Pisceans are anxious to please their partners, particularly in the first week of a relationship, so if you take your Piscean lovers to the New York subway and tell them to get lost, they'll be happy to oblige.

After six months: ****
After six months, the Piscean may start clinging to you, rather like a limpet. However, you should find that it's a relatively easy matter to prise them off, provided that you don't fall for their sob stories.

After three years: **
After a few years of a relationship, the Pisceans will get to know your emotional weak spots. You may therefore find it difficult to get rid of the Fish, unless you're prepared to be tough with them.

How to upset your lover

If you want to upset Pisceans, you must cut off all emotional contact with them. So when they laugh, or smile or cry, you must be utterly unmoved. If you do have to respond to them, make sure that you are logical and stick to the facts. You would, therefore, tell a tearful Piscean, whose pet catfish had just been turned into fish pie, that the family was hungry and that the fishmonger was closed for the day. As compensation for hurt feelings, you might offer them ten pounds' worth of luncheon vouchers.

Another way of upsetting Pisceans is to be completely in-
different to their mistakes; if they're late for an appointment,
or make a mess of your house, you should carry on as if
nothing has happened. By taking this approach, you're letting
the Pisceans know that you no longer have any interest in
them. If you can keep up this indifference for a period of
months, the Pisceans will inevitably start looking for a new
partner who is able to combine loving discipline with strict
compassion.

How to turn off your lover

Pisceans are very sensitive to atmosphere, so it is a good idea
to make your home as unromantic as possible. Fit 150-watt
light bulbs everywhere and replace all your carpets with lino-
leum. You should cover your walls with bus and train time-
tables and play 24-hour hardcore technorock through your
sound system. Your bedroom should have an industrial flavour
to it. There should be lathes and machine-tools all over the
place and the floor should be covered in wood shavings. The
bed should be of an institutional style: in other words, single,
made of steel and with a three-inch mattress.

It is also a good idea to keep your giant-sized incense
burner well stocked with rubber tyres and diesel fuel. When it
comes to having sex with the Piscean, take your clothes off,
rub engine oil all over your hair and your body, spray the
room with fly spray, lie on your bed, and say, in your most
unromantic drawl, 'I'm all yours, baby, do what yer like to
me.'

How to give your lover the final push

The best way of giving Pisceans the final push is to be submissive. Tell the Fish that you want them to take control of every
aspect of your life, including your sex life, your career and
your personal hygiene. You should instruct them to be a strict

master/mistress and to give you regular punishment. In most cases, this approach should get rid of your Pisces lover in seconds flat.

However, if your lover still refuses to go, take him or her to a car boot sale, and sell them to the lowest bidder.

If your Pisces lover still refuses to go, take him to a car boot sale, and sell him to the lowest bidder.

FINAL WORDS

MONICA: So, Sandra, what did you think of the book?

SANDRA: You mean *Sex, Stars and Seduction*? Mmm . . . well, it's brilliant. F— brilliant. Except what they said about Sagittarians.

MONICA: Oh, yeah?

SANDRA: That they make a lot of noise when they're having sex.

MONICA: Well, they do, don't they? You remember when we went on holiday to Cannes? You and . . .

SANDRA: Gary . . . or was it Jeff? No, it must have been Gary.

MONICA: You threw Gary and the bed through a wall, didn't you? Lucky you were insured.

SANDRA: French hotels . . .

MONICA: Sure. Anyway, Sandra, are you going to tell all your friends what a fantastic read *Sex, Stars and Seduction* is?

SANDRA: Of course. It's a fabulous book that has completely transformed my life. Thanks, Barbara and Archie, you've done an amazing job.

MONICA: Great. Oh no, I've a call coming through. I'll ring you back. Bye.

SANDRA: Bye.

By the same authors

LIFE, LOVE
AND DESTINY

Follow this practical, easy-to-use guide to find out the secrets of the stars, and you'll soon be able to draw up your very own horoscope and open up a personal hot line to the cosmos.

Discover all you need to look for in a lover – the stars can tell you what you don't already know!

New insights into everyday life at work and at home are revealed – say goodbye to confusion and misunderstanding. With *Life, Love and Destiny* as your closest companion, you can discover what the future will bring.